The Feminist Uncanny in Theory and Art Practice

Also available from Bloomsbury

Feminist Theory, Fourth Edition, Josephine Donovan
Feminist Theory After Deleuze, Hannah Stark
Listening to Noise and Silence, Salome Voegelin
The Trouble and Strife Reader, edited by Deborah Cameron and Joan Scanlon

The Feminist Uncanny in Theory and Art Practice

Alexandra M. Kokoli

Bloomsbury Academic
An imprint of Bloomsbury Publishing Plc

BLOOMSBURY
LONDON • OXFORD • NEW YORK • NEW DELHI • SYDNEY

Bloomsbury Academic
An imprint of Bloomsbury Publishing Plc

50 Bedford Square
London
WC1B 3DP
UK

1385 Broadway
New York
NY 10018
USA

www.bloomsbury.com

BLOOMSBURY and the Diana logo are trademarks of Bloomsbury Publishing Plc

First published 2016
Paperback edition first published 2017

British Library Cataloguing-in-Publication Data
A catalogue record for this book is available from the British Library.

ISBN: HB: 978-1-4725-1139-3
PB: 978-1-3500-6078-4
ePDF: 978-1-4725-0558-3
ePub: 978-1-4725-1402-8

Library of Congress Cataloging-in-Publication Data
Kokoli, Alexandra M., author.
The feminist uncanny in theory and art practice / Alexandra M. Kokoli.
New York : Bloomsbury, 2016. | Series: Bloomsbury studies in philosophy |
Includes bibliographical references and index.
LCCN 2016012320 (print) | LCCN 2016027808 (ebook) | ISBN 9781472511393 (hardback) |
ISBN 9781472505583 (epdf) | ISBN 9781472514028 (epub)
LCSH: Feminism and the arts. | Feminist theory. |
Uncanny, The (Psychoanalysis) | Feminism and art.
LCC NX180.F4 K65 2016 (print) | LCC NX180.F4 (ebook) | DDC 704/.042–dc23
LC record available at https://lccn.loc.gov/2016012320

Series: Bloomsbury Studies in Philosophy

Cover design: Clare Turner
Cover image © Su Richardson

Typeset by Deanta Global Publishing Services, Chennai, India

Contents

List of Figures

Acknowledgements

I wish to thank the Art & Design Research Institute (ADRI), Middlesex University, whose financial support reduced my teaching load in 2014–15, allowing me to complete this book. I am especially grateful to Dr. Valeria Graziano of ADRI for her assistance towards organizing and securing permissions for illustrations. I would also like to thank the Association of Art Historians (AAH) for their financial award towards licensing and reprographic costs, without which *The Feminist Uncanny* would have included far fewer illustrations.

For permission to reproduce some previously published material, I am grateful to KT Press and Tate Publishing.[1] I also wish to thank the artists whose work is reproduced here and their representatives for their support of this book project.

I have shared ideas that culminated in *The Feminist Uncanny* at various stages of development with colleagues past and present and a variety of international academic audiences and discussants, whom I thank for their feedback, encouragement and occasional reality check. Professors Deborah Cherry and Elena Gualtieri successfully introduced me to the ways of scholarship and academic writing some years ago, despite some resistance on my part; I thank them for their expert guidance and persistence. My gratitude also goes to all the anonymous peerreviewers who have engaged with my work, for their unpaid and largely invisible labour.

I was fortunate enough to have this manuscript reviewed by knowledgeable and busy colleagues, whose input has been integral to getting this text to publication. I am enormously grateful to Felicity Allen, Rosemary Betteron, August Davis, Catherine Dormor, Bronwyn Platten, Hilary Robinson, Suzanne van Rossenberg, Abi Schapiro, Anne Schwartz and Sue Tate for their time, attention and expertise. All errors and omissions of course remain my own.

The unwavering support and generosity of Monica Ross (1950–2013) and Susan Hiller saw me through some rough patches of casualized underemployment and confidence crises, while their friendship, conversation and integrity have been a steady source of inspiration. I am also grateful to Rosemary Betterton and Laura Mulvey for their positivity and encouragement, especially in the difficult early postdoctoral years.

There is more than a little irony in having fashioned an intellectual home out of the uncanny, since my first encounter with it through the courses in comparative literature of Professors Michalis Chryssantholpoulos and Elisavet Tsirimokou (School of Philology, Aristotle University, Thessaloniki), in the mid-1990s. As Martin Jay pointed out (1998), the 1990s were indeed an uncanny decade in more ways than one, but for me and I suspect for many others the uncanny holds fast twenty years on and doesn't look like it's going anywhere.

I am sure that I am not the only feminist academic to be suffering from anxiety of influence in reverse, namely the occasionally paralysing fear that I have failed to adequately acknowledge the range of ideas and practices that have fostered the development of my own. This, like all of my work, is built on the shoulders not of giants, nor of giantesses, but of many industrious, knowledgeable, brilliant and brave women, men, and those who don't identify with either. I hope to have acknowledged most of them but doubt that I have.

Last but not least, I would like to dedicate this book to the memory of my parents, Maria Vertsoni-Kokoli (1940–95) and Xenophon A. Kokolis (1939–2012), who managed not to dissuade me from becoming an academic despite knowing all too well what this path entailed. And to my own family, Aaron Winter, Matthew and Shane, for their unfailing support, their intelligent feedback (Aaron, mostly), and of course their love.

Introduction

Why witches? Setting the scene

In her editorial to the first issue of the French journal *Sorcières: Les femmes vivent [Witches: Women live]* (1976),[1] Xavière Gauthier explained the choice of the journal's title: witches dance, they sing, they steal/fly [*elles volent*], and have only historically appeared ugly and wicked because they 'pose a real danger to phallocratic society' (Gauthier 1981, pp. 199–203). Crucially, witches were announced to be back and ready to avenge the repression of their predecessors. Marginalized, oppressed and victimized but also representing the repressed underbelly of a rationalist and sexist – 'phallogocentric'[2] – order of things, witches emerged as a sorely needed bridge between social oppression and symbolic repression. Oppressed and marginalized groups have long had an affinity for the cultural unconscious and an interest in mining it; conversely, the culturally repressed is often perceived as threatening and socially subversive. It is therefore not surprising that Gauthier and the editorial board of *Sorcières* were not alone in symbolically deploying the figure of the witch as a specifically feminist revolutionary. In *The Newly Born Woman*, Catherine Clément singled out the witch as an emblem of emergent feminist womanhood, without, however, being blind to its risks: out of the bundle of contradictions, bittersweet transgressions, imposed sufferings and precarious victories with which every culture's imaginary space of otherness is fraught, Clément urged her readers to keep 'the witch's broom, her taking off, her being swept away, her taking flight' (Clément and Cixous 1986, p. 57). In 'The Laugh of the Medusa', Hélène Cixous' manifesto of feminine writing, it is not specifically the figure of the sorceress that is evoked but the powerful metaphor of the return of the repressed, already underlying the deployments of the sorceress by Gauthier and Clément. The Greek mythical monster Medusa, famously discussed by Freud in reference to the castration complex, became a cipher for intrepid femininity that made 'an explosive, *utterly* destructive, staggering return' (Cixous 1976b, p. 886, emphasis in the original). Feminine writing takes place when the culturally repressed return with a vengeance, when the long censored and (presumed) impossible erupts into language and the world, throwing it into 'chaosmos' (ibid., p. 888). Through the seventies and for the duration of the feminist second wave, a networked, collaborative manifesto appears to have been woven across a growing body of theoretical writing as well as visual art practices, in which witches and female monsters are not merely reclaimed but reimagined as symbols of resistance and even revolutionary agents.

Meanwhile, another network of formally trained and untrained women artists was emerging across England and, increasingly, internationally. In 1976, the year of the first publication of *Sorcières* and of the English translation of Cixous' call to feminine writing in *Signs* (1976b), a feminist postal art project was gathering pace through a growing number of participants and touring exhibitions. *The Women's Postal Art Event* (1975–77) and its installations under the titles *Feministo: Portrait of the Artist as a Young Woman* and *Portrait of the Artist as a Housewife* (ICA 1977) called into question the implicitly gendered hierarchy between art and craft by employing craft techniques, traditionally passed on from one generation of women to the next and now repurposed for a feminist art project inspired by consciousness-raising (Elinor et al. 1987; Goodall 1987; Walker 1980; Kokoli 2004).[3] In addition to crocheting, quilting and embroidery, simple DIY techniques like papier-mâché and collage were used to level the playing field between participants regardless of training or access to art supplies and designated studios. Most of the resulting works, small and cheap to post, turned the connotations of feminine craft on its head, aggressively debunking domesticity as an oppressive ideal founded on a patriarchal division of labour. In its more elaborate installations, a mock-domestic set-up was adopted for greater effect, including a kitchen and bedroom but also a memory room and a rape room, in which Kate Walker's *Rape Cup and Saucer* was displayed, an obvious homage to Meret Oppenheim's *Fur Cup and Saucer*, lined with newspaper clippings reporting incidents of sexual assault. Amputated female body parts were presented in chocolate boxes (Kate Walker), a full English breakfast was offered with burnt egg, as small, perhaps unconscious protest (Su Richardson), while a series of crocheted sandwiches (Richardson), arranged on a cutting board next to a load of real bread did not make packed lunches but eloquent statements about the experience of mothers and housewives. *Feministo*'s treacherous home installations were not merely anti-domestic but rather brought to light the suppressed discontents, silences, inequalities and even violence on which domesticity is founded.

This book's focus is neither on witches specifically, nor on artistic indictments of domesticity, but rather on an important dimension that the textual and visual practices outlined above have in common: the return of the repressed. Its starting point is the deliberate unsettling quality that many cultural artefacts informed by feminism continue to possess. The book proposes the term 'feminist uncanny' to best describe this quality, while also pointing at a *critical* encounter in both senses of the word, crucial and founded in critical discourse: the fraught but fertile relationship between feminism and the uncanny and, by extension, Freudian psychoanalysis. This relationship will be explored both in critical texts and in examples of feminist art practice.

Feminism and the uncanny

In the uncanny, which Freud famously described as the disturbing fallout of the return of the repressed, feminism discovered an unexpected ally in its attempt to forge subversive countercultural strategies, to claim a place in the canons of creative practice and critical theory, and to revolutionize them in doing so. Such strategies involve a process of defamiliarization, namely of uncovering the strangeness of what is assumed to be known, established or ordinary, which is tinged with an indictment of the division between the familiar and the unfamiliar in the first place, a division that is viewed as intrinsically hierarchical and imbued in the politics of power. In the context of the discipline of art history, divisions between the known (also assumed to be worth knowing) and the unknown (assumed to be minor, marginal, of lesser importance, or less representative of dominant tendencies, movements, traditions) are both the reflection and the vehicle of authoritative value judgements. Insidiously, such divisions filter down to mainstream, lay understandings of art, history and value, and get entrenched, validated and naturalized through repetition. Hence among the earliest tasks of feminist art, history has been the interrogation of the criteria operating within and through the discipline. Linda Nochlin's question 'Why Have There Not Been Great Women Artists?' (1989 [1971]) was met with a multitude of answers, ranging from the rediscovery of forgotten, marginalized or underrated women artists and traditions of female collective and anonymous cultural production, to the systematic unmaking of the implicitly gendered, classed and racialized construct of the solitary artistic genius. Either way, ignorance was stripped of its claim to innocence. In the exhibition catalogue of the ICA exhibition *About*

Time (1980), Lynn MacRitchie simultaneously underlines the timeliness of this women-only group show and acknowledges that it is 'a mere drop from the pool available. Thus the unfamiliarity of work by women artists does not lie in its rarity. It lies in its suppression' (MacRitchie cited in Parker and Pollock 1987, p. 39). If the strange bears the mark of its suppression, infecting the familiar with unsettling unfamiliarity can be a righteous turning of the tables – a justified act of overdue retribution.

The fairly straightforward proposition that feminism found in the uncanny an apt subversive strategy is not without its caveats. On the one hand, feminism and psychoanalysis do not always make a happy pairing: as with Marxism, their relationship has been troubled as well as productive.[4] On the other hand, the uncanny is among the most flawed and flickering critical formulations, already mutating within Freud's writings, which do not fully acknowledge previous attempts to pin it down, and becoming increasingly elusive in theoretical and practice-led reworkings thereafter. In acknowledgement of such issues, this book approaches the uncanny not merely as subversive strategy but as a cipher of the collaboration between feminism and the theoretical apparatus of psychoanalysis, a collaboration that is inherently compromised and compromising despite notable accomplishments. The uncanny makes ideal vehicle for an arrangement marked by ambivalence and acts as a constant reminder that, even though feminism ended up revitalizing psychoanalysis through their critical encounter, the two are never quite at home with one another. 'In every alternative practice, every elaboration in the other manner, including the present one, the one you are reading, *un peu de mal*, a bit of difficulty, a bit of maleness, returns' (Gallop 1982, p. 55).[5] One of the key advantages that psychoanalysis presents to feminism is not to minimize or contain this difficulty (on the contrary, in many respects it amplifies it) but rather to foster a fearless self-reflective capacity for acknowledging and working through it. Conversely, feminist thought has revolutionized psychoanalysis in too many ways to fully acknowledge here, from Melanie Klein's emphasis on pre-Oedipal development and the importance of the maternal function (Jacobus 1995; Kristeva 2001), to Bracha Ettinger's sustained attack on binaries and specifically the subjectifying/objectifying logic of the Lacanian gaze (Pollock 2006; Ettinger 2004). Rather than embracing the transformative potential of such radical revisions, this book is mired on the murky terrain of the close, adversarial dialogue between second-wave feminism and the *fathers* of psychoanalysis, suggesting that dangerous encounters can often be the most serendipitous. Rather than the model of a transformative overhaul, I am more interested in the minor mode of 'rhetorical catachresis' (Lyon 1999,

p. 198), a tactical misprision of master discourses by those excluded from and/or misrepresented by them.[6] Feminist catachresis, partly concurrent with the Situationist *détournement*, is an established form of feminist practice albeit not usually identified by name. In art informed by feminism, 'deflection, diversion, rerouting, distortion, misuse, misappropriation, hijacking, or otherwise turning something aside from its normal course or purpose' (Knabb 2006) have all organically and/or programmatically emerged as prominent creative and political strategies, from the mutually subversive mixing of women's craft and oil painting in Faith Ringgold's quilted canvases to the mock documents of *The Fae Richards Photo Archive* by Zoe Leonard, in which documentary and archival conventions are mimicked as an indictment for the gaps and silences in real archives and histories. It is my contention in this book that most feminist encounters with Freudian psychoanalysis are inherently and profoundly catachrestic, particularly since Lacan's revisions of Freud were not only eventually elevated to the highest echelons of critical theory, but have also been abused as academic litmus tests, thanks to their presumed opacity. In *Reading Lacan* (1987), Jane Gallop not only sidesteps but also challenges the orthodoxy of many of Lacan's followers, making the audacious revelation that her approach to the material under consideration was at once openly feminist *and* far from masterful, an admission that caused much trouble in the peer-review process of her book. Instead of intellectual inadequacy, of which she was accused, relinquishing 'the usual position of command' suggests a reflectively feminist attitude to the making and circulation of ideas:

> Though I have worked long and hard at Lacan's text and with the various commentaries upon it, rather than present my mastery I am interested in getting at those places where someone who generally knows the text well still finds herself in a position of difficulty. … My assumption of my inadequacy and my attempt to read from that position are thus, to my mind, both Lacanian and feminist. (Gallop 1987, pp. 19–20)

In my own attempt to stave off orthodoxies (Freudian, Lacanian, feminist), I have assumed not only the openness to interpretation and reinterpretation of all the texts with which I engage, both written and visual, theory and art, but also the inherent instability of their signification and significance, as well as accepting the specificity and limitations of my own perspective. I share Gallop's hope that the meeting of feminism and psychoanalysis 'can bring each other to its most radical potential' (Gallop 1982, p. xii). Over three decades later, I would venture further to argue that this hope has been realized in multiple forms and platforms. Significantly, while this encounter was originally hosted in the realms of critical theory and literature (and the many hybrid texts in-between), it gradually migrated to feminist approaches to visual art and culture, where it has taken roots and continues to flourish (Apter 2006, p. 329).

The book is loosely divided into two parts, the first of which examines the relationship between feminism and the uncanny focusing on theoretical texts, while the second approaches it in light of pertinent examples of feminist visual art practice. Although the distinction between theory and practice is questionable at best (after all, practice implicitly proposes its own theories, and theory can only be articulated through different types of practice), each part of the book operates differently. The first two chapters introduce the multiple definitions of the uncanny, as slippery concept, subversive textual/artistic strategy, and cipher for the ambivalent engagement of feminism and the theories it drew on and transformed. Chapters 3–6 are thematically organized around aggressively defamiliarized premises and platforms, and consist of new readings of prominent works as well as an engagement with less well-researched art projects.

Art and feminism: A disclaimer

For the purposes of this book, feminism refers not only to the historical Women's Liberation Movement, a.k.a. second-wave feminism, but also to contemporaneous and subsequent movements, individuals and practices that have been significantly informed by the changes brought about by feminist political and cultural activity. A positive identification of the artists under consideration with feminism is not essential as long as the impact of feminist theory and practice on their practice is evident. Most art practice under consideration spans the 1970s and 1980s, although later works are also included if they represent the culmination of processes that began earlier. In the case of the theory under discussion, it can be more straightforwardly placed at the moment of the tremendously productive meeting between psychoanalysis, post-structuralism and deconstruction that erupted in the early 1970s. Jacques Lacan's reinterpretation of canonical psychoanalytic texts was not limited to an insistence on the workings of language within them, nor the crucial role of the symbolic in the formation and definition of the subject, both revolutionary in themselves: 'The crux of Lacan's reading of Freud is that Freud's discovery of repression was itself necessarily and constantly threatened with being repressed' (Mehlman 1972, p. 5). In other words, as the textuality of psychoanalytic writing was restored and foregrounded, psychoanalytic ideas were subjected to (psycho)analytic scrutiny more than ever before. The return to Freud in the 1970s, through Lacan, but also through Jean Laplanche, Julia Kristeva and Luce Irigaray, among others, was singularly revisionist, self-reflective, and subversive from within.

Regarding feminism's waves (or lack thereof), it would be tempting to argue for an irreducibly diverse continuum of presence since the late 1960s, radically varied but at the same time connected in its shared multiplicity. Yet the existence of growing feminist legacies, however diverse, as well as the commitment to respond to current cultural and political contexts means that some differentiation is necessary. Writing in the mid-1980s, Dale Spender argues that there are important distinctions to be drawn even within the second wave, at the point in which feminism emerged as a body of knowledge as well as a political and activist practice:

> Coming to know through books is a qualitatively different experience from coming to know through the collective and creative process of consciousness-raising. The existence of a body of knowledge invariably means that knowing feminism is not the same for the 'second generation' of women in the contemporary movement, who must first learn before they can introduce their personal insights, and for whom there is an increased chance that they will be 'wrong' in a way that would have been extremely rare for the 'first generation' [of the late 1960s and early 1970s]. (Spender 1985, p. 121)

An academic habit has recently emerged of questioning the use of feminist periodizations for many good reasons, from challenging the illusion of linear progress, to dodging the dangerous reduction of feminist debates into intergenerational conflict, and, perhaps more abstractly, because the waves may 'stifle the writing of the kind of complex historical genealogy of feminisms' (McRobbie 2009, p. 156). Although the case against the waves is often persuasive, their rejection masks the privilege of being already fluent in the nuances of feminist critical idioms and practices, and knowledgeable enough of their histories to challenge and deconstruct them. The generalizations that neat periodizations both presume and perpetuate can be substantially enabling to those new to feminism and trying to get to grips with its rich history, if only as a first step on a hopefully long journey. After all, one can only break the rules that one already knows.

Returning to – and thereby outlining – feminist traditions in art and theory has emerged a big feminist issue over the past decade. Two major survey exhibitions, *elles@pompidou*, Pompidou Centre, Paris, and *Rebelle: Art and Feminism,*

Museum voor Moderne Kunst, Arnhem (both 2009), were predated by an explosion of events, exhibitions and publications in 2007 that sought to address the pasts and futures of feminism in visual art, including notably the MoMA symposium *The Feminist Future: Theory and Practice in the Visual Arts*, the exhibition *WACK! Art and the Feminist Revolution* (Museum of Contemporary Art, Los Angeles, and travelling), curated by Cornelia Butler, *Global Feminisms*, curated by Maura Reilly and Linda Nochlin, in celebration of the opening of the Elizabeth A. Sackler Center for Feminist Art in the Brooklyn Museum, NYC, and *Kiss Kiss Bang Bang: 45 Years of Art and Feminism*, curated by Xavier Arakistain, Bilbao Fine Arts Museum.[7] The year before saw the opening of *It's Time for Action (There's No Option): About Feminism*, curated by Heike Munder, at the Migros Museum of Contemporary Art, Zurich. The exhibition *Konstfeminism* [*Art Feminism – Strategies and Consequences in Sweden from the 1970s to the Present*] opened in Sweden in 2005, while in 2006 I organized, at the University of Sussex, the one-day conference *Difference Reframed: Reflections on Art and Feminism*, with a keynote by Griselda Pollock and presentations by emergent artists and art historians.[8] More important even than the diverse content and clashing assumptions of this 'revival' was that it happened, and that it responded to an emergent demand for a celebration of art in feminism and feminism in art, a call for a preservation of and ongoing reflection on the heritage of the second wave and a continuation of feminist practices in art and art writing. Ultimately, it was the search for 'feminist models' and enabling continuities that powered this revival. Katy Deepwell suggests that one of the principle continuities has been a commitment to asking similar, always difficult questions both of art history and of contemporary art about the visibility of women's practice, the re-evaluation of their representation in art history and criticism, and the representation of gender broadly defined (Deepwell 2007, pp. 198–9). The most important thing that remains constant, despite its ongoing transformation, is feminism itself (p. 208). And it is feminism's commitment to articulating, nurturing and ever-complicating difference that guarantees its coherence through change.

The artists and artworks under consideration have been selected through a variety of processes and for different reasons. Like many feminist writers, I have experienced the anxiety of influence in reverse, constantly worrying about the cultural producers, texts, theories and practices that I have failed to acknowledge, adequately or at all. It would be disingenuous to suggest that serendipity, the opportunity to visit some archives and not others, personal taste and even personal relationships did not inform the selection. The evident

Anglo-American bias (including 'French theory', which is to a large degree an Anglo-American invention), of both my scholarly and artistic references may not be excused, but can be explained by the fact that I came to know most of the artists under consideration through English-language books, and mostly through feminist art historical writing, which has only recently began to address its Eurocentricity in earnest, rather than in exhibition or on studio visits, although in most cases first-hand experience followed the initial mediated encounter. More importantly, this book contributes to feminist knowledge by reviewing and revising (seemingly) familiar ground, rather than by introducing heretofore neglected and/or geopolitically marginalized theory and practice. In doing so, it adheres to one of the tenets of the uncanny that situates the unknown and partially unknowable in the dark heart of the familiar. I have almost deliberately steered clear of artworks which explicitly reference the uncanny (or the related concepts of the abject and the – base – sublime) in their titles or texts, or which would be visually immediately identifiable as being connected to such concepts. On the one hand, I want to suggest that the uncanny permeates, in one way or another, all practice informed by feminism; on the other, I have often felt that artworks that announce themselves as uncanny aren't that uncanny after all. I hope that if the feminist uncanny has been as important and pervasive a concept and strategy as I argue here, then any insights coming out of this book could be transferred beyond its pages to different artworks, texts and debates. Going further, I aspire to demonstrate that the feminist uncanny, as an improper concept and cluster of strategies, is too widespread, diverse and protean to be exhausted in any single monograph.

(Dis)identifications

It has become increasingly common to question feminism's reference to 'women' as its principle if not exclusive constituency, particularly for students of feminism and/or those who, regardless of age, have only recently become involved. This is hardly a new issue in feminist thought and activism. Through a Foucauldian genealogical investigation into the category of 'women', Denise Riley not only charts its important transformations in and beyond feminist movements but also argues that the changeability and indeterminacy of this category needs to continue to be fully acknowledged in any current and future feminist thought (2003). Following Judith Butler, Alison Stone offers an alternative to 'strategic essentialism' (the simultaneous acceptance that 'women' is an inadequate and dangerously unifying descriptor and the recognition that it can also be an enabling identification towards common political action), in her conception of 'women as genealogy':

> Every cultural construction of femininity takes over and reinterprets pre-existing constructions, themselves the precipitates of still earlier layers of reinterpretation, so that all these constructions form overlapping chains. … Thus, although women do not form a unity, they are nevertheless assembled through their location within this history … amenable to collective mobilisation on a coalition basis. (Stone 2007, pp. 26–7)

It is true that many of the feminist texts and documents I have read do not appear to acknowledge gender positions beyond the binary of femininity and masculinity. However, I am not convinced that this makes them or their writers retroactively heteronormative, essentialist or transphobic. It is up to contemporary feminists and their allies to reinterpret past texts, documents and images and thus imbricate themselves in the overlapping chains that Stone mentions above. I do not have to turn to philosophical (Moi 2001) nor social theoretical (Gunnarsson 2011) defences of the category of 'women' to give myself permission to continue to use the term and even, with some reservations, to identify with it. The most convincing and perhaps simplest defence of keeping the term in circulation (rather than on a pedestal) comes from the practice of feminist art history. Writing in the mid-1990s, when feminism seemed 'so well established, maybe even old hat' (Wagner 1996, p. 4), Anne Wagner explains why she continues to write on artists who are women and to use the category of the 'woman artist'. In social and cultural contexts 'woman' continues to signify and resonate, as in art, whether it is actively claimed as an identification, avoided or externally imposed. Conversely, to be a 'woman artist' hasn't been nor will it ever be the whole story: none of Wagner's chosen artists represents 'women', let alone 'Woman'; 'just as images are not transparent to social identity (or anything else), neither are people' (Wagner 1996, p. 26).

Which psychoanalysis (what theory?): Some parameters and preliminary observations

It is important to point out that in the 1970s, the 'formative years' of the feminisms under consideration, psychoanalysis and Freud's writings in particular enjoyed a different status than they do today. Although their popularity may still be debatable, the idea that they formed part of popular culture at the time isn't.

The Pelican Freud Library (later Penguin Freud Library), based on the Standard Edition by James Strachey but omitting texts deemed of little interest to the general public, such as papers on technical aspects of the psychoanalytic method and early writings on neurology, was organized in fifteen thematic anthologies. Sometimes compared to a psychoanalytic Vulgate, the Pelican/Penguin Freud Library was widely available in bookshops and larger news agents alike across Britain in the 1970s. The idea of being able to buy some Freud at a train station or an airport may seem surprising to the contemporary reader, especially if she, like me, has a vague or no recollection of the 1970s, but it is necessary to keep in mind when engaging with feminist theory and art practice whose foundations lie in that cultural context. Freud was considered to be both a captivating and a politically important read, emphatically *not* reserved for the academically minded. Therefore, when Laura Mulvey (whose influential contributions to the academic journal *Screen* and feminist magazines such as *Spare Rib* are assumed to be emblematic of second wave's take on psychoanalytic theory) describes her own involvement with psychoanalysis as pop-Freudian, it is not out of false modesty but in recognition that, in the 1970s, Freud himself was pop.

Juliet Mitchell's founding text *Psychoanalysis and Feminism* (1974), also published by Pelican/Penguin drove this point home for me first and foremost, when I first read it twenty-five years after its original publication. Mitchell and her publishers clearly expected of her readership a working knowledge of some key texts by Freud as well as the work of anti-psychiatry founder R. D. Laing, Wilhelm Reich and feminist detractors of psychoanalysis, including Kate Millett and Shulamith Firestone. *Psychoanalysis and Feminism* unfolds as a series of carefully argued theses on the open-endedness of Freudian thought on matters of gender and sexuality and its value in articulating the ideological and psychological workings of patriarchy and the oppression of women (Part One), followed by a detailed discussion of the relationship between Freudian psychoanalysis and 'radical psychotherapy', represented by Reich and Laing (Part Two: I) and of 'Feminism and Freud' (Part Two: II). Mitchell demonstrates how feminist attacks on a 'debased Freudianism' by Simone de Beauvoir, Betty Friedan, Eva Figes, Germaine Greer, Shulamith Firestone and Kate Millett have been politically 'necessary' (Mitchell 1974, p. 356) but have not helped advance an understanding of the implications of patriarchy for women and men alike. An acknowledgement of the particular workings of the unconscious and an attention to Freud's textuality are essential in the productive – that is to say, revolutionary – deployments of psychoanalysis in the interests of feminism. They are also, incidentally, essential in freeing Freud of his imposed 'debasement'. In her effort to restore the complexity of 'Beyond the Pleasure Principle', Mitchell suggests that the perceived and much maligned 'dualism of drives', the death drive and the sexual drive, 'does not persist even at the moment of its inception', since the two are 'in constant battle', or rather in a 'dialectical relationship', as well as infinitely mutable and are thus likely to produce unforeseen changes in their dynamics as they attach to one another in shifting transformations (Mitchell 1974, p. 390). Mitchell's ambition for feminism, psychoanalysis and their interface is no less than to awaken this vibrant and generative ambiguity and exploit it not only for the analysis of the world as it is but towards effecting change. It is this feminist view on psychoanalysis, which recognizes that the texts reveal more than its author dared to acknowledge, that both inspires and shapes this book. In the feminist context, the vibrant and generative ambiguity of the text is not allowed to flounder in its own endlessly self-deferring indeterminacy, as in deconstruction, but often gets harnessed in polemics, subverted in consciousness-raising, revisited in art practice, experimented with and recycled, in various forms and to different ends, time and again.

The psychoanalytic traditions evoked in this book are very closely tied to Freud and his published works. Lacan, who unequivocally declared himself a Freudian, also makes constant reference to Freud's texts and brings to them an attention to language broadly defined, which is shared by feminist writers and artists, regardless of whether they directly cite Lacan's work. After all, Lacan and self-declared Lacanians do not hold the exclusive rights of mining Freud's textuality, and it would be hard to deny that paying attention to the silences and ambiguities of texts and images has been an intrinsically feminist issue. It is therefore thanks to a *shared* interest in cultural silences, rather than the mere influence of the master on the movement, that the meeting between feminism and Lacan's work has been such a productive one, and deeply enriching of the longer-standing ambivalent relationship between feminism and Freud. Introducing a selection of Lacan's work on sexuality, Jacqueline Rose maintains its relevance to feminism for outlining the psycho-cultural conditions by which 'woman' is assigned 'a definition in which she is simultaneously symptom and myth' (Mitchell and Rose 1982, p. 57)

Reading second-wave feminist theory in the present comes with the added bonus of catching glimpses of its primary materials. For instance, Judith Williamson's *Decoding Advertisements* (1978) serves as an invaluable introduction to the casual sexism of mainstream visual culture of the 1970s in the UK and, to some degree, in Northern Europe and North America, as well as a reminder of the *currency* of Freudian and Lacanian psychoanalysis, semiotics and structuralist and post-structuralist theory. Although such required background knowledge has since largely shrunk back into academia, it is essential to keep in mind that, thanks to the intellectual underpinnings of feminist and New Left activism and the emphasis on the habit of reading among those who considered themselves to be politically engaged, the conceptual and analytical frameworks of the artworks and texts under consideration in this book had a different cultural capital at the time of their production: both higher, because of the perceived timeliness, relevance and applicability of such frameworks to everyday life; and lower, because they weren't confined to academic settings.

After much consideration I decided to stick to Strachey's translations as they were published in the slightly updated Penguin Freud Library editions of the 1990s, which are those that introduced me to the most of Freud's work. Where necessary I refer to the Standard Edition for texts not included in the Penguin Library. Despite the many advantages of the new translations of Freud's works in the New Penguin Freud expertly edited by Adam Phillips, including, for instance, the elimination of many errors and oversimplifications in Strachey's original translations for the standard edition, I decided to stick to the Penguin Freud Library, as it is this which was read and is cited by the English-speaking writers with whom I engage. Revisiting Freud's texts in their new translations from a feminist perspective would make a potentially worthwhile project, which however falls outside the scope of this book.

Theory and/as practice, practice and/as theory: Chapter summaries

Josh Lyman: 'The art around here scares the hell out of me.'
Amy Gardner: 'That's what it's supposed to do.'[9]

The first two chapters consist of an examination of the common ground between the uncanny and femininity, not only because Freud clearly positioned femininity on the side of castration, the unspeakable and death but because both remained equally fascinating and mystifying in Freud's work. In addition to key texts by Freud (e.g. 'The Theme of the Three Caskets' and 'Beyond the Pleasure Principle'), Chapter 1, 'The Uncanny Feminine', considers relevant formulations by Jacques Lacan and Jean Laplanche and their relationship with theories of femininity.

Chapter 2, 'The Feminist Uncanny', provides an overview of feminist scholarship on the uncanny, by writers including Hélène Cixous, Jane Marie Todd and Sarah Kofman. Freud's eponymous essay has inspired a multitude of critiques and revisionist accounts that throw into relief the troubling contradictions at the heart of feminism's engagement with psychoanalysis. The specificity of my approach will be contextualized within and against a range of influential feminist concepts, including Julia Kristeva's 'abject', Barbara Creed's 'monstrous feminine' and Mary Russo's 'female grotesque', each of which evokes distinct cultural and critical practices. While mostly engaging with 'theory', the first two chapters also chart the discursive transformations of texts and intertextual relationships that have been repeatedly interpreted, debated, contested and, ultimately, activated in ways that draw attention to their status as (textual) practice.

Chapter 3, 'Moving sideways and other dead metaphors: Susan Hiller's Paraconceptualism', introduces the part of the book that deals more directly with art practice. Committed to a ceaseless excavation of the cultural unconscious, Hiller's oeuvre sits awkwardly within conceptualism for refusing to disavow visual pleasure and, even more importantly, for not succumbing to the inherent rationalism of much historical conceptualist practice. Just sideways of conceptualism and neighbouring the paranormal, a devalued site of culture where women and the feminine have been conversely privileged, Hiller's 'Paraconceptualism' opens up a hybrid field of radical ambiguity where neither conceptualism nor the paranormal are left intact: the prefix 'para-' allows in a force of contamination through a proximity so great that it threatens the soundness of all boundaries. This chapter includes critical readings of the automatic writing work *Sisters of Menon* (1972; 1979), the video installation *Belshazzar's Feast* (1983) and the short film and etchings of *The Last Silent Movie* (2007).

In Chapter 4, 'Squats and Evictions: The Uncanny as Unhomely', the uncanny (*das Unheimliche*) is translated verbatim as unhomely and restored to its literal meaning. Domesticity and the sexual division of labour were not only major issues in feminist activism and political debates but were also tackled in a range of feminist practices, including visual art. Installation has been used strategically and subversively to recreate domestic environments from the perspective of feminist dissent, overhauled and made uncanny to reveal that, for the homemaker, the home has always been marked by profound ambivalence. The chapter is principally devoted to a relatively unknown British postal art project and travelling installation, the aforementioned *Feministo* (1975–77), but also tackles some of the cultural and philosophical supports of the conflation between femininity and domesticity, notably in the work of Emmanuel Levinas.

Food preparation and the social potential of communing over a shared meal are interrogated through a series of works that target familiar genres, attitudes and activities. Chapter 5, 'Dinner Parties: Eating Out, Coming Together', examines some of the ways in which canonical representations of the Last Supper are evoked and disrupted in Mary Beth Edelson's collage poster *Some Living American Women Artists/Last Supper* (1972), a wishful representation of women artists in positions of power which they didn't in reality have, combined with a critique of the gender politics of organized religion. In her infamous *The Dinner Party* (1974–79), Judy Chicago celebrates iconic female figures by portraying them *as* table settings, the implications of which have barely been addressed in relevant critical writing. The chapter also explores the strategies of menacing defamiliarization in Martha Rosler's *Semiotics of the Kitchen* (1975), where a banal inventory of kitchen utensils gradually morphs into a performed threat of imminent violence, akin to Bobby Baker's only superficially light-hearted *Kitchen Show* (1991). *Housewives with Steakknives* (1985), an early painting by Sutapa Biswas, emerges as a visual manifesto for a feminist reclamation of the world starting with the kitchen, where the goddess Kali leads a revolution for artists/housewives and, most of all, against their distinction.

Like feminist sociocultural critique, art informed by feminism strove to uncover the patriarchal but also class- and 'race'-based underpinnings of the ideology of the nuclear family. Chapter 6, 'Family Albums: World-Making as Compensation', examines Jo Spence's funny and disturbing re-creations of the family album, in and beyond her involvement in phototherapy, which expose the performative nature of family roles. Probing, unsentimental and at least partially redemptive, *The Only Woman* (1985) by Marie Yates intersperses photographs from the artist's real family album with personal artefacts, news reports and cryptic textual fragments that teeter between the public and private; while addressing the mourning process of a daughter for her mother, the work also investigates the representational strategies and affective weight of family photographs and narratives. In *Rosa Alice: Ordinary/Extraordinary* (1980–81), May Stevens contrasts History with family narratives by overlaying two life stories, that of revolutionary leader and writer Rosa Luxemburg with the artist's mother's life, marred by poverty and mental illness. Rather than labelling each life as either ordinary or extraordinary, the work invites viewers to consider the extraordinary in the ordinary and vice versa. Building on Abigail's Solomon-Godeau's concept of 'tactical haunting', namely 'the conjuring of historical absences and silences' (Solomon-Godeau 2006, pp. 371–401), the chapter explores the process and ramifications of injecting history with the repressed stories of its oppressed. Faith Ringgold's series of narrative-quilted canvases *The French Collection* (1991–93) narrates the life and work of a struggling African-American woman artist in Modernist Paris, fictional and yet not entirely unlikely. Through her eyes, the gendered, racial and racist ambiguities of primitivism are teased out: referencing familiar paintings such as *Sunflowers* and *Demoiselles d'Avignon*, *The French Collection* renders the Modernist canon not exactly unrecognizable but rather contingent on the invisible contributions of its non-European others. In a similar vein, Zoe Leonard's *The Fae Richards Photo Archive*, a photographic biography of an fictional black lesbian actress whose life spans the twentieth century, boldly claims the status of a historical document of a life story that would have been most likely confined to oblivion. Archives haunted by lacunae are also at the centre of *Jeanne Duval: A Melodrama* (2003) by Scots-Ghanaian artist and poet Maud Sulter, in which the process of researching the biography of Baudelaire's famous yet elusive partner leads to a retelling of established stories of art from the angrily defamiliarizing perspective of the artist's muse.

The book closes with a double postscript that questions the ambiguity of endings, especially in the case of politically motivated cultural production, and the appropriateness of drawing conclusions. I propose that the feminist uncanny has been one of the most enduring legacies of the Women's Liberation Movement for contemporary artists. A wide range of feminist uncanny practices is evoked through a few representative works, from a spoof of early education books that bitingly comments on the role of contemporary art in the inculcation of middle-class identity in Britain, to the continuation of unsettling deployments of craft that underline its subversive potential, and the radical reconsideration of the remit of psychoanalysis and its relationship to popular and even low culture. The second part of the postscript considers some revealing temporal complexities in the work of Monica Ross and proposes a seemingly self-defeating but serendipitously uncanny feminist strategy: angry melancholia.

1

The Uncanny Feminine

The uncanniness of 'The "Uncanny"'

In her introduction to her book *The Female Thermometer: 18th Century Culture and the Invention of the Uncanny* (1995), Terry Castle draws the reader's attention to an absent text, which nevertheless haunts her book throughout. The text is, unsurprisingly, Freud's 1919 essay 'The "Uncanny"', 'magnificent, troubling, and inspired' (Castle 1995, p. 3), which Castle values for its fundamental paradox of attempting to shed light on a persistently dark corner of the Enlightenment project, and which she proceeds to mine as a theme index. What 'The "Uncanny"' demonstrates so powerfully is the powerlessness of reason in the face of both the individual and cultural unconscious, famously played out in the Enlightenment and its subsequent critiques from the Frankfurt School and 'a phalanx of historians and social theorists – from E. P. Thompson to Michel Foucault' (Castle 1995, p. 6). While most of the attackers of the Enlightenment focus on the authoritarian and oppressive compensations for the repressed powerlessness of reason, Freud both addresses and performs this powerlessness: first through the choice of the uncanny, 'an archaic fantasy of fear, long ago exiled to the unconscious, that nonetheless "returns to view"' (ibid., p. 7); and secondly and most importantly, by demonstrating, in his own (thinking/writing) practice, the inadequacies of reason, including his own reasoning. Castle finds in Freud's essay a template for her own scholarly work, which is framed by the knowledge that 'the more we seek enlightenment, the more alienating our world becomes' (ibid., p. 15). Although she doesn't quite spell out the instructive capacity of the flaws and contradictions in Freud's essay, she makes the important point that the object of the Enlightenment's faltering pursuit of knowledge is often cast as female or even femininity itself (ibid., p. 16). Alongside developing technologies of surveillance and spectacle, Castle relates the uncanny to major eighteenth-century preoccupations, including masquerade, sexual impersonation and a resulting blurring of strict categorizations in gender and sexuality (1995, esp. chapters 5 and 6). For Castle, the emergence of the uncanny is therefore presented as a side effect of the Enlightenment and its will to knowledge, both intellectual and technological, and is also tied to growing anxieties around threats to established economies of gender and sexuality.

'The "Uncanny"' haunts this book too, like so many others. And yet, like Castle, I hesitate summarizing the essay here, for a number of reasons. First and most obviously, it is unlikely that any reader of this text would not be familiar with Freud's essay (and if they aren't yet, *The Feminist Uncanny* will hopefully motivate them to read it first-hand and carefully, rather than providing them with pass notes). Secondly, 'The "Uncanny"' is awkwardly structured, starting with a lengthy and not altogether gripping discussion on the lexicographical oppositional pair *heimlich–unheimlich*; and culminating in a heavily manipulated and partial reading of a short story and an even more disappointing insistence on the prevalence of the castration complex, despite many suggestions of the complexity and ultimate undecidability of the uncanny. Freud's essay on the uncanny has always been more interesting to parse and deconstruct than to summarize.

Where does an infamous but unwieldy point of origin leave a concept as prevalent if not popular as the uncanny? In a rather nebulous place, as Anne Masschelein suggests in her ingeniously titled book *The Unconcept* (2011).[1] Masschelein's book offers a genealogical perspective on the 'uncanny', based on the recognition that, not only is Freud's formulation of the uncanny far from clear-cut, but that the position and function of the concept since Freud, through the decades and in different disciplines, is also widely divergent, further complicating an already convoluted picture. The quotation marks that cradle and suspend the 'uncanny' in Freud's essay title acquire a translocated and expanded meaning in Masschelein's book. Rather than a concept with a more or less defined meaning, the 'unconcept' of the 'uncanny' has often come close to becoming an empty signifier, whose accelerated circulation and eventual canonization in the 1990s is symptomatic of typically fin de siècle concerns, including alienation and anxiety on the precipice of all the influential 'post-'s, already then on the wane. Masschelein charts fluctuations in both significance and signification through the decades, convincingly proposing that the uncanny is '*a late-twentieth century theoretical concept*' (2011, p. 4, emphasis in the original). She thus demonstrates that the uncanny became a vehicle for a certain kind of post-structuralist theory which focused on 'the metaphorical nature of "scientific" concepts' (ibid., p. 5), aimed to show theory and practice – particularly of writing – as deeply intertwined, and which is 'uniquely characterised by a meta- or self-reflexive concern with concepts' (ibid., p. 7).

Gender, sexuality and feminism are all curiously absent from the wide range of disciplinary fields and schools of ideas under consideration in Masschelein's study, even though both Sarah Kofman and Hélène Cixous' treatments of the uncanny are discussed in detail. Following Masschelein's advice to not rely exclusively on indices and similar bibliographical tools (p. 17),[2] I would argue that the feminist uncanny is far more expansive than feminist texts and works that address it directly, as the second part of this book hopes to show. Writing on 'woman' and 'the feminine' as mutable concepts (though not quite 'unconcepts'), Alice Jardine examines the processes by which the anthropocentrism of humanism came to be replaced by a another, denaturalized model in modernity, not exactly empty but with 'woman' at its core (1985, p. 24). 'Gynesis', this process of denaturalization in the feminine, embraces alienation as a new existential dwelling or, in other words, makes a home of the condition of homelessness. In her book, Jardine lays the foundations for a hauntology, a hybrid of ontology and haunting, or a haunted ontology, that is implicitly gendered. 'It is a strange new world [that the writers of modernity] have invented, a world that is *unheimlich*. And such strangeness has necessitated speaking and writing in new strange ways' (Jardine 1985, p. 24). Alongside the great (male) Modernist masters, Jardine begins to chart the essential difference of gynesis by French feminist theorists, including Cixous, Irigaray and Kristeva. Without misrecognizing the real dangers of gynesis for women, notably being cast as 'poet and madwoman' (p. 49), Jardine prepares the ground for '*new* configurations of woman and modernity' (p. 264), which at the time of the publication of her book were yet to be undertaken. The feminist uncanny aims to contribute to this work by focusing on a distinctly feminist exploitation of the already established links between 'woman' and the unhomely 'strangeness', which Jardine addresses. There are grave risks involved in the project of the feminist uncanny, considering how closely it grazes against harmful stereotypes and received ideas and that it remains unwilling to turn its back on the compromised and compromising critical apparatus of Freudian psychoanalysis. Yet such recklessness is fundamental to the feminist uncanny, which meets Freud's insistence on a single explanation of the uncanny hinging on the castration complex with a vibrant and contagious ambivalence, not least towards the author of 'The "Uncanny" ' himself.

The uncanny core

In 'The "Uncanny" ' (1919), Freud sets out to investigate an area in which, as he claims, aesthetics has shown little interest. The uncanny, he argues, has been neglected because it is neither beautiful nor pleasurable. The essay proceeds with a *quasi*-lexicographical survey which succeeds in demonstrating, however, that there may be a better reason for this neglect. It transpires that *heimlich* is a word the meaning of which develops in the direction of such peculiar ambiguity that it finally coincides with its opposite, *unheimlich*. This uncomfortable semantic ambiguity – which is a trace of a deeper-ingrained, psychical ambivalence – plays a crucial role in the formation of the uncanniness of the feminine on the one hand, and the emergence of the feminist uncanny on the other.

Once the unpopularity of the uncanny 'in the specialist literature of aesthetics' is noted (Freud 1919, p. 339), Freud proceeds to uncover its banality. In opposition to Ernst Jentsch's interpretation of the uncanny as the result of intellectual uncertainty, especially as to whether something or someone is alive or dead, animate or inanimate (1995), Freud locates it in certainty. Uncanny is something well known and familiar that is deliberately forgotten, that is to say repressed. He traces the uncanny back to the dread of castration, the inconceivability of one's own mortality, childhood beliefs that have seemingly been overcome, as well as superstitions that should have been collectively grown out of. Childhood and primitive beliefs in the omnipotence of thoughts, sorcery and animism are quick to resurface in the face of what the evolved intellectual faculties of adult humans still find impossible to handle. Where repression is to be found, either in terms of the development of the individual or of the species (ontogenetically or phylogenetically), the uncanny *may* follow. Granted that not every instance of repression results in some form of uncanny manifestation (its traces may also, for example, emerge as symptoms, in dreams, etc.), the uncanny is always the belated mark of repression: the prefix 'un-' is the token of a repression already at work (Freud 1919, p. 368).

The uncanny is located at the 'very core' of psychoanalysis, at the point of convergence of all the principal and most radical psychoanalytic discoveries (Dolar 1991, pp. 5–6). Yet this doesn't make it any easier to grasp. On the contrary, it is too pivotal, too pervasive, too blurred and too commonplace, alluding, as it does, to both the beginning and termination of life. The uncanny remains alien, because it is too close to contemplate. Jacques Lacan translates the German term '*unheimlich*' as '*extime*' (extimate), to describe this condition of simultaneous extreme closeness and irreconcilable otherness. As Jacques-Alain Miller shows, the place of the extimate may be occupied by either the (big) Other, namely the locus of the symbolic and, potentially, of truth, or the small other, which is to say the *objet petit a* (Miller 1988, pp. 123–4). Lacan posits the *objet petit a* (untranslated at his own insistence, Lacan 1998, p. 282) as his alternative to the object in the vocabulary of psychoanalysis, where *a* is what fuels desire – *not its object* – precisely by being ungraspable. The *objet petit a* is also the unrepresentable remainder in every act of representation: *a* is the leftover of every articulation allowed in the symbolic and hence it is necessarily of the real (Zizek 1989, p. 132). Finally and most importantly, *a* is the symbol of the lacking phallus, the phallus as lack (Lacan 1998, p. 112). It is this very lack that the Lacanian woman is lacking. And yet it is also woman who 'serve[s] as the object *a*', as a 'bodily remainder' in the constitution of male subjectivity. 'The being that is sexualised female in and through discourse is also a place for the deposit of the remainders produced by the operation of language' (Irigaray 1985b, p. 90).

The purpose of this re-exposition of some uncanny principles is to show that the feminine is woven through the psychoanalytic uncanny from its inception. Freud also gives many thematic examples of femininity's implication in *Unheimlichkeit*. As his essay on fetishism clearly shows, the dread of castration can be virtually projected onto the female body, which is perceived as having been already punished with castration by the father (1927). It is in the presumably already perpetrated castration of the female body that Kristeva detects 'the universal partnership with death of the penis-lacking feminine (1992, p. 27)'. In 'The "Uncanny"' this link is elaborated further and more explicitly. Freud revisits the German saying '*Liebe ist Heimweh*' ('love is homesickness', 1919, p. 368), to point out that the female and, primordially, the mother's body is emblematic of a feeling of at-home-ness which has however been repressed, and which thereby renders this body un-homely. In an earlier essay, 'The Theme of the Three Caskets' (1913), Freud examines the mythological and literary *topos* of the three caskets/sisters/goddesses/Fates, between whom the hero is invited to choose. The third, most beautiful and seductive candidate who invariably gets chosen is bound to betray the hero's wish to return to his first home. 'But it is in vain that an old man yearns for the love of woman as he had it first from his mother; the third of the Fates alone, the silent Goddess of Death, will take him into her arms' (Freud 1913, p. 247). So while the compulsion to repeat is affirmed, so is its innate impossibility: one may never go back, especially not back home. Freud plays out this impossibility in his uncanny treatise on the death drive, 'Beyond the Pleasure Principle' (1920), where repetition is deployed in writing as if to stall its own conclusion and textual 'death'. While repetition wards off the end(ing) and allows the opportunity for each living being to reach it in its own way, it also affirms the inexorability of its arrival.

There is nothing straightforward about the death drive, and even less so about the text of 'Beyond the Pleasure Principle'. In the second part of *The Post Card*, Derrida deftly turns Freud's essay into a virtual kaleidoscope through which he awakens the essay's textuality and follows various intertextual threads that take him from Freud's personal correspondence to Lacan's reading of Poe's short story 'The Purloined Letter' and back (1987). However, as is the case with most of Derrida's writing, this is yet another elaboration on Derridean philosophy using the texts of others as pretexts. Unlike Derrida, Jean Laplanche grapples with 'Beyond the Pleasure Principle' with a psychoanalyst's conscientiousness that seems to frustrate even him, as Freud's essay refuses to make sense. While acknowledging the contribution of Daniel Lagache on the issue of aggressiveness, Laplanche also points out the shortcomings of any critique of a text as flawed as 'Beyond the Pleasure Principle':

> To criticize, in the etymological sense of the term, is to choose, to redistribute the cards, to 'air out' what has been mixed. ... It goes without saying that with the death drive, there was a poor deal of the cards; the hand is all wrong. But is it sufficient, in that case, to begin the deal all over again and to effect a more correct combination? We believe that it is insufficient simply to redistribute the cards without first attempting to interpret the previous 'deal'. (Laplanche 1976, p. 109)

Before concluding with a graph representing the 'strange chiasmus' of the sex and the death drives, placing face to face and against one another Freud's constitutive but fragile pairs of opposites (p. 124), Laplanche attempts to explain just what is wrong with the hand that 'Beyond the Pleasure Principle' deals. First, the essay is dominated by 'a theoretical exigency' or compulsion (*Zwang*, as in the composite *Wiederholungszwang*, the compulsion to repeat) (pp. 109–10). This compulsion can be witnessed in other of Freud's work and as a rule emerges whenever the opportunity for a theoretical leap appears, which might shed doubt on previous conclusions. Freud curiously does not follow some of his arguments through, interrupting them with dogmatic aphorisms that compromise the very specificity of the psychoanalytic approach. By tracing Freud's terms of engagement back to Breuer and neurophysiology, Laplanche calls attention to the death drive of, and within, psychoanalysis itself: the purely Freudian notion of the drive is nearly diminished to the biologist banality of the instinct (p. 123): 'Beyond the Pleasure Principle' shows psychoanalysis in the midst of an identity crisis and on the precipice of self-destruction. Laplanche suggests that the death drive may have also been contrived as a defence against the risk of psychoanalysis losing the edge of its negativity to be reduced to ego psychology, but in this case, the cure was almost worse than the disease.[3] If, ultimately, death is 'the most radical – but also the most sterile – principle' in the logic of the unconscious (p. 126), the deeply rooted link between death and femininity may start to become understandable, if no less damaging.

In the words of Elizabeth Bronfen, who views 'The Theme of the Three Caskets' as a gender-oriented foreshadowing of 'Beyond the Pleasure Principle', 'woman functions as privileged trope for the uncanniness of unity and loss, of independent identity and self-dissolution' (1992b, p. 56; and 1992a, esp. chapter 2 'The Lady Vanishes'). Yet as the dumbness of the chosen candidate suggests ('the silent Goddess of Death'), the connection between femininity and death is not exclusively based on the original homely site of the maternal body, nor of its evocation of returns. In 'Femininity' (1933), Freud laments the premature arrest of psychical evolution and flexibility in his female patients: 'A woman of [about thirty] … often *frightens* us by her psychical rigidity and unchangeability.' It is 'as though, indeed, the difficult development of femininity had exhausted the possibilities of the person concerned' (1933, p. 169).

Such unnerving rigidity is strongly reminiscent of Freud's reading of the myth of the Medusa. One of the Gorgon sisters, Medusa was a priestess of goddess Athena who was seduced (or raped, in other versions) by Poseidon, breaking her chastity vows. As punishment, Athena turned her beautiful hair into live snakes and cursed her so that she turned to stone anyone who met her gaze. According to Freud, Medusa's hair represents the threat of castration, as the proliferation of phallic snakes suggests the detachability of the male member, which is dreaded in the castration complex. Although the threat of the Medusa, represented in her uncanny snake hair, is clearly castratory,[4] the apotropaic uses of the decapitated (i.e. 'castrated') Medusa's head suggest that the psychical rigidity by which she punishes her victims offers them some degree of compensation by alluding to erectile function (1940). The psychical rigor mortis observed in female patients, which frighten 'us', may well offer *them* the compensation of vindictively causing alarm to their analyst. However, I would like to suggest that the source of uncanniness in the case of Freud's 30-year-old female patients, becomes uncannily unfixed and equivocal, if one follows Lacan's link between anxiety and the flipping of subject and object positions, as I do later in this chapter, in 'The Uncanny and Anxiety'. Is it the rigid unchangeability of female patients that is unsettling, or rather the fear of failure on behalf of their analyst to 'change' them through analysis? And could it be that their analyst's fear is projected onto these women of thirty years, whose bodies are imagined to be monstrous, turned into emblems of their assumed mental fixity?

Unsurprisingly, the myth of the Medusa has come under feminist scrutiny and has inspired numerous reinterpretations (e.g. Garber and Vickers 2003). Her complex Greek and Roman origins as one of the chthonic Gorgon sisters will not be discussed here, even though her recounted transgression (the breaking of chastity vows willingly or by force) and punishment (turning the beauty of her hair and face into something literally petrifying) are both exemplary of gendered expectations, infringements and disciplinary measures. Revisiting the myth of the Medusa in reference to visual representations of the female terrorist, Griselda Pollock points out that, prior to Freud's influential casting of the mythical figure as the illustration of 'castrating terror represented by the site of female sexual difference as anatomy' (Pollock 2013, p. 170), other, potentially empowering interpretations of the Medusa were in circulation. Pollock cites early twentieth-century classical feminist scholar Jane Harrison, who notes that rather than embodying terror herself, it was terror – the terror of her violent beheading – that turned the Medusa into its symbol. According to Harrison, the *Gorgoneion*, that is, the apotropaic amulet portraying the severed, grotesquely grimacing Gorgon's head that is found on ancient shields, urns and coins, came before the gendered narrative that, once again, tied horror to binary anatomical sexual difference (Pollock 2013, p. 171).

In addition to casting horror in the feminine and, more specifically, on the site of female genitals, the cultural transformations of the Medusa since

Figure 1.1 Coin with a Gorgon's Head, 550–546 BCE, Athens. Courtesy of the British Museum.

and under the tacit influence of Freud have conditioned otherness in general (emblematized but not exhausted by sexual difference) as horrific in and of itself. It is not, after all, incidental that the *Gorgoneion* is so often featured on weaponry: war as a context of the encounter with the other as mortal enemy shapes the significance of both the *Gorgoneion* and the Medusa, rather than the other way around. The association between the Medusa and war does not go unnoticed or unexploited in Cixous' rousing 'The Laugh of the Medusa', discussed in the next chapter. Feminist philosopher Adriana Cavarero views the Medusa as 'a feminist guide to understanding violence against the vulnerable' in Griselda Pollock's interpretation (Pollock 2013, p. 173), a mirror in which humans can contemplate their own terrifying dehumanization (Cavarero 2009, p. 16). However, I also find in Cavarero's words an outline of the feminist uncanny, specifically of the potential of turning the monstrous feminine into a terrifying instrument of feminist dissent. As the quotation below suggests, the gendering of horror is not necessarily a patriarchal afterthought but a feminist turn of the screw that both intensifies and renders horror uncanny – terrifying in its familiarity.

> Medusa belongs to the female gender. ... As in every theatre of violence that we know of to date, men continue to be the unchallenged protagonists. But when a woman steps to the front of the stage of horror, the scene turns darker and, *although more disconcerting, paradoxically more familiar*. Repugnance is heightened, and the effect is augmented, as though horror, just as the myth already knew, required the feminine in order to reveal its authentic roots. (Cavarero 2009, p. 14, emphasis added)

In spite of the convenient grouping of the feminine and the uncanny in psychoanalysis as two of its darkest subjects, Freud unhesitatingly concedes that psychoanalysis itself is perceived as uncanny for the same reasons that epilepsy and madness can potentially have uncanny effects on his contemporary 'layman'. Madness raises an awareness of 'hitherto unsuspected' forces in the psychical apparatus, which, once witnessed at work in others, are dimly sensed – remembered – in one's own self. Since psychoanalysis lays bare and deals with such *heimlich* (secret) forces, it also takes on an uncanny quality by association (1919, p. 366), as well as, I would add, through the implication of its own analytical and therapeutic faculties in the realm the mysterious and inexplicable, perhaps even the supernatural. Like a sorcerer, Freud boldly conjures what should have remained hidden in the psyches of his patients. His feminist undutiful and subversive apprentices return to his writings to unveil what he himself chose (or had) to forget, by exposing the uncanniness of his essay on the 'uncanny'.

The significance of the uncanny in the relationship between feminism and psychoanalysis consists of at least three levels. Conceptually, in Freud's work femininity and uncanniness intersect in multiple and complex ways, as this section shows, which automatically places the (un)concept of the uncanny centre stage in any discussion of psychoanalytic feminisms. Textually, because 'The "Uncanny"' is, ultimately, 'a great text for arguing with, for working out what is at stake in its variously problematic, confused, strangely paradoxical lines of argument and demonstration' (Royle 2003, p. 7) – and the relationship between feminism and psychoanalysis is one dominated by arguments, some of which are addressed in the next chapter. And intertextually because, as the next section 'Uncanny Couplings' suggests, the uncanny (or something uncanny) spreads through Freud's texts, as does femininity, and they cross paths, disappear and resurface time and again, in unexpected and unlikely places.

Uncanny couplings (An Interlude)[5]

For Freud, women remained largely a 'dark continent' because he at least (usually tacitly) recognized that his theories did not equally apply to the whole of the population. As so much feminist critical writing on the case of Dora also suggests (Bernheimer and Kahane 1985), the patient whom he failed to treat and who fired him in frustration, Freud's early failures with gendered disorders like hysteria shaped his career, his thinking on femininity and, subsequently, his critical reception. Yet Freud's famous and derided defeat has the potential to be radically reinterpreted and repurposed.

When someone first sets out to work on Freud and femininity, the list of relevant writings seems reassuringly straightforward to compile and short in comparison to the volume of his complete published works: his work on hysteria with Breuer and some of his case histories; all essays on sexuality (conveniently assembled in the eponymous tome of the Penguin Freud Library) touch on sexuation – the acquisition of a position and role in the sexual economy – and thus femininity; 'Femininity' in the *New Introductory Lectures on Psychoanalysis* (1933), where Freud revisits his main findings on the subject and takes stock; and a few of his writings on art and literature, including 'Medusa's Head' (1940) and 'The Theme of the Three Caskets' (1913), an elaboration on a scene from *The Merchant of Venice* and the mythological motif which binds femininity with death. Yet this is hardly the whole story: for Freud, it was not just femininity that was a dark continent; rather, it was darkness, the unknown, the unrepresentable that were feminine. Jacqueline Rose and Sarah Kofman, among many others, have explored the implications of this discovery, with Kofman going as far as to argue that femininity forms the unconscious of psychoanalysis (Kofman 1985). This has been the disturbingly mixed blessing of psychoanalytic feminism: femininity is at once excluded and constitutes the privileged terrain from which to critique the site of its exclusion.

This mixed blessing, one of the many to be found in Freud's life and work, raises the question of the interface between the centre and the margins and leads straight to a literally marginal – peritextual – space in Freud's writing, his footnotes. Freud never finished revising his ideas, amending and adding to his articles continuously, even if he wasn't pursuing their immediate republication. Adding footnotes was a favourite method, not necessarily out of laziness but possibly thanks to a desire to preserve his writings as historical documents charting the development of his ideas. As Darian Leader demonstrates, Freud's footnotes can be read as a roadmap of Freud's responses to vibrant debates in psychoanalytic circles (2000). In 1919, Freud finishes his long essay 'The "Uncanny"' by illustrating some of the limits and limitations of the concept. Although fairy tales often contain scenes and episodes that should normally strike an uncanny cord, they generally tend not to, he explains, because the whole genre of the fairy tale is exempt from the rationalist universe to which Freud's readership is assumed to be committed. He specifically names a story by the Brothers Grimm, 'The Three Wishes', as an example of 'the animistic standpoint of the omnipotence of thoughts and wishes'. 'All this is very striking', he admits, 'but not in the least uncanny' (Freud 1919, p. 369). In the same year, he also adds a footnote on nightmares to *The Interpretation of Dreams* (1900). Defending the main principle that dreams are fundamentally wish-fulfilment, he explains how and why they sometimes go wrong. While there is no question that wish-fulfilment must bring pleasure, what is less clear is to whom. The dreamer's 'relation to his wishes is quite a peculiar one', Freud explains (1900, p. 737, n. 1); a dreamer's wishes may be repudiated and censored, and thus their fulfilment would be a source of anxiety as opposed to pleasure. To illustrate 'the gulf between the unconscious and the conscious (between the repressed and the ego)' (Freud 1900, p. 709), he relates a 'familiar' central-European folktale – none other than 'The Three Wishes', which he cited as an example of where uncanniness evaporated in 'The "Uncanny"':

> A good fairy promised a poor married couple to grant them the fulfilment of their first three wishes. They were delighted, and made up their minds to choose their three wishes carefully. But a smell of sausages being fried in the cottage next door tempted the woman to wish for a couple of them. They were there in a flash; and this was the first wish-fulfilment. But the man was furious, and in his rage wished that the sausages were hanging on his wife's nose. This happened too; and the sausages were not to be dislodged from their new position. This was the second wish-fulfilment; but the wish was the man's, and its fulfilment was most disagreeable for his wife. You know the rest of the story. *Since after all they were in fact one – man and wife –* the third wish was bound to be that the sausages should come away from the woman's nose. (Freud 1900, p. 737, n. 1)

It is baffling that the same example of the absence of the uncanny is used, in the very same year, as an illustration of how a dream may turn into a nightmare. There are a few gender-specific observations to make in response to this folkoric introjection. First, the wife is predictably cast in the role of the unconscious: childlike in her impulsiveness, she is seduced by her own appetites, is quick to change her mind and opts for instant gratification. The husband-ego is left to clean up the mess, even though this is at least half-due to his own angry impulse in the story. Yet the most crucial implication of the use of this folktale as example is also the most explicitly stated: man and wife are one – just as the ego and the id are, and should remain, one,[6] or at the very least in the same locale,[7] in the marital home, together. But what if the wife decided to leave the husband after his humiliating punishment? Or what if she took the third wish for herself, made her resentful husband disappear and learnt to live happily ever after, forever enveloped in the aroma of the sausages permanently (and phallicly) swinging from her nose? Freud was perhaps right that there is nothing uncanny in the story as such. Uncanniness only begins to flicker through the cracks of this comically unhappy marriage; it emerges only when one focuses on the split in and between the couple, the momentary but momentous wobble in their oneness.

Feminism undertook the rewriting of this and many other stories that Freud called on to illustrate his principles; they did so not only to set the record straight, or give their side of the story, but because they knew – from Freud – that to do so had the potential of overthrowing the carefully maintained balance of psychoanalytic theory and practice, of unfixing the subject, turning the dream of the talking cure into a countercultural nightmare. There is a significant aesthetic side to this upheaval inspired by and against psychoanalysis, which the second part of this book examines, as well as social and material consequences, in regard to care-giving and domesticity, defamiliarizing language and the recasting of fact and fiction as a messy continuum rather than an opposition.

For feminism, Freud's most valuable legacy consists of an attention to language in its broadest sense – from the work of representation to the workings of becoming a speaking subject – inflected by the acknowledgement that the most acute reading is one inspired by antagonism. This is not the same as bad faith, and the deconstructive adage of interpretation 'against the grain' doesn't quite cover it. Just as he studied slips of the tongue and of the pen, Freud exemplifies in practice the fecundity of blind spots. Amazingly, Freud has helped fashion some of the analytical tools by which to unpick even his own work. More disappointingly (and yet even more provocatively), Freud's repeated failure to live up to the full groundbreaking potential of some of his key ideas, exemplifies how revolutions go awry, and provides a roadmap for at least spotting, if not escaping, the gravitational pull of established models of thought and practice (cf. Laplanche 1999, pp. 52–83).

In representing the ego and the id as husband and wife, Freud reveals more than a reliance on heteronormative sexual economies, or the gendering of the unconscious and the repressed. Intended or not, there is more than a little critical dig at the institution of marriage in this laden illustration. The marriage metaphor has also been used by psychiatrist and academic Thomas Szasz, where this small dig blossoms into an explicit attack. In 'Psychiatry and Matrimony: Arrangements for Living', Szasz parallels the institution of marriage with institutionalized psychiatric practice, in which he casts the psychiatrist as husband and the patient as wife. In a non-expert but rhetorically powerful linguistic investigation that smacks of the first few pages of Freud's essay 'The "Uncanny"', Szasz notes that the meaning of the phrase to 'put away' (one's wife) has evolved from divorce, in biblical English, to 'a euphemism for committing her to a madhouse' (Szasz 1976, p. 146). The word 'commitment' 'betrays the idea that not only is the patient committed to the hospital, but that patient and psychiatrist, like wife and husband, are also "committed" to each other' (ibid., p. 156). With the creation of asylums and later of hospital psychiatry, 'madwoman' emerged as a viable career choice for women, alongside the longer established old maid, wife or nun (i.e. 'bride of Jesus') (ibid., p. 148). Even the imagery and rhetoric of lengthy psychiatric hospitalization with all its frustrations and complaints from both parties, resemble the tedium of long years of marriage (ibid., p. 160). In a breathtaking footnote that could have come straight out of a radical feminist pamphlet, in content if not in tone, Szasz spells out the power inequalities that govern marriage and psychiatry alike:

> In American slang, the two most common vulgar terms for sexual intercourse – namely, 'fuck' and 'screw', both of which are used in the sense of the male doing 'it' to the female – also mean cheating or taking advantage of someone. Homely language thus reflects more honestly than does technical language the frequently exploitative nature of the sexual, and marital, relationship. These terms are also commonly applied to the psychiatric relationship by those who disapprove of the psychiatrist's uncontrolled power over his patient. (ibid., p. 170, note)

'Homely language' spells out the casual acts of oppression and violence that other formal – notably scholarly and scientific – languages strive to gloss over. The heteronormative couple of the patriarchal marriage emerges as a powerful metaphor for women's oppression and also for the critical continuities between oppression in the home, in the public sphere and in the symbolic; and between female oppression and the repression of the feminine.

The uncanny and anxiety

Lacan begins his seminar on anxiety (1962–63) in a manner that is reminiscent of the awkwardness of 'The "Uncanny"'.[8] It is not in Lacan's style to express hesitation, but he chooses to share with his audience the surprise of a colleague at hearing Lacan's choice of seminar topic. Indignantly and with a hint of menace, Lacan insists that rather than an unlikely or odd choice, anxiety is 'very precisely the meeting point where everything from my previous disquisition is lying in wait for you' (Lacan 2014, p. 3). He proceeds to literally bring anxiety home to his audience: if psychoanalysts (think they) don't feel anxious, they probably should be (p. 5). He turns to Freud's 'Inhibitions, Symptoms and Anxiety' to point out that it doesn't actually address anxiety, identifying a gap (p. 9), like Freud did when he claimed that experts in aesthetics neglected the uncanny at the beginning of his essay. Lacan continues with a discussion of the linguistic origins of 'inhibition' and 'embarrassment', pre-emptively and somewhat defensively noting that 'looking up the etymology doesn't imply any superstition. I help myself to it when it's helpful to me' (p. 10). Just as the uncanny is at the core of Freud's psychoanalytic edifice, anxiety finds itself at the intersection of Lacan's most important concepts and is always already there, at home, in his seminar room, instilled (or simply awakened) in each of his listeners, psychoanalysts and students of psychoanalysis. Importantly, Freud and Lacan set the scene in very similar ways: identifying gaps where they hoped to find answers (or so they claim), turning to language, being defensive and killing time. Tempting though it may be, I will not continue with a close interpretation of Lacan's seminar focused on its telling marginalia, reading it for the plot and not the story, to paraphrase Peter Brooks (1992). Instead, I will try to articulate where and how anxiety meets with the uncanny and consider the significance of their meeting in terms of gender.

At the end of the third meeting, Lacan sets 'The "Uncanny"' as essential reading for the seminar participants. The *Unheimliche*, he explains, appears in the place where the minus *phi* ($-\varphi$) should be (Lacan 2014, p. 42). Minus *phi*, the phallic signifier also stands for imaginary castration since it is inherently lost, an emblem of absence or a negative object. Lacan defines the uncanny as the affect triggered by the absence of minus *phi*, namely the lack of Lack. So the uncanny and castration are indeed linked, Lacan suggests, but not because the uncanny exposes castration anxiety, as Freud argues, but because it replaces it: the uncanny steps in, in minus *phi*'s stead. Strictly speaking, the uncanny therefore represents the minus *phi*, insofar as representation rests of the absence of what is represented and its substitution with a signifier; or, it is a metaphor for minus *phi*, since metaphor rests on the substitution of one signifier with another. Once again, Lacan, the Freudian, and Freud find themselves so close and so far away from one another at once. It is far from accidental that Lacan introduces the relationship between anxiety and the uncanny by alluding to the much admired, widely discussed and fundamentally untranslatable Freudian aphorism 'wo es war, soll Ich werden' (Lacan 2001), which places the id and ego in the same location but not present at the same time. The ego will be where the id was, and the uncanny emerges where castration cannot be found – or, as I'm tempted to suggest, where castration is found to be lacking. The apparent contradiction between casting the uncanny as the representation of castration (Freud) and as a metaphor of its failure (Lacan) dissolves when one considers representation not in terms of exposition but as a necessarily incessant deferral and obfuscation of meaning. At the risk of oversimplification, I would suggest that (Lacanian) anxiety is the affect tied to the phenomenon of the (Freudian) uncanny, which is of course already steeped in affect. However, Lacan is tellingly selective in his reading of 'The "Uncanny"'. If Lacanian anxiety and the Freudian uncanny are indeed inextricably linked, they are only so through the Lacanian uncanny, which I attempt to outline below.

Lacan interprets Freud's lexicographical exploration of the uncanny in the eponymous essay as proof of the importance that Freud attaches to language, arguing that this essay alone would justify the prevalence that Lacan himself gives to the functions of the signifier in his commentary on Freud's work (Lacan

2014, p. 47). For Lacan, the extreme ambiguity of the *heimlich–unheimlich* pair of apparent opposites that eventually merge into one, which Freud notes but doesn't feel the need to elaborate on in too much detail, resonate with the provisional, topological definition that he has already given to anxiety. 'The *Unheim* is poised in the *Heim*' (ibid.), an idea commensurable with the concept of extimacy (Miller 1988), in a manner that mirrors the mirror stage: 'the specular image becomes the image of the double', pointing to a fundamental absence in one's core, or, to put it differently, 'the presence that lies elsewhere' (Lacan 2014, p. 47). While the mirror stage is pivotal in the process of becoming subject, it paradoxically makes the subject appear as object to itself as well as other, highlighting its uncanny lack of autonomy. The uncanny is here cast as the specular shadow of the mirror stage and its conceptual outfall; it is perceived not when the mirror stage doesn't work but when, for a moment, it sees itself for what it is, whenever the interface between the ego and the reflected image is perceived as fissure rather than suture (Lacan 2014, p. 59; and Lacan 2001, pp. 1–9).[9] Lacan, among many others, highlights the role of vision in E. T. A. Hoffmann's 'The Sandman' as well as 'The Devil's Elixir' (which Freud only briefly mentions, despite insisting on its relevance) and notes the convoluted nature of Freud's engagement with both stories. Losing one's way is instrumental to the explication of the uncanny, since it suggests the function of the labyrinth: 'In following each of these twists and turns, however, it's clear that the subject only gets to his desire by always substituting himself for one of his doubles' (Lacan 2014, p. 48).

Further on in the seminar, Lacan elucidates another dimension of anxiety, still in terms of vision, or rather an apparition, in space and time: the uncanny always enters 'suddenly, all at once' (Lacan 2014, p. 75). Now the mirror becomes a frame, a window and also a stage for anxiety, in which the uncanny makes its abrupt entrance. Lacan corrects Freud's borrowed definition from Schelling as that which should have remained hidden but has come to light, as 'that which *may not* be said' (ibid., emphasis in the original), putting prohibition centre stage. It is the framing, the stage that plays the role of the '*un-*' of repression here: 'Anxiety is the appearance, within this framing, of what was already there, at much closer quarters, at home, Heim' (p. 75). As soon as the *Heimliche* enters the frame of the stage, it becomes *Unheimliche*. What kind of change does the frame of anxiety represent? Again, as in the mirror stage, it is a normally imperceptible, sutured, shift that all of a sudden becomes unravelled as it gets seen and heard. Edging closer to castration but also using what seems to me to be a (pre-digital) cinematic metaphor, Lacan describes anxiety as 'the cut', 'without which the presence of the signifier … is unthinkable' (p. 76), but which is normally kept 'off stage'. This kind of cut enables an alternative reading of Freud's dictum 'anatomy is destiny': not anatomy in terms of possessing certain external sexual characteristics but 'ana-tomy' in its etymological sense of dissection, is indeed essential in the process of becoming subject (pp. 236–7). Lacan coins the term 'separtition', not (just) separation but 'partition on the inside' as a more accurate alternative to castration, which unhelpfully alludes to emasculation. The anxiety-inducing effect of uncovering the hidden supports of the subject is iterated, this time as an explanation of 'the topological division between desire and anxiety': anxiety lies 'at the level of the Other, at the level of the mother's body', while desire 'remains forever elided and hidden' (p. 237).

A glimpse behind the scenes of the most fundamental psychical processes, therefore, causes anxiety. In support of this interpretation, Lacan later notes in reference to the subject's relation to the phallus that the subject does not have it as much as he [*sic*] is 'not without' having it. The detour of the double negative is a necessary protective buffer. 'The phallus mustn't be seen to be involved. If it gets seen, then there's anxiety' (Lacan 2014, p. 89). Writing about the analysis of a male patient by a female analyst, Lacan describes the patient's breakthrough as successfully mourning the absence of castration in his wife, her lack of Lack, at which point the Oedipus complex turns into 'the Oedipal comedy' (Lacan 2014, p. 199). Like the uncanny, anxiety borders both laughter and horror (see also Freud 1919, p. 359).

One final and most important iteration of Lacanian anxiety elaborates a Freudian idea in a more specific direction. One manifestation of the omnipotence of thought is the coming to life of something inanimate, comforting and pleasurable in childhood, common in the animism of 'primitive' cultures as well as in fairy tales, but uncanny to the rational white European adult that Freud had in mind (1919, p. 369). Lacan develops the notion of animation in his own terms of subjectivization. The uncanny doesn't emerge when the inanimate is animated, but when the object becomes subject – of desire. This turning of the tables takes place in the field of vision, which normally helps keep it at bay.

> The eye institutes the fundamental relationship of the *desirable* inasmuch as it always tends, in the relation to the Other, to lead one to misrecognise how beneath the *desirable* there is a *desirer*. … Imagine that you're dealing with the most restful *desirable*, in its most soothing form, a divine statue that is just divine – what would be more *unheimlich* than to see it come to life, that is, to show itself as a *desirer*? (Lacan 2014, p. 271, all emphases in the original)

As the mirror stage reveals the object hidden within the subject, this exchange of gazes between this 'divine' statue and its human admirer (named as Pygmalion and his statue in Freud 1919, p. 369) uncovers the desiring subject in the object of desire. The repercussions of this structure for second-wave feminist debates around the 'objectification of women' and, conversely, women becoming (writing/making) subjects of culture, against the odds, are immeasurable. Not only are such reversals radical, but Lacan inadvertently names them among his definitions of the uncanny, very nearly prefiguring the idea of a feminist uncanny or, more pessimistically, (fore)seeing the uncanny in feminism.

The uncanny feminist

In *Cultural Semantics: Keywords of our Time*, cultural theorist and historian Martin Jay devotes three essays to the uncanny, broadly defined. The framing of this anthology of his columns for *Salmangundi* since 1987, a Humanities and Social Sciences quarterly published by Skidmore College since 1965 and addressed to a general public, is in part inspired by Raymond Williams's *Keywords: A Vocabulary of Culture and Society*, insofar as it also acknowledges 'the ideological charge on certain pivotal terms' (Jay 1998, p. 2). Such terms are subjected to 'a kind of semantic defamiliarisation … until they reveal at a least a few of their secrets' (p. 5). At the same time, the original publishing context allows Jay to use 'a voice … more colloquial and personal – at times also irreverent and flippant' compared to standard academic conventions (p. 5). It is significant that the uncanny constitutes the focal point of three out of seventeen selected essays and is referenced in at least another two, while it also appears to inform Jay's analytical perspective in general.

'The Uncanny Nineties' (Jay 1998, pp. 157–64) provide a well-rounded introduction to the uncanny and particularly its importance to the critical theory of the end of the twentieth century, as well as its interweaving with deconstruction. Jay argues that although the uncanny comes up time and again in discussions of the political, it has often done so in a worryingly depoliticized manner. For instance, the celebration of Derridean hauntology, namely the idea that all hegemonies are haunted by their own repressed, does not prompt or indeed accommodate a distinction between utopian and dystopian ghosts, revolutions and dictatorships, welcome and unwelcome revenants (p. 162). Furthermore, Jay takes issue with the etymological root of the *Unheimliche* as unhomely to point out the thoughtlessness of the uncanny slippage between the literal and the metaphorical when it comes to real homelessness and statelessness (p. 163; see also Vidler 1992, p. 13). Finally, the uncanny is portrayed as a victim of its own success: it has emblematized *fin-de-siècle* concerns with 'the troubled interface between history and memory', (p. 163) so smoothly and with such ease that it is beginning to lose its uncanny edge. 'Abjection Overruled' (Jay 1998, pp. 144–56)[10] takes the Whitney Museum's exhibition 'Abject Art' as its starting point and Kristeva's elaboration of abjection in *Powers of Horror*, to make a similar argument about abjection as about hauntology. Whereas the abject rests on the valorization of pollution and contamination as, at the very least, revealing an uncomfortable truth at the core of the subject, if not actually making a new kind of (non-)subject possible, it also conveniently represents emergent theoretical and cultural orthodoxies in deconstruction, queer theory and feminism, to which it owes its popularity. Jay juxtaposes metaphorical contaminations with threatened real ones, notably HIV, to evoke the ethical and political limitations of the abject, and concludes that even if the abject does propose an alternative to the subject (which it actually does not do), it leaves a lot to be desired in terms of the potential for new communities and collective action. To sum up, Jay shows himself profoundly knowledgeable in uncanny theory but also jaded and ultimately unconvinced by the radical potential of the uncanny, which at the time had become too trendy to remain truly eccentric. However, I believe that there is still an authentically disturbing facet of the uncanny to be found in Jay's essay collection, and it presents itself under the guise of the feminist star academic.

'The Academic Woman as Performance Artist' (Jay 1998, pp. 138–43) begins with an arresting image of an unnamed female academic who, according to an also anonymous report, once walked into the classroom 'wearing nothing but warpaint and a tampax' (p. 138). Her nakedness, aggressively emphasized by *war*paint, is amplified by the evocation of her body's interior thanks to the hanging string of her tampon. This figure introduces a newly emergent, firmly gendered kind of intellectual presence who poses a series of challenges to the academic establishment. In Jay's analysis, the educational models and social conventions that are being defended against this presence come across as positively traditional, especially considering Jay's level of comfort within the discourses of deconstruction in his other two essays on the uncanny, as well as the rest of his academic work (cf. esp. 1994). The academic performance artist blurs the persuasiveness of what she says with the impact of her self-presentation, thus eroding the academic values of objectivity and even meritocracy. In her attack on academic conventions, she mobilizes identity politics on a literal level by 'getting personal' and/or deploys a range of female stereotypes, including, tellingly, 'the woman as avenging virago, castrating Medusa' (p. 140). Jay cites a self-reflective passage from Jane Gallop's *Thinking Through the Body*, in which she explains how she arrived at the look that Jay describes as 'sexual predator' (p. 139) but which she views as a 1940s femme (p. 141). What is at stake is a struggle for power fought on many fronts:

> No longer the passive object of male gazes, they look back shamelessly and without apology, as if the role of the hysteric in Charcot's celebrated amphitheatre at Salpêtrière is now to be played by Manet's brazen Olympia. (Jay 1998, p. 141).

The range of images and archetypes evoked is revealing and inherently uncanny: the hysteric made into a simultaneously instructive and titillating spectacle; the virago; the Medusa; a menstruating amazon; and a 'brazen' sex worker, who upsets the conventions of the female nude by looking back. Jay sees some value, or at least some purpose in these performances, but also fears their excesses (represented by none other than Camille Paglia), which, he believes, would lead to the trivialization of the important issues they purport to tackle. While attempting to defang the uncanny, to show how it has become a trend and a politically liberal one at that, Jay stumbles across a current and genuine source of it – not femininity, nor women, but the feminist female academic, in her eccentric, aggressive and insistent embodiment.

In his readings of Toni Morrison and Nadine Gordimer, Homi Bhabha casts the uncanny as intrinsically connected with femininity, not for any essentialist, biological or reproductive reasons but because of the privileged and culturally overdetermined association between woman and the domestic sphere. Bhabha draws a connection between Freud's citation of Schelling's definition of the uncanny as what ought to have remained secret but has come to light and Hannah Arendt's description of the distinction between private and public along the lines of 'things that should be hidden and things that should be shown' (Arendt cited in Bhabha 1994, p. 10). Since the private sphere, inextricably mapped onto domesticity, is thus systematically repressed, if not disavowed, the figure of woman becomes marginalized and edited out alongside it. By making such divisions visible and attempting to challenge them, feminism, thus

> disturbs the symmetry of private and public which is now shadowed, or uncannily doubled, by the difference of genders which does not neatly map on

> to the private and the public, but becomes disturbingly supplementary to them. … the personal – *is*-the political; the world-*in*-the-home. (ibid., p. 11).

This chapter has not been an overview of literature on the uncanny but a selective outline that teases out its gendered foundations. Had it been a comprehensive overview it wouldn't have failed to mention Mike Kelley's exhibition *The Uncanny* (Sonsbeek, Arnhem 1993 and Tate Liverpool 2004) and its intellectually ambitious catalogue, which includes a selection of writings on the subject, most notably an incisive essay by John C. Welchman that examines the history of the uncanny as a concept, Kelley's contribution, the uncanny in the practice of collecting and in contemporary 'human-scaled polychrome sculpture' (Welchman 2004, p. 39). Maria Walsh's concise book *Art and Psychoanalysis* (2013), suggests that almost any encounter between art and psychoanalysis at the very least brushes against uncanniness, even if the uncanny and the death drive are only named in two out of eleven chapters. It is not merely the uncanniness of psychoanalysis, due to its focus on the repressed and the unconscious and its peculiar methods that are ultimately too intuitive and poetic to qualify as science; rather, art viewed through a psychoanalytic lens is emphatically defamiliarized and brims with uncanny potential. Mirrors, real and metaphorical, the obsessiveness barely masked in collections of objects and images, the ambiguous compensations offered by objects, (dream) screens, opportunities for re-enactment and repetition, all make art seem inexorably uncanny at its core. Once considered through psychoanalysis, the uncanny in art 'sticks'; once observed, it cannot be unseen.

Another set of contributions addresses not the revolutionary potential of the uncanny, which is assumed and elaborated in a body of feminist theory and will be discussed in the next chapter, but rather the uncanniness in (any) revolution (Zizek 1989, pp. 136–7; Vidler 1992, p. 14; and particularly Mehlman 1977, pp. 3–7 and *passim*), due to cycles of repetition in both (and in between) political practices and texts. Derrida's return to Marx consolidates and has, to a degree, 'branded' this approach through the widely circulated term 'hauntology', a composite of ontology and haunting to underline that no (id)entity is ever completely free of the ghosts it must exorcise in order to protect its boundaries (Derrida 1994). The implication of 'hauntology' is precisely that 'haunting belongs to the structure of every hegemony' (ibid., p. 37) yet, on the other hand, it also means that all haunting is complicit in hegemonic structures. An unhappy but curiously loyal couple, haunting and ontology are stuck together whether they like it or not. All hegemonies have the seeds of revolution in them but also, conversely, all revolutions are on the brink of becoming hegemonic. It is useful, in this context, to be reminded that there is no such thing as pure repetition. 'Repetition demands the new. It is turned towards the ludic, which finds its dimension in this new' (Lacan 1998, p. 61). The devil is always in the playful but crucial detail. In his incomplete psychoanalytic revolution, Freud returns to the Romantic tradition to revisit and revise the *Unheimliche* in light of his discovery of the unconscious. The very name of the 'second wave' posits it as the return of the women's movement, a Second Coming of sorts. In addition to its own past, the second wave also revisits, revises and revives psychoanalysis.

The next chapter homes in on feminist approaches to the uncanny feminine, in which textual blind spots and omissions take centre stage. More often than not, the uncanny continues to be gendered feminine, but with markedly different agendas and consequences. Either a revolutionary force or the manifest spectacle of the monstrosity of the splits and divisions perpetrated by phallogocentrism, the feminist uncanny retains and amplifies the troubling potential of *Unheimlichkeit*, while bearing the scars of its troubled encounter with psychoanalysis. Despite its exposed gender bias (or perhaps thanks to it), the uncanny must be counted among the psychoanalytic contributions to the second wave. Juliet Mitchell demonstrates how psychoanalysis and especially Freud's writings may serve as a descriptive and analytical system of patriarchy (1974). Jacqueline Rose discovers in Freud not only a growing awareness of the vicissitudes of gender performance, but also the acknowledgement that the assumption of the feminine role by women is neither straightforward nor enviable (1986, pp. 83–103). Sarah Kofman casts the idea of penis envy as Freud's makeshift means of mastery of the untameable feminine, which once unpicked, threatens to unravel the whole fabric of psychoanalysis. In Kofman's view, the feminine stands for the unbearable, which is obsessively covered up and insufficiently managed throughout Freud's work (1985, p. 122ff.). While maintaining that the feminine subject is systematically written out in and by psychoanalysis (in other words, that subjectivity, like the libido, is a male prerogative), Irigaray does not hesitate to model her interrogation of the philosophers after Freud and especially Lacan's style (1985a and 1993, for example). To this list, which could be considerably longer, I would add the uncanny. The feminist second wave did not miss its genderedness, but saw in it great potential for the development of a dissident mode of critiquing and ultimately transforming the social, cultural and political structures from which it emerged.

2

The Feminist Uncanny

Doomed from the start

Maintaining that the feminist uncanny is both (properly) uncanny and (fiercely) feminist is not stating the obvious. The feminist uncanny alludes to, displaces and revises the psychoanalytic concept of the uncanny in transformative and profoundly masterful ways, so much so that, this book argues, the feminist uncanny, in theory and in practice, should claim its place within the expansive (art and) literature on the uncanny, as a major player. On the other hand, the particular uncanniness of the feminist uncanny stems from the margins of the uncanny canon: it results from hauling back – in anger – the systemically unrepresentable into the position of a culturally productive subject. It is not simply defamiliarizing but deeply unsettling, as it exposes the presumed familiarity of the field of culture as a fraud and, worse, a crime of symbolic violence. In the uncanny, the return of the repressed is not horrifying due to what has been repressed but due to the unearthing of the event of repression. In feminism, the feminine that returns is not monstrous or grotesque in itself, although both monstrousness and grotequeness have been used as vehicles for exploring the effects of its repression. The return of the feminine bears the mark of its imposed exile, from which it broke free; its scars are what is uncanny and its return against the odds is terrible. The feminist uncanny is thus perpetually suspended between revision and revenge.

There are good reasons why feminists have been seduced by even (or especially) the least flattering psychoanalytic ideas on sexuality and sexuation, namely the acquisition of a gendered subject position in the symbolic. Laura Mulvey suggests that feminists discovered a certain 'beauty' in Freudian and Lacanian accounts of castration and feminine sexuality thanks to their

> exact rendering of the frustration experienced under the phallocentric order. [Psychoanalytic theory] gets us near to the roots of our oppression, it brings

> closer an articulation of the problem, it faces us with the ultimate challenge: how to fight the unconscious structured like a language (formed critically at the moment of arrival of language) while still caught within the language of patriarchy? (Mulvey 2009, p. 15)

This appropriation of psychoanalysis by feminism, also advocated by Juliet Mitchell (1974), is only one of second-wave feminism's contributions to a long-standing relationship that has often been too close for comfort. Shulamith Firestone brands psychoanalysis as the 'misguided feminism', making note of their considerable common ground: both 'came as reactions to one of the smuggest periods in Western civilisation, the Victorian Era … but Freud was merely a diagnostician for what feminism purports to cure' (Firestone 2003, p. 41). Eventually, '*Freudianism subsumed the place of feminism as the lesser of two evils*' (ibid., p. 56, emphasis in the original). Both responded to 'centuries of increasing privatisation of family life', the resulting intensification of the oppression of women, and the concomitant ill effects of sexual repression (ibid.). Yet whereas Freud 'questioned the given reality' (ibid., p. 64), subsequent incarnations of psychoanalysis as a therapeutic method were repurposed as a weapon against feminism in the 1960s and thereafter.

Moreover, psychoanalysis in its inception faced struggles similar to second-wave feminism in their common effort to articulate what did not yet exist, struggles which are shared with (other?) avant-gardes. Masud R. Khan's description of Freud's predicament prefigures some of the practices of the feminist uncanny:

> To say what he was discovering, Freud was compelled to borrow the vocabulary of the language as it existed; but Freud had *to distort and extend it* to yield the meanings and insights he meant it to communicate. (Khan cited in Laplanche and Pontalis 1973, p. v, emphasis added)

And even more intriguingly, it appears that Freudian psychoanalysis and feminism come under a comparable threat as their familiarity and influence increases:

> A completely new language gradually crystallised in Freud's hermeneutics of human epistemology. Freud himself was fully and painfully aware that in time the concepts he had so diligently created to establish a new instrument of self-discovery, would get taken over by the vulgar zeal of shallow familiarity. (Khan, ibid.)

On the one hand, the feminist uncanny is that force of perpetual unrest that doesn't allow feminism to 'crystallise' or succumb to 'the vulgar zeal of shallow familiarity'. On the other, feminists have sometimes been counted as among those who misuse, oversimplify, or simply do not comprehend the complexities of psychoanalytic discourse, particularly since its transformative encounter with post-structuralism (e.g. Gallop 1985, p. 19). So although similarities between the aspirations if not impacts of feminism and psychoanalysis are evident, it would be a mistake to assume that they have enjoyed the same status, especially in their relationship with one another.

The long established links between feminism and psychoanalysis may be undeniable but painful to acknowledge for the reasons that Mulvey and Firestone foreground. While strategically useful and even seductively eloquent in regard to women's oppression (as Mulvey suggests), Freudian psychoanalysis colluded in this very oppression (as Firestone argues).

> The notion that there is an intimate, perhaps even fated, historical link between the two [psychoanalysis and feminism] has haunted one substantial section of feminist thought in the last twenty years, even when the specific content not only of Freud's theories of femininity but of many other aspects of psychoanalytic theory have been censured. ' "We were made for each other" says one partner in the flush of rapture; only to be followed at a later, more bitter stage by a transformed insistence that "the relationship was doomed from the start" ... neither side ever lets go ... psychoanalysis and feminism seem to be locked into combat or copulation unto the death.' (Appignanesi and Forrester 1992, p. 460)

The most radical feminist response to the choice between endless combat or fatal copulation comes in the psychoanalytically argued assertion that the insights of psychoanalysis may well speak to (straight) *man*kind but have little relevance to anyone else. One such example is the films and writing of Laura Mulvey in the 1970s, in which she boldly appropriates psychoanalysis 'as a political weapon' (Mulvey 2009, p. 14). The evocation of Bob Dylan's 'Balad of the Thin Man' (1965) in the title of the essay 'Fears, Fantasies and the Male Unconscious *or* "You Don't Know What's Happening, Do You, Mr. Jones?" ' (first published in *Spare Rib*, 1973) on the *Women as Furniture* sculpture series (1969) of Allen Jones, deals a devastating blow to what Mulvey outlines as fundamentally patriarchal structures of spectatorship, not by challenging its aesthetic or political legitimacy (which would be far too obvious), but by confidently pointing out the enormity of the blind spots of its visual – sexual economy. In Dylan's song, Mr Jones comes across as an eminently educated establishment figure, possibly a media critic, who is ultimately defeated by the counterculture, represented by

Dylan's elastic metaphor of the circus or sideshow, with which Mr Jones tries desperately but unsuccessfully to engage. In this song, as in others, Dylan's circus has an equivocal and shape-shifting quality that is intensely disturbing because of its unknowability to outsiders. Mulvey's critique of the deployment of 'woman as spectacle' reveals it as a defensive strategy, a phallic substitute for the male narcissistic fear of castration: although symbolically already castrated, woman's objectified body beautiful comes to stand for the phallus as signifier. In Mulvey's careful interpretation, Allen Jones's work becomes the bridge between the layperson's understanding of sexual fetishism and the feminist theoretical recasting of it as a mass media representational strategy of the female body. In retrospect, this political use of psychoanalysis and the resonance of 'fetishism' in countercultural discourse were equally inspired by Marxist ideas around commodity fetishism, at once following and contributing to the almost alchemical fusion of Marx and Freud in the cultural politics of the New Left (Mulvey 1996, pp. 1–6; Pollock 1999b; Kokoli 2012a, p. 145). While female objectification via phallocentric fetishism is no doubt undermining to women, its power over them is significantly limited:

> Women are constantly confronted with their own image in one form or another, but what they see bears little relation or relevance to their own unconscious fantasies, their own hidden fears and desires. They are being turned all the time into objects of display, to be looked at and gazed at and stared at by men. Yet, in a real sense, women are not there at all. The parade has nothing to do with woman, everything to do with man. The true exhibit is the phallus. Women are simply the scenery onto which men project their narcissistic fantasies. (Mulvey 2009, p. 13)

The essay ends by announcing not the end of male fears and fantasies, which are already rendered irrelevant and thus symbolically neutered, but the dawn of a new era in which feminist ones would finally be spoken, shown and explored. With this conclusion in mind, the essay's epigraph from Freud's ' Medusa's Head' (1922; published posthumously in 1940), which upon first reading appears to simply serve as a snappy definition of castration, acquires a hint of menace: 'To decapitate is to castrate.' Medusa, with her head of snake-hair that suggests the detachability of the male organ and therefore, following Freud's rationale, spells out the threat of castration, may well come from that still underexplored terrain of female fears and fantasies, an appropriated mythical figure that is simultaneously ancient and of the future.

The return of the Medusa

Medusa's potential as a feminist heroine or a metaphor for a repressed feminine creativity that has bounced back with a vengeance is famously demonstrated in Hélène Cixous' essay 'The Laugh of the Medusa' (1975; rev. 1976b), the most cited though far from unique exposition of the concept of feminine writing (*écriture feminine*) and one of its most incandescent literary performances.[1] Feminine writing is never straightforwardly defined, nor could it be, as it represents the violent and vengeful eruption into the symbolic of the culturally repressed, which is gendered feminine but whose expression isn't limited to women, including also male writers such as James Joyce, Heinrich von Kleist and Jean Genet. 'When I say "woman", I'm speaking of woman in her inevitable struggle against conventional man' (Cixous 1976b, p. 875). To underline the borderline unrepresentability of this newly liberated perspective, Cixous creates a series of neologisms and endows common terms with specific meanings and connotations, to populate the living semiosis of feminine writing. Thus, feminine writing throws the world into 'chaosmos' (p. 888), enveloping the cosmos into chaos, while 'sext' wilfully conflates sex and text, suggesting simultaneously the symbolic charge of gendered bodies but also the bodily nature of writing: 'Let the priests tremble, we're going to show them our sexts!' (Cixous 1976b, p. 885). Other key terms remain untranslatable in their punning polysemy: 'dé-penser', combines 'to think' and 'to spend/expend' (p. 882, n. 4, translator's note), casting 'woman' as a scandal of impropriety in both semiological and economic terms, particularly if economy is returned to its etymological roots in 'oikonomeia', the Law of the house (Derrida 1982, pp. 219–20). More famously, the double meaning of the verb 'voler', to steal and to fly (away), becomes a concise figuration for 'woman's attitude to all respected canons and established cultural practices of 'biblico-capitalist society' (ibid, p. 886), from which she takes what she will in order to, ultimately, abandon it for something entirely new and heretofore unthinkable. The evocation of the Medusa has the at least double function of conjuring psychoanalysis as one of 'woman's' phallogocentric enemies and of specifically exploding the Freudian link between woman, castration and death. Cixous' Medusa is no more than a cipher for the patriarchal fear of women; it is that fear that renders her ugly and deadly, while in truth, 'She's beautiful and she's laughing' (p. 885). The 'dark continent' of femininity 'is neither dark nor unexplorable' but merely marginalized, neglected and unexplored – not unrepresentable but systematically un- and misrepresented. Cixous takes pains to untangle the uncanny from the monstrous and its gendered mythologies: it is not the repressed that is ugly or horrible; only its repression makes it appear so. The most exciting, at once joyous and menacing aspect of this text is that the revolution that is announces has already started to take place within it and, against all odds, has always been bubbling under the surface.

The site of actual horror shifts from (the sight) of the Medusa's head to 'the arid millennial ground', which will be destroyed and from which the 'unforeseeable' will finally be foreseen and projected onto an implicitly feminine futurity (Cixous 1976b, p. 875). The rhetorical flourish and blissful excess of 'The Laugh of the Medusa', typical of the discourse of the manifesto, mark it out as a predecessor to the 'ironic' poetics of 1980s feminist manifestos, in which 'the manifestic pronoun "we"' is foregrounded as 'an index of multiplicity rather than as a signifier of univocality' (Lyon 1999, p. 171). Admittedly, 'The Laugh of the Medusa', like other of Cixous' texts written at this time and to some degree since, oscillates between a heroic tour de force by an imposing feminist voice, embodied in a famously arresting female presence known for wearing heavy eyeliner and real fur, and the opening up of a horizon for a genuinely diverse and perpetually revolutionary 'writing in the feminine' to emerge. Considered in isolation, one might be justified to conclude that Cixous' proclamations remain Modernist in tone and delivery despite their distinctively postmodernist aspirations, and that their style, typical of the elite albeit left-wing intellectual circles to which she belonged, including the group *psychanalyse et politique* (*psych et po*), makes them too hermetically individualist to represent their contemporary (let alone inspire any future) feminist social movements. Critics have also doubted the potential for radical poetics to bring about social change, suggesting that the notion of a profoundly disruptive feminine shouldn't be conflated with feminism (Felski 1989; Jones 1994). I would argue that Cixous' writing and especially 'The Laught of the Medusa' has been the victim of its rhetorical might and great quotability, which encourages fragmentation and decontextualization.

If, in 'The Laugh of the Medusa', the feminine is cast in the role of the uncanny, as the repressed whose return is as devastating as it is radical, in 'Castration or decapitation', a text based on an interview with the editors of *Les Cahiers du GRIF* conducted the same year as the first publication in French of 'The Laugh of the Medusa', Cixous' poetics find an equally potent but more sober expression, simultaneously more densely referenced and scholarly, more (conventionally) political, and reflective on other, more equivocal texts, including 'The Laugh of the Medusa' and her contribution 'Sorties' to *The Newly Born Woman* (Clément and Cixous 1986). Here, Sun Tse's manual of military strategy furnishes an evocative anecdote in which the king sets General Tse an impossible task: to make soldiers out of the king's wives. When they fail to obey the language of the drumbeat, to which they are instructed to march, they lose their heads. Decapitation can only be avoided on condition of total silence and submission, of being turned into automatons, with heads but no minds of their own (Cixous 1981, pp. 42–3). Woman's relationship to the phallus and Lacan's reconfiguration of the castration complex opens up a realm of blissful possibility, which is however perpetually out of reach, already consigned well beyond this life, let alone the symbolic, as indefinite as it is indefinable (p. 46). The price of 'lacking The Lack' (ibid.) is death, in more ways than one: representing death for/to men; being sentenced to the living death of imposed silence; and being put to death on a whim, as they have nothing else to lose but their lives, no property or power stakes from which they can be deprived as punishment. In this essay, Cixous begins to point to some real-life ramifications of the conditions so evocatively articulated in the language of psychoanalysis. The silencing of women and the culturally widespread threat to their lives, after all, are not just metaphors. 'Coming to Writing', gives more concrete forms to this threat of annihilation in an autobiographical account of her early life in Algeria, European anti-Semitism and colonial violence. For 'Jewoman' Cixous (Cixous 1991, p. 7), her (maternal) mother tongue, German, bears the mark of threatened extinction and imposed exile from the start, not metaphorically but literally.

> I had the 'luck' to take my first steps in the blazing hotbed between two holocausts, in the midst, in the very bosom of racism, to be three years old in 1940, to be Jewish, one part of me in the concentration camps, one part of me in the 'colonies'. (ibid., p. 17)

Originally published in 1977, *Angst* constitutes a novelistic performance of 'coming to writing' through 'great suffering'. Dedicated to 'la Vivante', 'The Vital Woman', *Angst* gives birth to a new – writing and reading – subject in the feminine, prompted by the 'horriginal' separation of the narrator from a/the mother/lover/god, at which moment she is split into at least two (an 'I' and a 'you') and is hurled into an infinitely painful 'waiting'. Through a thick tissue of biblical references, pagan myths and psychoanalytic parables punctuated by allusions to the familiar plotlines of heteronormative romance, *Angst* charts its female narrator's transition from a jilted, frustrated, perpetually judged but unfailingly adoring companion, to a female Prometheus[2] who 'breathes doubt' on her lover/

god's scars and scratches his wounds open. While waiting to be summoned, she develops the dangerous habit of reading and becomes an undutiful daughter/mother/lover/believer/prophet. To the lover/god's accusing question 'Are you Medusa?', her convulsive laughter comes as an appropriately blasphemous response (Cixous 1985, pp. 205–8). It wouldn't be an exaggeration to suggest that *Angst* outlines the unavoidably painful process of a separation, not of the infant from its (m)Other and her/his entry into civilization (even though the language of the psychoanalytic sacrificial economy is heavily evoked) but rather a split within patriarchal marriage and the abandonment of the treacherous ideal of heteronormative romance. The narrator-Medusa's laughter[3] in the closing of the novel resonates with the devastating assertion of one of Cixous' peers, socialist-realist author Christiane Rochefort: 'After all, we [women and men] don't belong to the same civilisation' (1981, p. 186).

The Uncanny in/as fiction: Feminist readings too close for comfort

As the previous section suggests, Cixous' engagement with the uncanny return of the repressed feminine is not only extensive but fundamental to her poetics of feminine writing. However, there is one essay that directly addresses the uncanny in/of the text and which is customarily discussed among the most pivotal deployments of the uncanny, as a model for future re-readings of Freud's essay and thus contributing to its canonization (Masschelein 2011, p. 127). In 'Fiction and its Phantoms' (French orig. 1972; English translation 1976a), Cixous postulates that Freud's essay never quite takes off, remaining trapped in knotted case studies and 'suitable' examples (Cixous 1976a, p. 531), jumping from one reference to the next, because it is itself bound by the repression of the hybridity between theory and fiction, science and literature. By describing 'The "Uncanny" (1919) as 'less a discourse than a strange theoretical novel' (Cixous 1976a, p. 525), Cixous points to a 'wildness' and provocation of Freud's text, which is sadly not fulfilled. 'The "Uncanny"' is haunted by 'its hesitating shadow', and its author by a mysterious double who leads the reader down a labyrinthine path from which there is no way back (ibid.): 'It is certain that the use of the *Unheimliche* is uncertain,' since what is at stake is 'a concept whose entire denotation is connotation' (ibid., p. 528). E. T. A. Hoffman's short story 'The Sandman' is condensed and retold linearly, 'as a kind of "case history", going from childhood remembrances to the delirium and the ultimate tragic end' (p. 533). Freud's misconstruction of fiction as psychoanalytic document goes hand in hand with his dismissal of Ernst Jentsch's interpretation of the uncanny as the affective outcome of intellectual uncertainty. Through expelling intellectual uncertainty, Freud also reduces his own conclusions to an unsatisfactory and restrictive affirmation of the castration complex (p. 535). Fear of castration, masked under the fear of losing one's eyes in 'The Sandman', is taken by Freud to be the most profound 'secret', the innermost nucleus of truth of both Hoffman's story and of the definition of the uncanny. The castration complex therefore acts as a superficial suture for the narrative gaps that the uncanny promises to pry into rather than fill in: without Freud's partial emphasis on arbitrarily chosen aspects of 'The Sandman', 'the narration would be castrated. The fear of castration comes to the rescue of the fear of castration' (Cixous 1976, p. 536). To Freud's famous identification of the prefix 'un-' in the uncanny as the token of repression, Cixous adds, 'Any analysis of the *Unheimliche* is in itself an *Un*, a mark of repression and the dangerous vibration of the *Heimliche*' (p. 545) This 'dangerous vibration' chips away at the preciously erected wall between stories and real life, that is, narrated experience; for Cixous, the uncanny is tantamount to an earthquake that threatens the collapse of heavily invested divisions, revealing a truth of/in the text that Freud could not face:

> Neither real nor fictitious, 'fiction' is a secretion of death, an anticipation of nonrepresentation [sic], a doll, a hybrid body composed of language and silence that, in the movement which turns it and which it turns, invents doubles, and death. (ibid., p. 548)

'Fiction and Its Phantoms' exemplifies second-wave feminism's ambivalence towards psychoanalysis and the/its father. While using the tools of psychoanalysis, such as the ideas of repression and compensation and its elevation of works of fiction into revealing documents worthy of analysis, it challenges Freud's intellectual ability and willingness to tackle difficult aesthetic, philosophical and, ultimately, also political questions.

In a similar vein, Jane Marie Todd focuses her reading of Freud's essay on an instance of its author's paramnesia, by which the first published version of 'Das "Unheimliche"' wrongly cites Schleiermacher instead of Schelling as the source of the definition of the uncanny as that which 'ought to have remained hidden but has come to light' (Todd 1986, p. 521). According to Todd, this confusion between two major nineteenth-century German writers with somewhat similar sounding names points to an act of repression. 'Schleiermacher' literally means 'veilmaker'.

> Not only does Schelling's definition involve hiding and uncovering, the primary function of a veil, but the phrase immediately following Schelling's in the dictionary entry quoted by Freud is: 'To veil the divine, to surround it with a certain *Unheimlichkeit*'. (Todd 1986, p. 521)

The significance of the veil, and specifically the veiling and unveiling of the human body to be seen, is linked to the castration complex, which is offered as the ultimate albeit flawed explanation of the uncanny. In their respective analyses of Hoffman's tale, Ernst Jentsch focused on Coppola's beautiful automaton, Olympia, since he argued that uncanniness emanates from uncertainty as to whether something (in this case, the automated doll) is animate or inanimate (Jentsch 1995, p. 11), whereas Freud seeks to differentiate himself from and correct Jentsch by insisting on Olympia's lack of importance. In doing so, 'Freud failed to see that the question of woman is inextricably connected to Nathanael's fear of castration' (Todd 1986, p. 523) and, going deeper, he appeared to repress the fundamental gender asymmetry of the castration complex. 'By passing over the theme of the doll Olympia, Freud failed to see the social meaning of castration' (ibid., p. 525). Todd next singles out another example of uncanniness from Freud's essay, or rather its absence, also involving dolls. In reference to the omnipotence of thought, Freud relates the repressed childhood wish of a female patient of bringing her dolls to life by looking at them in a special, intensely concentrated manner. If eyes are of as great significance in terms of both the uncanny and the castration complex, why does Freud forget about this formidable, life-giving young female gaze (pp. 526–7)? The female gaze is too frightening to contemplate, even in an essay that deals with the frightening. Rather than castration, it is women themselves that turn out to be uncanny, either because their bodies are perceived as already mutilated and thus provoke the fear of castration in men; or because their gaze reminds them of penis envy and the precious thing they have to loose; or because the fear of being buried alive, 'the most uncanny thing of all', is explained as the repressed wish to return to the mother's body (ibid., p. 527). Echoing Mulvey's essay on Allen Jones's *Women as Furniture*, Todd concludes that Freud's essay 'tell[s] a story about men's fear of women and the social consequences of that fear' (ibid., p. 528). In other words, 'The "Uncanny"' has everything to do with women as objects and nothing to do with women as subjects, although it also points to the instability of subject/object positions.

In 'The Double is/and the Devil: The Uncanniness of *The Sandman*', Sarah Kofman also begins by noting the peculiarly hesitant and incomplete structure of Freud's essay: 'In it the work of Eros', namely Freud's stated intention to get to grips with an ill-defined concept, 'is always undermined by the silent activity of the death instincts' (Kofman 1991, p. 121), namely by the unwieldiness of the topic to conform to the author's desire for a re-affirmation of a pre-prepared thesis on the connection between castration, the uncanny and death. Kofman uncovers Freud's strategic choices and rhetorical devices by which he disguises the colonization of the uncanny by psychoanalysis as an earnest, if not entirely competent, scholarly investigation. By selecting Schelling's definition of that which should have remained secret but has come to light, Freud already casts the uncanny in terms of the return of the repressed, before even announcing this typically psychoanalytic definition in his text. The order of exposition is thus used for deliberate rhetorical effects. Furthermore, the idea that the opposite of the uncanny, '*heimlich*', develops in the direction of ambivalence until it coincides with its apparent opposite (Freud 1919, p. 347) is only enabled by a deliberate selection of a specific range of meaning of each of the two terms (Kofman 1991, p. 124). Other logical flaws are pointed out, including crucially that the uncanny is not 'convertible', that is, that although most of what is deemed uncanny may be 'something which is secretly familiar (*heimlich-heimisch*), which has undergone repression and then returned from it', there are many situations and cultural artefacts that fulfil this condition and are yet not generally perceived to be uncanny (Kofman, ibid.). In wishing to assert a unified and uniquely psychoanalytic definition of the uncanny, Freud ignores important distinctions between reality and fiction (p. 125) and, within the latter, differences of genre (p. 127), even though he superficially takes pains to signpost such divisions to his reader. In Kofman's reading of E. T. A. Hoffman's 'The Sandman', an ambiguity around genre is of paramount importance, especially as it is dramatized in the competing perspectives of the different characters, specifically Nathaniel's romantic, visionary, dream-like and possibly mad point of view, versus his fiancée Clara's level-headed groundedness and realist clarity, as her name suggests (pp. 132–3). These competing perspectives are clearly represented in the three letters that form the first half of the story, two from Nathaniel to his friend and Clara's brother Lothaire, and one from Clara to Nathaniel. Kofman argues that in Freud's thematic reading of Hoffman's story, the effect of the uncanny is too hastily and too exclusively attached to Nathaniel's father figures, to the obfuscation of the crucial roles played by female characters. In response,

Kofman's essay enacts the return of the repressed in Freud's reading of 'The Sandman' and, to some degree, in Hoffman's story itself, by drawing attention to Nathaniel's fiancée and the occluded figure of his mother. What is glossed over in Freud's summary of the story is that the sight that drives Nathaniel mad when viewed through the Coppola's spy-glass is *not* Coppelius himself, mysteriously appearing in the crowd below the tower but Clara's familiar face, now looking like 'a veritable Medusa's head' (Kofman 1991, p. 133). One of the main sources of uncanniness in Hoffmann's tale is that madness and reason emerge not as polar opposites but as merely 'a matter of perspective' (p. 134):

> Clara's superiority over Nathaniel lies in the fact that she realises that everything is a matter of perspective; every point of view is exactly that: making him see reason, for her, is convincing him that his external vision reflects an internal reality. (Kofman 1991, p. 136)

Drawing on Clara's superior perspective (superior because it sees perspective for what it is), Kofman identifies the main flaw of Freud's essay as the attempt to identify uncanny *themes*, missing out on the realization that 'it is really the *form* of the narrative … which plays a decisive role in the production of uncanny effects' (p. 137, emphasis added). Literature is therefore not a textual illustration of the uncanny but its origin, nor a mirror, but its 'mother'. In the 'Postscriptum' to her essay, Kofman returns to the figure of Nathaniel's mother, occluded both by Hoffmann and by Freud, and suggests that 'The Sandman' could be read as a 'screen-fantasy concealing the incestuous desire for the mother', punishable by death. I would add that, although there are few informative references to Nathaniel's mother in the text, she regularly appears as a moral and affective barometer: 'My mother, I am sure, is angry' (Hoffmann 2010) reads the second sentence of Nathanael's first letter to Lothaire and of the story as a whole. Concealed behind the uncanny father and his even uncannier doubles (Coppola, Coppelius, Spalanzani), it is the identification with the mother that remains too unbearably uncanny to spell out (Kofman 1991, pp. 161–2). The stakes for Freud in his flawed and peculiar essay (and arguably also for his many obsessive commentators) are high, personal and self-referential: 'to master the incestuous and deadly function of writing' (p. 162).[4] This metatheoretical return to writing is typical of the preoccupation with language and textuality of Kofman's cultural and intellectual milieu but should not obfuscate her insight about the uncanniness of a cross-gender identification with the mother, particularly one who, typically, remains in the margins of the tale as well as Kofman's essay, barely within the frame but rather as the frame, inconspicuous and paramount at once.

The maternal also emerges as the pivot of an extremely influential subgenre of the uncanny, the abject, which is discussed in the next section.

The abject

For Julia Kristeva, the abject is that which is 'ejected beyond the scope of the possible, the tolerable, the thinkable' (Kristeva 1982, p. 1): it is the messy unrepresentable, the base sublime. Neither subject nor object, the abject has 'one quality of the object – that of being opposed to I'. It is 'the jettisoned object … where meaning collapses' (p. 2). Unlike the uncanny, the abject does not evoke something that is forgotten or censored (the return of the repressed) but predates the ego, order and differentiation, including that between the conscious and the unconscious. With the abject, Kristeva returns to an arena that she has previously explored in linguistic and literary terms, of the pre-Oedipal, pre-linguistic *chora* (Kristeva 1984), a term she borrows from Plato to describe a space before form but in which forms emerge, a state of being before identity but in which identity will come into being: 'Abjection preserves what existed in the archaism of pre-objectal relationship, in the immemorial violence with which a body becomes separated from another body in order to be' (p. 10). Defined also as a narcissistic crisis, 'The abject confronts us … within our personal archaeology, with our earliest attempts to release the hold of maternal entity before existing outside of her, thanks to the autonomy of language' (p. 13). Despite its roots in the pre-symbolic, abjection is not incommensurable with language but rather manifests as a break, an inter-/dis-ruption within it.

> Contrary to hysteria, which brings about, ignores, or seduces the symbolic but does not produce it, the subject of abjection is eminently productive of culture. Its symptom is the rejection and reconstruction of languages. (Kristeva 1982, p. 45)

Taking into account its disrespect for 'borders, positions, rules' (p. 4), it is not surprising that the relationship between the abject and both the uncanny and the feminine remains ambiguous. Kristeva first defines the abject in reference to the uncanny, as 'a massive and sudden emergence of uncanniness, which, familiar as it might have been in an opaque and forgotten life, now harries me as radically separate, loathsome' (p. 2). Consequently, this disparity in degree is amplified and reinterpreted as a qualitative difference: 'Essentially different from "uncanniness", more violent, too, abjection is elaborated through failure to recognise its kin; nothing is familiar, not even the shadow of a memory'

(p. 5). Unlike the uncanny, the abject has no reference to the unconscious, and therefore does not participate in its 'dialectic of negativity' (p. 7). Repression and its correlatives, denial and repudiation, become inoperative faced with the abject, which/who isn't subject to a functioning or even a mal-functioning psychical apparatus, but rather to 'the fundamental opposition … between I and Other or, in more archaic fashion, between Inside and Outside' (p. 7). Food loathing, vomiting and repugnance are the abject's – always bodily – exemplary manifestations.

The pre-symbolic provenance of the abject would suggest that it remains beyond or before gender, but this isn't exactly the case. On the one hand, the (nearly) metaphorized feminine as the emblem of 'unnameable otherness – that solid rock of jouissance and writing as well' (p. 59) stays on the limits of the abject. Confrontation with the feminine is 'enunciated as ecstatic' (ibid.) and kept clean of the horrors of abjection. On the other hand, the abject is inconceivable without reference to the maternal, an abstracted designation for procreativity and the pre-symbolic/pre-Oedipal chora, which is nevertheless embodied, to some degree, by women. The figure of the mother is absolutely central to the definition of the abject, at least on the level of the imaginary: 'If it is a jettisoned object, it is so from the mother' (p. 73). The third chapter of *Powers of Horror*, 'From Filth to Defilement', draws on Georges Bataille and Mary Douglas's *Purity and Danger* to elaborate on the risk of boundaries and thresholds and their links to 'mother phobia' (pp. 56–89). There Kristeva proposes a gendering and hierarchy among pollutants on the grounds of their potential of abjection. Menstrual blood is singled out as particularly dangerous since it represents 'the danger issuing from within' and, furthermore, it both complicates the relationship between the sexes and confronts them with (a procreatively defined, binary) sexual difference (p. 71). In addition to menstrual blood, other major defilement, excrement, is also implicitly gendered for two reasons. The 'anal penis' stands for the maternal phallus in the infantile imaginary in Freudian psychoanalysis; and because, due to the sexual division of labour that places the care of small children in the hands of the mother or her usually female substitutes, women tend to have both responsibility and authority over sphincteral training. Rather than feminine, the abject is maternal, which makes it a more appropriate term of comparison, contrast and resistance to patriarchy. Kristeva notes that pollution rituals are more widespread wherever and whenever patrilinear power finds itself under threat, as a potential defence against female fecundity (p. 78) and as 'a support against excessive matrilineality' (p. 77).

Although Kristeva views literature as the 'privileged signifier' of the concept of the abject since it 'represents the ultimate coding of our crises' (Kristeva 1982, p. 208), since the first publication in English of *Powers of Horror*, the abject has acquired far greater resonance and influence in the visual arts. In 1993, the Whitney Museum exhibition *Abject Art: Repulsion and Desire in American Art*, consolidated 'abject art' as the name of a transhistorical genre that comprises work from Surrealism, abstract expressionism, art informed by second-wave feminism, body art and various strands of late conceptualism. The exhibition included body-focused works by artists as diverse as Marcel Duchamp, Jackson Pollock, Robert Morris, Andy Warhol, Louise Bourgeois, Robert Golub, Mary Kelly, Eva Hesse, Yayoi Kusama, Paul McCarthy and Cindy Sherman (who has since emerged as the principal representative of 'abject art'). Even though the concept of abjection is founded on feminist theory, Rosemary Betterton points out that some 'abject art' lacks a sexual politics of its own, eliding important questions as to how the gender of the artist may affect the interpretation of how they treat 'taboo issues' in their art practice (1996, p. 136). Whatever its sexual politics of lack thereof, 'abject art' has taken root. The Tate website includes 'abject art' in its online Glossary, while it is also used as a tag on many user-generated content websites, including Tumblr. Although it is clear that abjection in art is as indebted to Surrealism as art informed by second-wave feminism, this book proposes a wider framework for considering the latter which may or may not involve the subversively graphic imagery and potential to spark immediate gut reactions associated with abjection, but which more often than not provokes a more slow-burning disorientation and insidious undermining of certainties by allowing the psychically and culturally marginalized to step forth.

In terms of visual culture and art practice, abjection seems closer to the grotesque, explored in great detail by Mary Russo in her book *The Female Grotesque*. Russo's most significant contribution from the perspective of this study was to attempt a difficult but necessary juxtaposition between Freudian psychoanalysis and its revisions in feminist theory on the one hand, and Bakhtin's concept of the 'carnivalesque' on the other. Russo assesses the socio-cultural potential of the radical poetics exemplified in Kristeva's 'semiotic chora', Deleuze and Guattari's 'lines of escape/flight' (and, I would add, Cixous' 'forays' and the double meaning of 'voler', to fly/to steal), to conclude that, although such poetics do not actually serve as symbolic alternative, they present an ever-renewable opportunity and remain a 'ludic space' of instability, potential and becoming (Russo 1994, p. 37). Through its choice of case studies, including visual and narrative representations of pioneering women aviators, and its methodological affinity to Michael Balint's 'philobatics' ('the field of activities and sensations organised around the thrills of seeing, feeling, or imagining the self-supported human body in space', Russo 1994, p. 34), *The Female Grotesque* further erodes the distinction between metaphorical and literal uses of language, which remains an important feminist issue.

In *Strangers to Ourselves*, Bulgarian-born Kristeva inflects the uncanny through a consideration of the representations of the stranger in the Western canon of theory and fiction. Rather than insisting on the endless deferral of meaning in Freud's essay, its blind spots, evasions and frustrations, Kristeva discovers in it a succinct inscription of a key psychoanalytic principle with rich, and as yet unmined, political potential. The foreigner is no stranger that threatens to invade from the outside but rather (s)he is already part of you/us, a mark of the extimate contamination of identity from the beginning (Masschelein 2011, pp. 136–7).

> I am a foreigner, there are no foreigners. … The ethics of psychoanalysis implies a politics: it would involve a cosmopolitanism of a new sort that, cutting across governments, economies and markets, might work for a mankind whose solidarity is founded on the consciousness of its unconscious – desiring, destructive, fearful, empty, impossible. (Kristeva 1994, p. 197)

Re-reading Kristeva's embrace of the risks and darkness involved in a 'consciousness of the unconscious' in the present moment, when terrorist violence from an obsessively but poorly circumscribed 'outside' is experienced both as reality as an imminent threat, throws into relief the radicalness of her intervention, particularly in view of the instability of metaphors discussed above, in reference to Cixous' *Angst*. Kristeva suggests that 'the deferral to a universal imperative of rights is no longer possible, arguing that a multicultural politics can no longer simply refer to a secular ethics' (Sjöholm 2005, p. 66). This politicized uncanny acts as a reminder that, one way or another, the war is (always) at home. In the final chapter of *Powers of Horror*, Kristeva asks, not entirely rhetorically: 'In these times of dreary crisis, what is the point of emphasizing the horror of being?' (1982, p. 208). The response that she indirectly proposes prefigures *Strangers in Ourselves*. The abject 'bespeaks the incompleteness of the speaking being' but does so with an unexpectedly 'comic gleam', because 'it is heard as a narcissistic crisis on the outskirts of the feminine' (Kristeva 1982, p. 209). It is the special relationship between the abject and the feminine that exposes, humorously but also uncannily, the inadequacy and hypocrisy of 'the religious and political pretensions that attempt to give meaning to the human adventure' (ibid.). At this point the abject reveals itself as not quite the same as but a sister to the semiotic chora, 'an unsignified free space, anterior to language and culture, but nonetheless powerfully remaindered within symbolization as an ambivalent … Otherness' (Russo 1994, p. 56; see also Kristeva 1980).

Critics have pointed out that, rather than gendering the threat to borders and (singular, self-possessed) identity, eminently exemplified in the maternal body, the abject posits a threat to maternal bodies in real life. In her article 'Against Abjection', sociologist Imogen Tyler expresses the concern that Kristeva's model of abjection 'risks reproducing histories of violent disgust towards maternal bodies' (2009, p. 77). She identifies abjection as the cornerstone of a genre of feminist writing that she terms 'abject criticism' (ibid., p. 79), a movement that consistently overestimates the subversive potential of feminine negativity without seeking any real-life evidence and by always privileging the study of representation over social, embodied experience. Despite a close reading of *Powers of Horror*, Tyler does not operate in the same terms of engagement, since she doesn't account crucially for the role of fantasy, the imaginary or the unconscious. By not acknowledging the imaginary, this essential mediator between the external and the internal world, in which first relationships between the ego and images, as well as correlations between entities originally perceived as images are formed, Tyler fails to convincingly establish a circuit in which representations and experience, theory and life, are not and cannot be entirely separate, let alone mutually opposed. Thus, when Kristeva writes of matricide as a precondition of individuation (1992), Tyler interprets it as a dangerous pronouncement open to misinterpretation and misuse. Tyler also makes much out of Kristeva's reluctance to be labelled a feminist, ignoring her germinal contribution not simply to feminist thought but also to strategic considerations of the futures of feminism, as in her famous article 'Women's Time' (1986 [1979]). In Tyler's hands, Barbara Creed's *The Monstrous-Feminine: Film, Feminism, Psychoanalysis*, the book-length study of common horror genre motifs that hinge on the procreative function of the female body (discussed below), 'furnishes [Kristeva's] theory of abjection with new cultural evidence' (Tyler 2009, p. 83), rather than demonstrating (as I believe it does) how the founding fears and fantasies of patriarchal culture simultaneously exhibit a well-established disgust towards and a desire to manage, control and punish the maternal.

In addition to not accepting Kristeva's terms of engagement, Tyler makes contradictory demands of Kristeva's texts. On the one hand, Kristeva is accused of speaking in metaphors, ignoring lived realities; on the other, her theory is assumed to have the potential to impact on the real world by affirming – rather than challenging, through detailed analysis – the link between femininity and abjection. The second half of Tyler's article includes a pastiche of sociological data on intimate partner violence and its exacerbation during pregnancy, as well as testimonies by battered pregnant women, collected primarily from social networking websites. Reading these harrowing narratives did not shake my confidence in Kristeva's analysis, nor did it make me consider whether feminism's engagement with the abject bears any responsibility for this kind of physical and psychological violence. Tyler does not seek to prove that abusers are familiar with Kristeva or Creed's work, which is arguably unlikely, but assumes that the two are somehow connected. It is difficult not to feel patronized by statements such as 'abjection has effects on real bodies; abjection hurts' (Tyler 2009, p. 90), especially when one knows that the motivation behind feminism's concern with abjection stems from an intense awareness of women's oppression, the cultural repression of the feminine and their deep-seated interconnections. In the course of critiquing the abject, and through the cited testimonies of battered pregnant women, Tyler abjectifies a body of feminist theory. Her article does more than misunderstand or dismiss it: it jettisons it beyond any feminist or academic credibility, beyond any hope of redemption, let alone debate.

Feminists who reject psychoanalytic theory have often pointed out the alienating complexity of its style and its propensity towards mystification (Jackson 2010, p. 126 and passim; Waddell and Wandor 1987, p. 204). Although it would be hard to deny that psychoanalytic writing since Lacan often puts up prohibitively high barriers through its style, and psychoanalytic theory can't be conceived independently of the language in which it is written, critics of feminist psychoanalytic theory fail to appreciate its contribution to parsing 'the reality and consequences of ideological struggle' (Adams et al. 1987, p. 205). Without psychoanalysis, another important thing that can get missed is the inscription of feminist desire in feminist theory and practice, which is always present and operative regardless of whether it is openly acknowledged (Pollock 1999a, pp. 16–18 and passim). While committed to truth-telling, to evoke Susan Hiller, feminist cultural producers should and usually do also strive to reflect on how their own desire shapes both their labour and their works.

The monstrous and the demonic

Among the most influential interpretations and applications of the concept of the abject has been Barbara Creed's writing on horror film and particularly her analysis of procreative motifs in *Alien*, first published in *Screen* (1986) and consequently revised for the monograph *The Monstrous-Feminine: Film, Feminism, Psychoanalysis*.[5] Creed views the horror genre as an exemplary illustration of abjection and treats the abject in specifically gendered terms. Horror films are dominated by representations of different aspects of the abject, notably bodily waste (blood, vomit, decomposing flesh), while dangerous thresholds and borders (between the human and inhuman; normal and supernatural, good and evil) remain central to the genre's construction of the monstrous (Creed 1993, pp. 10–11). Most importantly for feminist theory, horror film relies on and contributes to the construction of the maternal as abject. One pervasive manifestation of the abject maternal is the monstrously possessive mother, who refuses to let go of her offspring to the degree of smothering her/him not just socially but at the most fundamental psychical level. The blissful pre-Oedipal dyadic relationship between mother and child thus petrifies into an abject nightmare that (re)produces dangerous psychopaths rather than healthily independent adults (e.g. in *Psycho* and *Carrie*) (Creed 1993, p. 12). The boundaries of the clean and proper body are repeatedly, almost ritualistically, threatened with exaggerated defilement in 'scenes of blood and gore, deliberately pointing to the fragility of the symbolic order in the domain of the body where the body never ceases to signal the repressed world of the mother' (Creed 1993, p. 13). According to Creed, the inherently conservative genre of the horror film takes on the role of religion first, and later of art and literature, in performing the work of purification, 'that catharsis *par excellence*' (Kristeva 1982, p. 17).

> The horror film attempts to bring about a confrontation with the abject … in order finally to eject the abject and redraw the boundaries between the human and the non-human. As a form of modern defilement rite, the horror film attempts to separate out the symbolic order from all that threatens its stability, particularly the mother and all that her universe signifies. In this sense, signifying horror involves a representation of, and a reconciliation with, the maternal body. (Creed 1993, p. 14)

Creed successfully brings out the ambiguity of abjection, which Kristeva first identified but which is arguably stifled by the affective clout of the abject in *Powers of Horror*. While staging and restaging the abject maternal in all its/her gory monstrosity, horror film also strives to re-establish socio-psychical order to its fictional universe, which it offers as reassurance and compensation to its audiences for having frightened them. Furthermore, the monstrous mother cannot be wholly separated from the symbolic order and even has an important role to play in her child's passage to the symbolic order and in negotiating castration anxiety – however, garbled, perverse and occasionally literalized such a passage and negotiation may become (Creed 1993, pp. 14–15).

Creed's reading of *Alien* (1979) opens up the gap between the feminine and the maternal, often glossed by Kristeva in *Powers of Horror*. The archaic mother is the parthenogenic mother, that is to say, a profusely reproductive body (or sentient assemblage of body parts) before and beyond sexual difference. Unlike the pre-Oedipal phallic mother and the Oedipal castrated mother, the archaic mother remains beyond the control of patriarchal gender economy, even though she is often conflated 'with the mother of the dyadic and the triadic relationship', that is, with the maternal function before and after the introduction of the infant into the symbolic order (Creed 1993, p. 25). In his examination of fetishism in horror film, Roger Dadoun underlines the affinity of the archaic mother to a wholly undifferentiated universe, ever-present even in her narrowly defined absence, 'totalising and oceanic', 'a mother-thing' (Dadoun cited in Creed, p. 20). Ridley Scott's original science-fiction horror film offers multiple and layered representations of the monstrous feminine as archaic mother and at least four representations of the primal scene, some of which, such as the ejection of crew members from a spaceship, sometimes still attached to it by an umbilical lifeline, are conventional visual motifs of the science fiction genre (p. 19). In *Alien*, the crew of Nostromo interrupt their journey to investigate a transmission from a planet on their intergalactic path, where they discover a derelict spacecraft in a field of strangely fleshy, egg-shaped growths. There, one of the crew, Kane, is attacked by an alien life form that violently attaches itself to his face. Breaking quarantine protocol despite the protestations of Ripley (eventually, the only survivor), the crew brings the casualty back on board. Once the alien life form 'hatches' in Kane's body, it is 'born' out of his erupting stomach and proceeds to attack and kill all the crew bar one.

At once evasive and omnipresent, shape-shifting and – literally – slippery in its revolting viscosity, the alien obliterates structural oppositions that are important both linguistically and in specifically psychoanalytic terms, in a way that is reminiscent of the collapsing of the pair of opposites *heimlich* and *unheimlich* in Freud's 'The "Uncanny"'. The alien is both infant, when it emerges from Kane's stomach and emits a terrifying but strangely endearing cry before disappearing into the ship's recesses, and parent, having presumably laid the 'eggs' in the egg chamber and inside Kane; it is both inseminator and womb, 'rapist' and mother; it is both phallic in shape and possesses multiple, viscous and toothy mouths; it both gives birth and brings death. More than anything else, it is this obliteration of structural difference, allegorized but far from exhausted in the threat of dissolving the bodily boundaries of the subject, for which the 'mother-thing' stands. More thing than mother, the alien represents the 'archaic mother' but also gives the viewer an even more unsettling glimpse of the demonic. Creed refers to the demonic in her conclusion as the point where meaning collapses, the place of death (pp. 29–30).

There is another, more expansive and devastating definition of the demonic, which Creed does not reference. Revisiting Freud and Émile Benveniste, Jean Laplanche discusses 'primal words', which lack antithetical meanings, such as the Latin 'altus', which means both 'high' and/or 'deep', simply designating the vertical dimension (Laplanche 1999, p. 246). Rather than representing any radical linguistic ambiguity, 'altus' is pre-ambivalent, 'prior to the moment when the observer takes up a fixed position, whether at the bottom of the well, or at the top' (ibid.). Here, in the realm of the demonic, there is no repressed to make its uncanny return, no abjection even, but the flickering horizon of the chthonic (Verhaeghe and De Ganck 2012), which is not measurable by human consciousness, nor therefore the unconscious. It is intriguingly ironic that in *Alien*, the chthonic, meaning of or from beneath the earth, subterranean, is located on another planet. The implication is perhaps that this over-civilized earth has pushed away – repressed or even disavowed – its own chthonicity.

In *Phallic Panic*, the sequel to *The Monstrous-Feminine*, Barbara Creed turns her attention to male monsters and what she here terms the 'primal uncanny', 'that is, woman, the animal and death' (Creed 2005, p. vii). While the monstrosity of many male monsters is founded on features associated with the maternal body in its procreative capacity, male monsters can amplify the threat they pose to the symbolic by being male. The contradictions, slippages and failures of masculinity at a deep level create 'a disturbance around the phallus', resulting in 'phallic panic' (p. xvi). In other words, *Phallic Panic* bridges the horror genre with 'masculinity in crisis' films, or, yet more provocatively, classifies wildly aberrant masculinities as abject in their own right.

Feminist writers have elaborated on the subversive potential of feminine uncanniness from different disciplinary positions. From the field of religious studies, Diane Jonte-Pace mines Freud's texts, their polysemies and silences, to discover a 'counterthesis' that haunts his oeuvre and challenges the supremacy of the Oedipal paradigm. Freud's essay on the uncanny alongside 'Mourning and Melancholia' and 'On transcience' unwittingly decentre and subvert 'the

Oedipal masterplot' (Jonte-Pace 2001, p. 4), as do his cultural texts on religion and mythology, particularly in 'images and metaphors' (p. 2) that reveal more and sometimes something different than what was intended. In a re-reading of 'The "Uncanny"' drawing on Cixous and Kofman, Jonte-Pace charts the intricacies of Freud's simultaneous initiation to and resistance of 'an inquiry into the interrelatedness of mortality, immortality, and maternity' (p. 72), in which heaven (a spiritual home in the *Unheimlichkeit* of existential anxiety) and the mother's genitals (a first home now rendered uncanny) are reflected in one other. Psychoanalytic ideas about death and the afterlife are inflected and infected by the lingering presence not just of the (m)Other but specifically of the maternal body, in its insistent physicality.[6] In the field of American history and film studies, Susan Linville turns to the uncanny for its intrinsic ambiguity stemming from ambivalence and its aptitude for exploring dormant ambiguities in cultural texts. While moments of cinematic historical erasure 'often reduce women to eerie dolls and monsters, beings stirring repressed memories of both womb and tomb … the uncanny can alternatively serve as a springboard to unconventional cultural critique and to the engendering of less masculinist depictions of the past' (Linville 2004, p. 3). Specifically, in Linville's monograph the uncanny awakens the repressed of women as historical agents within cinematic allegorizations of Woman as mother and motherland (p. 30). Both Jonte-Pace and Linville's work exemplify how the uncanny for feminism has been a gateway for exploring the feminine repressed, manifestations of the oppression of women in cultural texts, and an unstable and equivocal yet incisive methodological instrument for exploring blind spots and mining the unspoken and the unspeakable. The next sections home in on the uncanny within feminism, first in matters that have and continue to be central to it, namely identity and identification, and then in amnesia, hauntings and returns of feminism's own past.

Identity inside out

The perceived unknowability and multiplicity of the feminine are interconnected in both Freudian psychoanalytic and feminist discourses and cited as grounds for its marginalization, its inherent uncanniness and, conversely, its subversive potential. I have already considered how the figure of the Medusa gets recast as revolutionary agent by Hélène Cixous, while Luce Irigaray's ambiguous formulation 'this sex which is not one' turns a censure on its head (1985b).

Femininity may not be a 'proper' sex, since it has been exiled from the 'empire du propre', the Empire of the Self-Same (Cixous 1986), but it is also much more than that, always at least double, emblematized by the two sets of (two) lips in the female anatomy, always in touch with one another, trumping the solitary monism of the phallus. From a post-second-wave feminist perspective, this multiplicity, which has been assumed to define the feminine, spills over into a proliferation of different theoretical articulations of the significance of identity and the processes of identification, both within feminism and also, of course, *as* feminism, since the Women's Liberation Movement has been consistently defined in reference to its identity politics. The complexity, discord, dissonance and, ultimately, the instability of identification processes have not only been at the heart of feminist scholarship (Mitchell and Rose 1982; Rose 1986) and art practice informed by feminism and psychoanalysis, but also help distinguish them from feminisms which do not engage with psychoanalytic ideas.

In her book-length study on identification in art, *Seeing Differently* (Jones 2012), which attempts to bridge feminist and queer theories and practices, Amelia Jones returns to a term that she originally coined in *Self/Image* (2006): 'parafeminism', an antidote to postfeminism, which is tantamount to its negation, as she has previously argued (1994):

> Through the term parafeminism – with the prefix 'para-' meaning both 'side by side' and 'beyond' – I want to indicate a conceptual model of critique and exploration that is simultaneously parallel to and building on (in the sense of rethinking and pushing the boundaries of, but not superceding) earlier feminisms. (Jones 2006, p. 213)

Understanding gender 'as a question rather than an answer', contextual, non-prescriptive and inherently intersectional, parafeminism sheds 'some of the closures and limitations' of the second wave and particularly its thinking around identity, including the collapse of the distinction between feminine subjectivities and female persons (p. 213). In *Seeing Differently*, parafeminism is enriched through a consideration of durationality (Jones 2012, pp. 170–217) and a more systematic effort to integrate feminist and queer perspectives on identity, although it is usually the latter that is shown to compliment and complicate the former. Despite appreciating and being inspired by Jones's models of identification, I hesitate to embrace the term parafeminism as an emblem for overcoming the impasses that she describes, despite the clear uncanny potential of the prefix 'para-', which is explored in the chapter on Susan Hiller's Paraconceptualism and has already been identified in the critical canon of the uncanny (Weber 1973).

Parafeminism is presented as a new hybrid, which Jones doesn't claim to have invented but which she names and to which she substantially contributes, and which incorporates the old but also manifests novel and serendipitous mutations, redolent of super-hero(ine) origin stories. Parafeminism implies that the old feminisms that have been assimilated did not benefit from such mutations, had either never mutated or at some point ceased to mutate and were incapable of doing so, having been – uncannily – turned to stone. I would like to argue instead that both the impasses, closures and limitations that Jones tackles and their always provisional and possibly temporary overcomings emerged in the same slippery, patchy and treacherous terrain; that they were, like the uncanny in psychoanalysis, at feminism's very core from the beginning, whenever that was; that feminism, at least partly thanks to its compromising bedfellows, has always been beside itself: the 'para-' has always already been implied.

The twisted specificity of feminist research in the visual arts is succinctly articulated in Katy Deepwell's editorial statement for the noteworthy international feminist art journal *n.paradoxa*, in which she elaborates on her choice of title. A composite of 'para' and 'doxa' (i.e. accepted opinion and/or common belief),

> n.paradoxa is a play on Donna Haraway's discussion of a parasite which lives in the gut of a termite in South Australia called *mixotricha paradoxa*. This parasite has paradoxical and unexpected habits of survival and reproduction. As a paradigm for feminist research it seemed apt for three reasons: 1) it survives by attracting others to live on it; 2) it reproduces by division and 3) its discovery reveals the value in seemingly obscure forms of research and the time and effort needed for interesting discoveries. (Deepwell 1998–)

Committed, drawn to the obscure, relying on symbiosis and division for its survival: this list of characteristics does not apply only to feminist research but feminism itself. The feminist uncanny as a concept draws attention to these fundamental attributes and their paradoxical ways. Returning to José Esteban Muñoz's *Disidentifications: Queers of Color and the Performance of Politics*, which is also a key reference for Jones (2012), I was struck by the section heading 'Identification *beyond and with* Psychoanalysis' (1999, p. 13, emphasis added), which delves into the work of critics like Diana Fuss and Teresa de Lauretis, who position themselves within and against psychoanalysis in an attempt not to overcome but to queer it. Muñoz describes his book as a whole as 'an argument with psychoanalytic orthodoxies' (p. 12), a para-psychoanalytic project much like the feminist uncanny. Both de Lauretis and Fuss (1995) regard the dichotomy between desire and identification in Freudian psychoanalysis as false and one that is, furthermore, motivated by the taboo of homosexuality. Fuss famously proposed vampirism as an alternative model of identification and the formation of subjectivities:

> Identification … invokes phantoms. By incorporating the spectral remains of the dearly departed love-object, the subject vampiristically comes to life. To be open to an identification is to be open to a death encounter, open to the very possibility of communing with the dead. (Fuss 1995, p. 1)

The most provocative ramifications of Fuss's formation is that identity politics are also recast in terms of a politics of desire, which, for feminism, is at the very least homosocial and potentially homoerotic, if not altogether queer. An always already haunted and vampiristic identification theory and identity politics comes in support of the feminist uncanny as it emphasizes the darkness, precariousness and risks in the very foundations of subject formation. From the perspective of contemporary feminist positions, nevertheless, from which the second wave is (re)viewed, assessed, admired and critiqued, vampiric identification raises some difficult questions: Do feminist foremothers have to be 'dead' in order to be identified with and thus also, at the same time, desired?

The relationship between different moments and camps of feminism, if feminism is to be viewed as a paradoxical continuum that not only accommodates but relies on change, could perhaps be better addressed through not identification but *transference*, that most transferable of all psychoanalytic concepts, beyond the clinic and into culture (Laplanche 1999, pp. 221–2), and *ambivalence*, which is already tied to the figure of the mother in Freudian psychoanalysis, as Kristeva has explored (1982). In her study of transference in Freudian and Lacanian psychoanalysis and its role in the making and reception of contemporary art by women, Mignon Nixon charts the telling omission of women in Freud's reflections on ambivalence, an omission concomitant with the exclusion of femininity from 'the Oedipal arrangements of patriarchy' (2006, p. 278). Nixon argues that the emergence of the figure of the 'woman artist' as a figure of transference at the time of the 'death of the author' was no accident. 'The emergence of new figures of transference might be seen to instigate new transferences: rather than the death of the author, it might be possible to imagine the transformation of authorship' (p. 282), as well as challenge the link between knowledge, cultural production and authority.

To return to Diana Fuss, nevertheless, there is more to vampirism than the desire for and death of the (m)Other.[7] In an excerpt on which Muñoz also draws, Fuss casts vampirism as an inversion of identification; it is 'identification pulled inside out – where the subject, in the act of interiorizing the other, simultaneously reproduces externally in the other' (1992, p. 730). Interestingly, inversion also relates to the uncanny, even without Fuss's vampiric twist. In their entry on 'The Return of the Repressed', Laplanche and Pontalis note that Freud originally proposed that 'the repressed, in order to return, makes use of the same chains of association which have served as a vehicle for repression in the first place. The two operations are thus seen as being intimately connected, each presenting the mirror-image of the other' (Lapanche and Pontalis 1973, p. 398) Later Freud retreated from this provocative idea, as he had done on many other occasions, to insist that the return of the repressed follows a completely separate and specific path. Considering Freud's own repressed original thought, however, suggests that the dregs of any identification process, that which is edited out, may find their way back into consciousness in the shape of uncanny identity formations. In visual art, 'mirror-images' and mimicry are mined for their potential to imitate identification while undermining it from within.

Lorraine O'Grady's series of performances as *Mlle Bourgeoise Noire* (1980–81) uses inversion as one of its strategies. The persona of Mlle Bourgeoise Noire, an ageing, (literally) self-flagellating beauty queen who has not so much forgotten but deliberately dispensed with her manners, was developed in (angry) response to Eleanor Antin's fictional persona of African-American ballerina Eleanora Antinova (1979–89).

> I liked the concept, it made me think of my mother, Lena, of what might have happened had she emigrated from Jamaica to Paris as an eighteen-year-old …. But my mother was tall and willowy, the black ballerina type. And neither this short, plump white woman in blackface nor her out-of-kilter vision of the black character's experience could compute for me. That was the moment I decided I had to speak for myself. (O'Grady 2012, p. 10)

Dressed in a gown and cape stitched together out of 180 pairs of white gloves, the symbols of oppression, both external and internalized, Mlle Bourgeoise Noire gave out white flowers while whipping herself with a white cat-o-nine-tails. She wore a tiara and sash identifying her as 'Mlle Bourgeoise Noire 1955', won in Cayenne, French Guiana, thus casting black bourgeoisie (or rather, bourgeoise-ness, i.e. the ideology, not merely the class position) as an international condition. 1955, the year of O'Grady's graduation from Wellesley, the elite women's college whose alumnae include Madeleine Albright and Diane Sawyer, conveys that 1980, when the persona first performed, was a jubilee year, 'a year in which she would enact a new consciousness' (O'Grady 2012, p. 13). Mlle

Figure 2.1 Lorraine O'Grady, *Untitled (Mlle Bourgeoise Noire Beats Herself with the Whip-That-Made-Plantations-Move)*, 1980–83/2009. Silver gelatin fibre print in 13 parts. 9 11/16 in. × 7 1/2 in. Courtesy Alexander Gray Associates, New York. ©2014 Lorraine O'Grady/Artist's Rights Society (ARS), New York.

Figure 2.2 Lorraine O'Grady, *Untitled (Crowd Watches Mlle Bourgeoise Noire Whipping Herself)*, 1980–83/2009. Silver gelatin fibre print in 13 parts. 9 11/16 in. × 7 7/8 in. Courtesy Alexander Gray Associates, New York. ©2014 Lorraine O'Grady/Artist's Rights Society (ARS), New York.

Figure 2.3 Lorraine O'Grady, *Untitled (Mlle Bourgeoise Noire Shouts her Poem)*, 1980–83/2009. Silver gelatin fibre print in 13 parts. 9 5/8 in. × 6 1/2 in. Courtesy Alexander Gray Associates, New York. ©2014 Lorraine O'Grady/Artist's Rights Society (ARS), New York.

Bourgeoise Noire was a dedicated space invader,[8] party crasher and spoil sport, marching into private views and protesting against the apolitical abstraction of some African-American art and the continuing segregation in the art world. Shouting poems against (self-)oppression, caution, and for breaking literal and metaphorical boundaries, Mlle Bourgeoise Noire was also an exorcism of O'Grady's own breeding and elite education, even while being partly enabled by the latter. Following the performances of 1980–81, Mlle Bourgeoise Noire became a curator of events and exhibitions, including *The Black and White Show* (1983) at Kenkeleba, a black New York gallery, in which an equal number of white-and-black artists were selected and all exhibited work had to be in black and white. 'To a blindingly obvious situation, sometimes you made an obvious reply,' O'Grady comments (2012, p. 13), yet the ragingly inappropriate Mlle Bourgeoise Noire performs an uncannily violent unmaking/remaking of identity that is both effective and complex. A revenant, crasher and spoiler of celebrations, she draws attention to the emblems and material supports of identity formation and performance (white gloves; tiara; whip), awakens their disturbing historical baggage (slavery and servitude; debutante balls and beauty pageants) and reconfigures them in an unsettling spectacle and a resonant voice that continues to haunt the history of contemporary art.

In the next section, I consider the uncanny in and of feminism and introduce some broad groupings of its manifestations in art practice: the revival of dead (i.e. lexicalized) metaphors, which is already operative in many of the theoretical texts discussed above; genre-fuck, which not only blurs the boundaries between established genres but also questions the separation between fiction and experience, reading and living; and world-making, which, similarly, places culture and subculture on an even keel, not out of a misrecognition of power inequalities but out of an acknowledgement that the repressed will always, somehow, return.

Dead metaphors, genre-fuck, world-making

Contemporary feminisms have arguably acquired an uncanny aura anew. In *Feminism and Popular Culture: Investigating the Postfeminist Mystique*, Rebecca Munford and Melanie Waters examine notable occurrences of postfeminist amnesia, in which feminism, I would argue, lives on as a classic instance of the uncanny, as that which should have remained secret but has come to light, due to its continuous, persistent but always incomplete repression. In this context, postfeminism is not an overcoming, watering down of or backlash against feminism, but simply a 'ghost feminism' (Munford and Waters 2013, p. 17). It haunts popular media though its name is rarely uttered (although this had already radically changed by the time of the book's publication); stars as well as fans are endlessly grazing against it, rarely acknowledging its presence: 'The postfeminist mystique – like the feminist mystique before it – works by mobilizing anachronism … In anachronism, the past is revisited upon us: what we thought to be gone returns, confirming its ability to influence the present' (Munford and Waters 2013, pp. 10–11).

For Mira Schor, amnesia has become an insidious ailment of contemporary feminist practices in the visual arts. In a scathing critique of *Future Feminism*, an exhibition and series of events that took place over the month of September 2014 in The Hole, NYC, published on her blog *A Year of Positive Thinking*, Schor shares her frustration at witnessing a hackneyed replaying of well-rehearsed feminist debates without any acknowledgement of their history. Becoming aware of this erasure of memory and rediscovery of what should already be known – 'the feminist wheel' – causes more than frustration: 'The toxic paint fumes or the perilous effects of *déja vu* on the brain made me freeze' (Schor 2014). In other – Freud's – words, discussing an unnerving episode of getting lost in an unfamiliar town, where his efforts to find his way kept taking him back to the same spot, 'an unintended recurrence of the same situation … result in the same feelings of helplessness and of uncanniness' (Freud 1919, p. 359). This repetition of the same masquerading as new, deals a double blow that has disturbing repercussions in terms of politics, the psyche, as well as the cultural unconscious; this isn't the feminist uncanny but the uncanny in feminism.

In this book, I want to revisit and revive the revolutionary capacity in the feminist uncanny, not because I don't agree with Munford and Waters that, despite a feminist resurgence, feminism is still often strangely disavowed, nor do I question Schor's assessment of the nefarious consequences of feminist amnesia. In its resonance as a bold, disquieting, funny and learned strategy, the feminist uncanny picks out the threads of continuity with the past both within and of feminism; in its acknowledgement of the inevitable messiness, even the dark side, of dialogues and negotiations, attempting allegiances and forging ways forward, the uncanny immunizes feminism against both amnesia and the risk of becoming a master discourse and keeps it wilfully unsanitized and majestically 'scandalous', to echo Jacqueline Rose (2014, p. x). The feminist uncanny makes feminism proud of its scars and baggage; it awakens a dangerously unstable ambiguity in feminism's own perceived familiarity; and it refuses to put seemingly settled questions to bed.

The rest of this book explores the feminist uncanny in art practice. I have attempted to stay away from work that could be read as too obvious an illustration of the concept of the uncanny from gendered perspectives. In fact, I endeavour to avoid discussing art practice as if it were an illustration of theory altogether, against which Susan Hiller also advises (1996, pp. 103–10), in recognition of art practice as an autonomous form of knowledge making. In art practice, the feminist uncanny manifests through a range of modalities that could be grouped into three broad categories: the literalizing of metaphors, genre-fuck and world-making. Each of these three categories may be more obviously relevant to some works than others but the art practice under consideration cannot be divided up into three neat groupings to match them one by one. For example, Maud Sulter's collages *Jeanne: A Melodrama*, physically place one of the few photographs of Baudelaire's famous but elusive 'muse' within the history of technologies of the spectacle and Western art's representations of the black female body, thus performing both genre-fuck (by mixing documentary and fiction; by referencing melodrama in an otherwise non-melodramatic visual art work) and world-making (by creating the incommensurably hybrid environments in which Jeanne comes out of Baudelaire's fantasy and into her own). *Womanhouse* and *Feministo* (Chapter 4) both rely upon and enact a verbatim translation of the German original '*Unheimliche*' as 'unhomely', in the creation of disturbing domesticities, but they also participate in world-making insofar as they collectively and collaboratively explore the construction of alternative social realities both in their installations and, even more importantly, in the dialogical processes of their making. Conversely, the verbatim translation of '*unheimlich*' as 'unhomely' resonates with the feminist uncanny in all its manifestations and, arguably, with the feminist project as a whole, since the gendered organization of domesticity and the patriarchal structure of family life, along with the sexual division of labour on which they hinge, remain paramount feminist issues. The unhomeliness of the uncanny is but one instance of the literalization of metaphors, further explored in Chapter 3, in which the awakening of dead (lexicalized) metaphors is specifically examined as a site of a deliberate and subversive summoning of the repressed. The origins of genre-fuck and world-making are usually traced back to foundational texts of queer theory, although by using them in this context I would like to suggest that both terms are applicable to feminist art and thought and that, furthermore, the ideas behind them may have pre-existed the celebrated queer acts of their coining.[9]

Charles E. Morris III and Thomas K. Nakayama, editors of *QED: A Journal in GLBTQ Worldmaking*, argue both for the currency and foundational importance of world-making in queer cultural and sexual practices and trace its conceptualization to the essay 'Sex in Public' by Lauren Berlant and Michael Warner (Morris and Nakayama 2014). Berlant and Warner evoke a queer cultural context in which physical intimacy is disengaged from the domestic sphere, which isn't necessarily the case for feminism, but whose 'radical aspirations' for decentring assumed referents or 'privileged examples' of sexual cultures feminism shares (Berlant and Warner 1998, p. 548). World-making exceeds the collaborative construction of social realities that social theory explores because queer worlds – just like feminist ones – 'do not have the power to represent a taken-for-granted social existence' (Berland and Warner 1998, p. 559, n. 22). Queer and, I would add, feminist worlds include 'more people than can be identified, more spaces than can be mapped out beyond a few reference points, modes of feeling that can be learnt rather than experienced as a birthright' (p. 558). In its bold imag(in)ings of places, people and events as they never existed, feminist art practice, such as Faith Ringgold's *The French Collection*, indicts the conditions of their impossibility and actualizes them retrospectively, by charting networks of 'entrances, exits, unsystematised lines of acquaintance, projected horizons, … alternate routes, blockages, incommensurable geographies' (ibid.). Despite not using the term, I believe it is world-making that is at stake in feminist philosopher Marilyn Frye's casting of women's anger as an instrument of cartography in the realm of identity and, by extension, as a valuable strategy in identity politics. Women's anger is performative and generative: it expands the range of women's experience and action by stretching the limits and challenging the limitations of normative gender identity (Frye 1983, pp. 84–94; see also Scheman 1980). 'Rethinking "woman" ultimately meant remaking the world' (Bammer 1991, p. 54).

For Sara Ahmed, the 'feminist killjoy' is explicitly linked with world-making: 'Being a killjoy can be a knowledge project, a world-making project' (2010, p. 4), while 'wilfulness', the killjoy's defining feature, is described as a form of creativity (p. 6). It seems that feminist theorists tap into the negativity in world-making, which is inherent in the concept even though Berlant and Warner only graze against it, for example in discussing the work of Leo Bersani against redemptive sexual pastoralism (Berlant and Warner 1998, p. 566). Lee Edelman's *No Future* (2004) is arguably the negative apex of a specifically queer world-making, in which he advocates 'an insistence on the negativity that pierces the fantasy screen of futurity, shattering narrative temporality with irony's always explosive force' (p. 31). Although I have been inspired by this book's at once nuanced and polemical engagement with Freud and Lacan, in which the child is elevated into the figure that embodies futurity and against which 'the queer' is always positioned, it also represents an example of queer theory that sits awkwardly with feminist thought and practice. This is because feminism remains embroiled in the politics of reproduction, regardless of the sexual and reproductive capacities and choices of individual feminists or feminist groups. In other words, just as the child can never be wholly metaphorized in feminist theory, children are likely to continue to be feminism's problem and one that cannot ever be fully bracketed off.

As a term, 'genre-fuck' is obviously modelled on 'genderfuck', which involves, according to June Reich, 'a reinvigorated reading of the discontinuity between sex and gender, during sex, in my performance as a "girl" on the streets, and in intellectual pursuits in the realms of phallocentrism' (1992, p. 113). In his reading of Pat Califia's unclassifiable text *Macho Sluts*, Ian Barnard concentrates on 'violations of the integrity of identity (of genres, characters, readers, and communities)' (1994, p. 267), which take place through deliberate slippages 'between author/character/reader and between author/narrator' (p. 276) as well as on the confounded status of the text as fiction *and* theory, fantasy with a safe-sex message in acknowledgement of the reality of HIV/AIDS, but also erotica and pornography (p. 277). While such violations are here presented as metaphorical, as breach of classification borderlines, it is crucial to point out their simultaneous literal manifestations as 'psychological and physical violences' on the bodies of the characters in *Macho Sluts* (p. 267). Ultimately, both Califia's and, in turn, Barnard's texts, cannot help but return to the relationship between fantasy, fiction and reality as they are complexly mediated by BDSM and the act of 'reading' (p. 282). This is famously a well-trodden terrain (at least in regard to the relationship between reality and fiction) and leaves little scope for genuinely new insights, let alone disentanglements. Yet Barnard insists on confronting it again and concludes with the following observations, whose relevance is far from limited to Califia's hybrid text, nor even BDSM:

> The relation of fantasies of desire to the political is simultaneously very convoluted, highly charged, and significantly formative. In exploding the distinctions and borders between the phantasmatic and the 'real' by showing how it is exactly the phantasmatic that produces ever heightened realities, I demand that these distinctions cannot – and should not – hold in the realm of political action either. This is not to repeat quietist assurances that revolutionising *language* or *imagining* a different order is sufficient political work .... This is to recognise the place of the unconscious in the political. (Barnard 1994, p. 288)

In evoking once more the place of the unconscious in the political, the imbrication of feminist and queer theory is revealed. Barnard does not cite it but he, as are many of the writers he does cite, is clearly indebted to feminism's engagement with psychoanalysis, all the more enlightening for drawing attention to blind spots (including those of psychoanalysis *and* feminism), all the more fruitful for being fraught. Barnard may well be expressing the weariness of some kinds of post-structuralist feminisms, such as the one represented in Julia Kristeva's *Revolution in Poetic Language*, in which it would appear in retrospect that the belief in the powers of 'signifiance', namely the 'unlimited and unbounded generating process, this unceasing *operation of the drives* toward, in, and through language' (Kristeva 1984, p. 17, emphasis in the original), were not only exaggerated but possibly misplaced. Yet he simultaneously recognizes that previously held distinctions between the psychical and the political don't hold and should no longer be assumed to do so. It was – and still is – feminism, in its multiplicity of theories and practices, through its heightened attention to the everyday, its recognition of identification as a continuous and troubled process, its mindfulness of tacit power relations and its persistent cross-contamination between what was and what could be that pioneered an attention to the unconscious in and of the political.

3

'Moving Sideways' and Other Dead Metaphors: Susan Hiller's Paraconceptualism

Sleeping metaphors[1]

While it is a truism that the boundaries of art movements are neither hermetic nor fixed, the fact that, at specific moments, these boundaries are heavily guarded by exclusive orthodoxies is also widely recognized. The exhibition *Romantic Conceptualism*, which unearthed central yet long-neglected aspects of the conceptual, such as 'cultural techniques of emotion', 'the fragmentary and the open' (Heiser 2007, p. 135), included an important early work by Susan Hiller, *Dedicated to the Unknown Artists* 1972–76 (and ongoing addenda). In an interview with curator Jörg Heiser, Hiller noted that some artists were excluded from Conceptualism 'proper' because they wouldn't purify their work of what was deemed 'sociological, psychological, personal', nor would they exorcise the unconscious. This exclusion is all the more important to highlight because it has since been erased:

> Retrospectively it is difficult to overlook the importance of Hiller's early decision to work with and on cultural materials whose meanings have been repressed, suppressed, censored or simply ignored. Her early works function perfectly as starting points for an art history traced backwards from now. (Szymczyk 2006, n.p.)

Looking back, Hiller spots a gender-specific pattern of marginalization and alternative practice in which the unconscious was not repudiated in favour of theoretical legitimation (Hiller 2009, p. 129). While taking advantage of the considerable insights and possibilities for self-reflection opened up by what Hiller calls the first generation of conceptualism, she made work that drew analytical attention to its media and languages but also opened up a space beyond language:

> [We] moved sideways. … We wanted to say other things … other than what's already in language … not necessarily feminist political things, but other kinds of things, and you couldn't do that without inventing other ways of going about the whole procedure of making art. (Hiller 2009, pp. 129–30)

Moving 'sideways' in order to act and be otherwise, sidestepping instead of turning away calls to mind countercultural strategies that were enabled by the Women's Liberation Movement, if not always developed within it, as well as earlier radical projects of the 1960s, such as the peace movement and the Black Liberation movement. It evokes critiques of progress and linearity and the rejection of vertical hierarchies in favour of the equality that lateral connections suggest. While it places her oeuvre in a historical canon from which it had been excluded, without erasing its previous exclusion nor its specificity, 'moving sideways' also signposts Hiller's affinity with second-wave feminist thought at its nascent, avant-garde moment. Furthermore, it alerts the reader/viewer to the importance of metaphors in Hiller's art and texts, the weight they hold in her perception of the world and their analytical and transformative function in her practice.

Concerns of self-reflexivity, the role of theory, impurity and not quite fitting in, are woven through Hiller's thought and practice. In 'Women, Language, Truth', a contribution to a panel discussion on 'Women's Practice in Art' organized by the Women's Free Art Alliance in London, she deployed the same metaphor, albeit in disguise:

> Each of us is simultaneously the beneficiary of our cultural heritage and the victim of it. I wish to speak of a 'paraconceptual' notion of culture derived from my experience of ambiguous placement within this culture. This placement has been painful to recognise and difficult to express. (Hiller 2009, p. 115)

In retrospect, the neologism 'paraconceptual' does more than signify the ambiguous, ambivalence-inspiring mixture of belonging and not belonging, of simultaneous victimization and complicity. These ambiguities have been extensively explored arguably in all of Hiller's oeuvre as they describe her poetics, and politicized in her texts on the rejection of anthropology and the implications of primitivism in art (Hiller 1991; and Hiller 2009, pp. 93–113). Elsewhere, it is the possibilities opened up by this precarious self-positioning that are emphasized: 'Like being a foreigner, being a woman is a great advantage' (Hiller 1993, p. 99). Just sideways of conceptualism and neighbouring the paranormal, a devalued site of culture where women and the feminine have been conversely privileged, the 'paraconceptual' opens up a hybrid field of radical ambiguity where neither conceptualism nor the paranormal is left intact: the prefix 'para-' allows in a force of contamination through a proximity so great that it threatens the soundness of all boundaries. In this way, 'paraconceptualism' (if I may turn the adjective into the '–ism' that I believe it to be) evokes a familiar trope of violent defamiliarization typical of the uncanny: 'nothing new or alien, but something which is familiar and old-established in the mind and which has become alienated from it only through the process of repression' (Freud 1919, p. 364). In his oft-cited essay 'The Sideshow, or: Remarks on a Canny Moment', Samuel Weber argues that the 'off-beat, off-sides' (*abseits*) fate of the concept of the uncanny in critical theory suggests an innate feature of the uncanny itself (1973, p. 1103). When Freud, in his essay of 1919, approached the topic from the margins (through semantics and etymology, while he claimed to be focusing on aesthetics), seemingly digressing from his thesis (the rather deflating assertion that the uncanny hinged on castration), and with the apprehension of someone who has veered off their area of expertise (a psychoanalyst commenting on aesthetics), he did not merely examine a concept but outlined a manner of investigation that is haunting because it is haunted by its troublesome subject matter.[2] Considered through this sideways approach, nothing is what it seems:

> Uncanny is a certain undecidability which affects and infects representations, motifs, themes and situations, which … always mean something other than what they are and in a manner which draws their own being and substance into the vortex of signification. (Weber 1973, p. 1132)

Curiously, the uncanniness of the uncanny hasn't been tempered by its growing popularity since the publication of Weber's essay in the early seventies. Banality feeds the uncanny by bolstering its deceptively familiar disguises.

In the expression 'moving sideways', the spatial metaphoricity of the 'paraconceptual' is drawn out and nearly literalized thirty years later, in Hiller's discussion with Jörg Heiser and Jan Verwoert. Here lies yet another important layer of the significance of metaphors in Hiller's work: by translating the Greek prefix 'para-' verbatim (as 'beside') and stripping it, for a moment, of its acquired connotations (such as irregular, secondary, derivative), Hiller slows down language and deprives its users of the conceptual shortcuts they are accustomed to. She turns a dead metaphor, one that has had its figurative value entirely suppressed through common usage, into live, vigorous signs. The poetic function of dropping grit in the flow of everyday language was originally noted by the Russian Formalists, while its radical potential has been mined in feminist theory and creative practice.

> One clear feminist challenge is to wake up sleeping metaphors.... Although the literary convention is to call such metaphors 'dead', they are not so much dead as sleeping ... and all the more powerful for it. ... Waking up such metaphors, by becoming aware of their implications, will rob them of their power to naturalise our social conventions about gender. (Martin 1991, p. 501)

The photograph and text installation *10 months* 1977–79 conjures up a pair of heavily interconnected and, historically, mutually exclusive concepts, that of creation/creativity and procreation (cf. Battersby 1989; Korsmeyer 2004, esp. ch. 3). The raw materials of the work were full-body photographs of Hiller herself in the nine calendar – ten lunar – months of her pregnancy and a kind of journal she kept during the same period, 'a huge plastic carrier bag full of scraps of paper' (Hiller cited in Liss 2009, p. 13). The photographs were cropped to extreme, nearly abstracted close-ups of the artist's expanding belly that not only obliterate her identity but no longer resemble a(ny) body at all, evoking instead moonscapes. If femininity is the 'dark continent', the female body in its precarious, dangerous and hence often consecrated pregnant state is ironically represented as another planet. By documenting and working through 'her observations of the bodily and psychic journeys she underwent during this fecund period' of pregnancy (Liss 2009, p. 12), Hiller also charts, scrutinizes and, by doing so, resists the operation of a gender-specific silencing, and exorcizes a writer/artist's block exacerbated by women's procreative function. The text eloquently probes the mechanisms by which gestation, this pervasive metaphor for artistic and intellectual endeavour since Romanticism, enforces a sexual division of labour that neatly maps out male and female onto its metaphorical and literal significations. Women/mothers literally produce offspring, men/artists metaphorically give birth to ideas/art. 'There is nothing she can speak of "as a woman". As a woman, she cannot speak' (Month Six). By writing in the third person, Hiller wards off the sentimentality that would stereotypically be read into a woman's artwork about pregnancy, yet also creates a more ambiguous lag between what is written and what remains outside/beside representation, not for lack of means but, on the contrary, due to a confining proliferation of multiple, incommensurable 'ways of knowing' (Month Ten). The work concludes on a positive note, by documenting the arrival not of a baby (although that came eventually too) but of the epiphany that contradictions and inconsistencies need to, and will be, embraced. The (pro) creator artist/mother occupies the difficult yet also privileged subject position from which this becomes possible and necessary. While seemingly being 'about' a pregnancy, *10 months* also crucially represents the symbolic birth of what Hiller has often referred to as 'fruitful incoherence'.

'Your Sisters from Thebes'[3]

The automatic writing project, installation and artist's book *Sisters of Menon* 1972–79 deals with voices, automatism and the culturally repressed.[4] The work operates in (at least) two registers, consisting of twenty pages of automatic writing, typed transcripts and *Notes*, each of which reflects on the work in a different style and tone while also forming part of it. Completed in 1979, when Hiller undertook the transcription of the retrieved automatic scripts made seven years earlier and wrote the accompanying *Notes*, *Sisters of Menon* spans a crucial decade for feminist art practice and extends into the 1980s, with its publication as an artist's book in 1983 by Gimpel Fils. In installation, the scripts are arranged in cruciform, with the *Notes* and typed transcripts positioned at the edges of the horizontal axis. The shape of the cross is repeated in the background of the typed transcripts and appears again as a grapheme within the automatic script. In the transcripts all automatically produced marks that do not correspond with letters are replaced by dashes, apart from the encircled 'X', a Cathar symbol which is copied intact. This symbol provides a link between the work and the location where the scripts were made, the French village of Loupien in the Cathar region, where Hiller was staying in 1972: 'Cathars followed a Gnostic tradition, which leads to interesting ideas about religion and gender.'[5] Certain Gnostic sects 'speak of the feminine element in the divine, celebrat[ing] God as Father and Mother' (Pagels 1979, p. xxxv). *Notes I* serves as an introduction to the work, explaining its method (automatic writing combined with gestural automatism, resulting in hybrid letter-drawings) and its history: the scripts were produced 'automatically', in a state of altered consciousness (which, however, as Hiller insists, 'didn't seem freaky')[6] during the artist's stay in Loupien. The scripts had been lost and only 're-appeared … almost exactly seven years after their transmission' (Hiller 1983, 'Notes II'). They were not rediscovered, but found their way back from oblivion 'automatically', as if of their own accord. The Greek word 'automatos' contains the meaning 'self-acting' (Liddell and Scott 1940), with the 'self' being, however, devoid of consciousness. The handwriting and 'voice' in which the inscriptions were made are not Hiller's typical style, even though her hands did the writing. When used, the possessive pronoun ('"my" hands') is suspended in quotation marks. Whereas the automatic scripts stand for the artist's participation in an altered state of consciousness, the *Notes* that frame it reveal a systematic and informed reflection on automatism and the work itself: *Sisters of Menon* proposes that these two positions (scientist and artist vs. medium and lunatic) need not be incommensurable but can be occupied alternatively and at will, while at the same time acknowledging that social and cultural conditions rob certain social groups of such flexibility. The work, which may or may not be read as 'primitive' self-expression or an '"occult" phenomenon', poses and responds to the question: 'Who is this one?' (Hiller 1983, Notes IV). Already embroiled in the dissolution of subject positions, Hiller tackles this question in the first-person singular, which is however again provisional, enclosed in quotation marks: '"I" feel more like a series of activities than an impermeable, corporeal unit … or rather, "I" AM NOT A CONTAINER' (ibid.).

If the *Notes* constitute the rational periphery or theoretical framing of *Sisters of Menon*, the name 'Menon' forms its indecipherable navel. 'Menon' remains ungendered and is never identified apart from through undefinable shifters

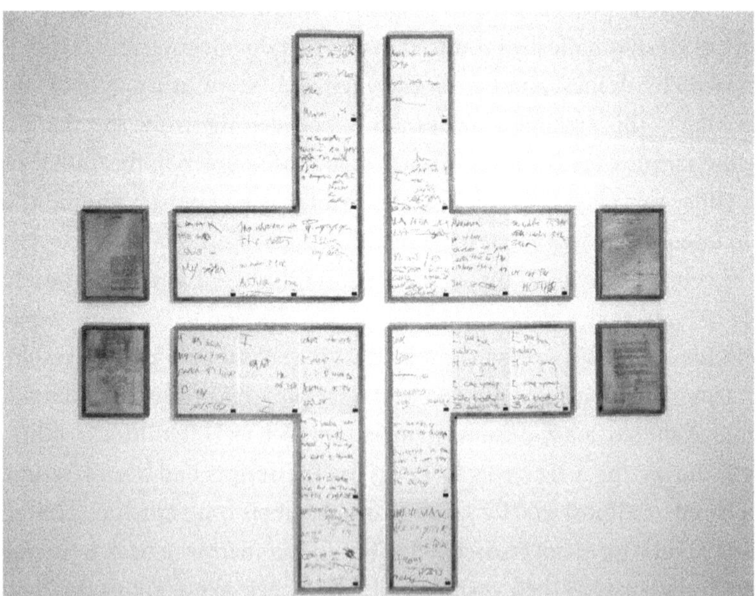

Figure 3.1 Susan Hiller, *Sisters of Menon*, 1972/79, installation view. Blue pencil, typescript and gouache on paper. Courtesy of the artist.

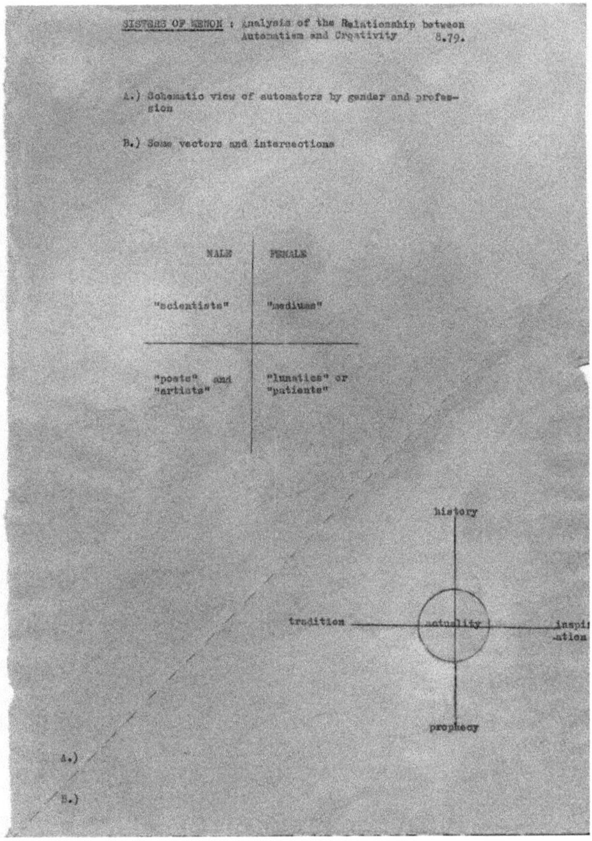

Figure 3.2 Susan Hiller, *Sisters of Menon*, 1972/79, 'Analysis of the Relationship between Automatism and Creativity.' Blue pencil, typescript and gouache on paper. Courtesy of the artist.

(i.e. personal pronouns but also terms such as 'here/there', 'now/then', that only acquire meaning in the context of a known situation) and self-referential predicates:

1. —/who is this one/I am this one/Menon is
2. Menon is this one/you are this one/

Menon is introduced only relationally and, crucially, not in terms of either patrilineality or matrilineality but laterally, on an equal plane, along sibling lines:

3. I am the sister of Menon/I am your sister/the sister of – everyone's sister/I am Menon's sister

18. we are the sisters of Menon/everyone is the sister/everyone is the sister/love oh the sisters/

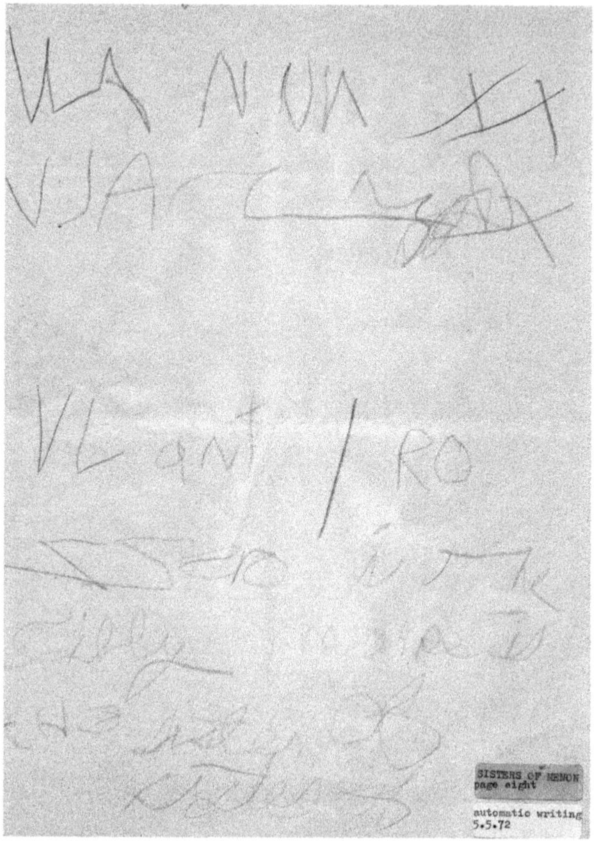

Figure 3.3 Susan Hiller, *Sisters of Menon*, 1972/79, automatic writing, page 8. Blue pencil, typescript and gouache on paper. Courtesy of the artist.

Lucy Lippard has noted that 'Menon' is an anagram of 'nomen', Latin for 'name' (1986), while Hiller has playfully suggested 'no men' (Morgan 1996, p. 42). The automatic message indeed reinforces the vacuity of the Lacanian Name of the Father by not literally excluding men but by challenging the symbolic function of patrilinearity. Moreover, the allusion to the historical second-wave 'sisterhood' cannot be denied (Betterton 2004, pp. 18–19). In this kinship network, there is no marriage, no exchange of women and thus no economy, either in social terms or on the level of the symbolic, culture and language (Irigaray 1985b, pp. 192–7).

> 9. Menon/we three sisters are your sister/this is the nothing that we are/
> 10. the riddle is the sister of the zero/we are the mother
> 11. of men/we are the sister of men/o the sisters

Automatic transmission and the reception of automatically produced texts break with rationalist codes of interpretation to create a semiotic inflation where seemingly contradictory propositions are valid at the same time. Lacan ties kinship and especially the exchange of women to language, as they are both 'imperative for the group in [their] forms, but unconscious in [their] structure' (2001, p. 72), in other words, simultaneously dominant and opaque. Kinship lays down not only the social but also the symbolic law. On the level of kinship, such semiotic inflation becomes almost incestuous: we/you/I are both the mother and the sister of men (or of Menon: 'We are the sister of *men/o* the sisters'). Such clues, including the reference to a 'riddle' in the tenth instalment, foreshadow the strongest allusion to the myth of Oedipus, dramatized by Sophocles and upon which Freud based the Oedipus complex, one of his most criticized yet fundamental theories of the construction of desire and the human subject. The last instalment of the automatic script locates this anarchic network of relations at the site of the Oedipus myth:

> 20. —/we are your sisters from THEBES/thebes[7]

In an interview with Rozsika Parker, Hiller concedes that *Sisters of Menon* 'reformulates the encounter between the Sphinx and Oedipus' (Hiller and Parker 1996, p. 51). Yet there are (at least) two Thebes. Elsewhere, she identifies Thebes without hesitation as an ancient Egyptian burial ground: '[It] is of course the necropolis in Egypt which undoubtedly I had already read about' (Morgan 1996, p. 42). In the Egyptian Thebes, now Luxor, there is a precinct dedicated to Memnon, son of Eos (Dawn), a Greek mythological hero whose name is only a letter away from Menon. Legend has it that the Northern statue of the two 'Colossi of Memnon' flanking the gateway of the mortuary temple of Amenhotep III emits a high note at daybreak in salutation of Memnon's mother. In the second interview, Hiller slips from the locus of the Oedipal drama to the Egyptian necropolis, from Oedipus's arrogant eloquence to the inarticulate lament of a son for his mother, unearthing a near-homonym between the mythical hero and the obscure navel of *Sisters of Menon*.

In *Oedipus Philosopher*, Jean-Joseph Goux proposes that the formulation of the Oedipus complex in psychoanalysis is constitutive of the 'conscious/unconscious cleavage' (1993, p. 201), a cleavage that is no mere partition but institutes a range of hierarchical relations, sacrificing the pre-Oedipal affinity with the maternal body for the sake of networks of kinship, privileging logos over what lies beyond representation and logic over the paranormal, and instituting the divided and polarized 'mode of subjectivity that characterises Cartesian societies' (ibid.). In tracing the Oedipean 'autocentred' subject in the Western philosophical tradition, Goux pays special attention to Hegel, who is credited with the transformation of Oedipus into 'a shadowless, fully inaugural figure' (1993, p. 159) and of his encounter with the Sphinx into 'the primitive scene of philosophy' (p. 163). Hegel casts Oedipus's encounter with the Sphinx as a confrontation between two different discursive regimes, out of which the rational hero emerges triumphant, but having sacrificed otherness: 'The light of consciousness, which is consciousness of self, obliterates all enigmatic alterity, suppressing the dimension of the unconscious'; the birth of Western philosophy coincides with 'the exit of Egypt' (Goux 1993, pp. 165–6). *Sisters of Menon* revises the encounter between Oedipus and the Sphinx by giving voice to a different kind of disarticulated subjectivity and by prying open the lag between the Greek and the older Egyptian city, the locus of Oedipus's intellectual victory and the burial site that gets buried by Oedipus and his family romance. The implications of this piece are not only feminist but also psychoanalytic, philosophical and postcolonial.

In invoking the two cities and at least two different ways of knowing, Hiller wakes up another sleeping metaphor, 'metaphor' itself. 'Metaphora', Greek for transfer, conveyance, transition, is transformed into a journey crossing the Mediterranean southwards, coasting from the master's discourse to the repressed aspects of the Freudian episteme, oscillating between automatism and theoretical and political reflection, connecting THEBES to thebes. As the lateral conceptualist that she is, Hiller draws attention to the ordinarily repressed truism that all language is metaphorical, not by striving after the unrepresentable sublime but by blurring the boundaries between the terrain of representation and what lies beyond it. Suspended between writing and drawing, knowing and sensing, the familiar and the uncanny, her work populates the world with 'enigmatic signifiers' (Laplanche 1989, p. 45) and intertextual rivets where resonant aesthetic, theoretical and political insights converge.

Dead President

Although far from a straightforward exercise in self-portraiture, *Sometimes I think I'm a Verb Instead of a Pronoun* (1981–82) is quite clearly an autobiographical work. It belongs to a series of photomat self-portraits produced mainly in the early 1980s, consisting of blown up passport pictures partially

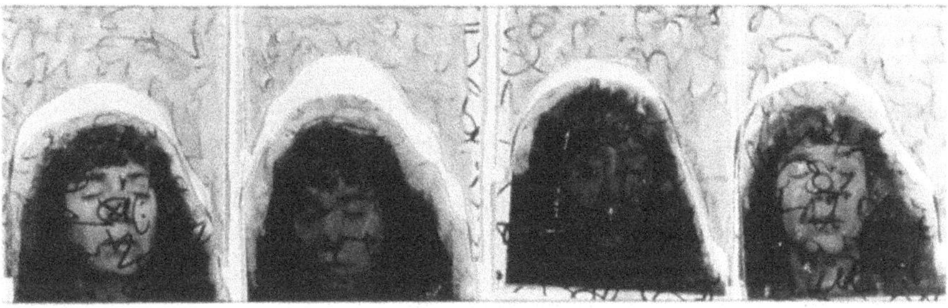

Figure 3.4 Susan Hiller, *Midnight, Tottenham Court Road*, 1982. C-type prints enlarged from handworked photobooth images. Courtesy of the artist.

covered by automatic script and paint. *Sometimes I Think I'm a Verb Instead of a Pronoun* consists of twelve panels, each comprising eight frames (two foursomes of photomat pictures) that have been layered with script and paint, and were consequently rephotographed. The conventions of identification photography are thwarted on two levels: the photographed subject either averts her gaze or, as in this work, presents body parts other than the face to the camera, while the photographic print is purposely veiled in writing and colour. The automatism of the illegible script is relayed by the absence of a seeing, conscious agent behind the camera of the photomat.

> Clearly what's happening here has got to do with the question of, say, presence or absence of the female subject, the female person who is the subject of these works, namely me. (Hiller 1996, p. 63)

Hiller identifies the title as a quotation by American General and Eighteenth President Ulysses S. Grant. Once again, the question of self-identity passes through the other in a most pronounced way: the artist encounters a dead father – of a nation – not simply a sovereign figure but a symbol of sovereignty. Yet Grant carves out an odd patriarchal figure. Emerging from the American Civil War as hero (his initials were said to stand for 'unconditional surrender'), his presidency was marred by numerous financial scandals. In late life, unwise investments 'impoverished the entire Grant family and tarnished Grant's reputation' (Biography.com Editors, 2015). His presidency has even been described in terms of confusion, inefficiency and impotence: he is said to have 'provided neither vigour nor reform' and 'seemed bewildered. One visitor to the White House noted "a puzzled pathos, as of a man with a problem before him of which he does not understand the terms"' (Whitehouse Historical

Association 2015).[8] The trajectory from the Greek to the Egyptian Thebes, from Oedipus to Memnon and then to President Grant, also marks another transition. Hiller's automatic script morphs from relative decipherability in *Sisters of Menon* to a primordial cryptolinguistic mark-making that seems closer to drawing than writing but is probably neither and both. This new script principally documents the physical act of mark-making that produced it and, in this sense, it is indexical, as it conveys little other than the act of mark-making.[9] The index does not only sidestep language but, in doing so, disrupts the authorial function of the subject and dispels its authoritative aura. Ulysses Grant, serendipitously named after another mythological fortune-seeker, becomes the anti-Oedipus, marking the point of dissolution of the Western subject just like Oedipus marked its emergence. A year before his death and while struggling to complete his memoirs that were to be such a big success that they nearly made up for his family's bankruptcy, Grant was diagnosed with throat cancer that resulted in the complete loss of his voice. Reduced to communicating principally through writing and in considerable pain, he wrote in a note to his physician:

> I do not sleep though I sometimes doze a little. If up I am talked to and my efforts to answer cause pain. The fact is I think I am a verb instead of a personal pronoun. A verb is anything that signifies to be; to do; or to suffer. I signify all three. (Grant cited in Sebeok 1986, p. 2)

On the brink of death, the index overtakes the symbol, the intelligible sign, the body overwhelms the subject, verbs take over from pronouns. In *Sometimes I Think I'm a Verb Instead of a Pronoun*, sensations speak louder than words – the subject is flesh again, beneath and beyond language. Just as the script devolves into indecipherability, the body parts replacing the face in the photomat frames now remain just that, fragmented, barely identifiable, not stapled together by the 'I'. More than any work from the series of photomat self-portraits, *Sometimes I Think I'm a Verb Instead of a Pronoun* celebrates the sensual pleasures of painting with thick, textured layers of colour – pleasures believed to have been prohibited in orthodox conceptualism and (some) second-wave feminist art practice alike. As Judith Mastai whimsically put it, 'the Law of the Mother' was 'thou shalt not paint' (1995). Hiller does, but her stance does not coincide with lawlessness or having no rules. For her performance-lecture 'Duration and Boundaries', for example, Hiller imposed two rules on herself, in acknowledgement of the opportunities and limitations of language: 'to tell the truth' and 'to speak without using any first-person pronouns' (editor's note, Hiller 1996, p. 170). Neither on the wrong nor on the right side of the law, 'fruitful incoherence' is always beside(s) it.

> Although 'I' must be in some sense co-determinate with this culture, and my expression, *to be comprehensible to any degree*, merely an aspect of it, … I can find myself ONLY in refusing to speak in readymade terms as an example, representative or instance. (Hiller 2009, p. 116)

Uncanny Voices

Sometimes I Think I'm a Verb Instead of a Pronoun resonates with the ghostly traces of a dead president's lost voice. Hiller has often made use of voice recordings, notably in the twenty-minute film and series of etchings *The Last Silent Movie* (2007).[10] Through its title at least, the video belies expectations. Replete with the recorded voices of people mostly now dead, speaking languages that are also dead or endangered and that are not only likely to be unfamiliar to most viewers but, in many cases, even completely unknown by name, *The Last Silent Movie* isn't as much silent but 'blind', non-visual, not a movie at

Figure 3.5 Susan Hiller, *The Last Silent Movie*, 2007. Single-channel projection with sound, 20 mins, installation view. Courtesy of the artist.

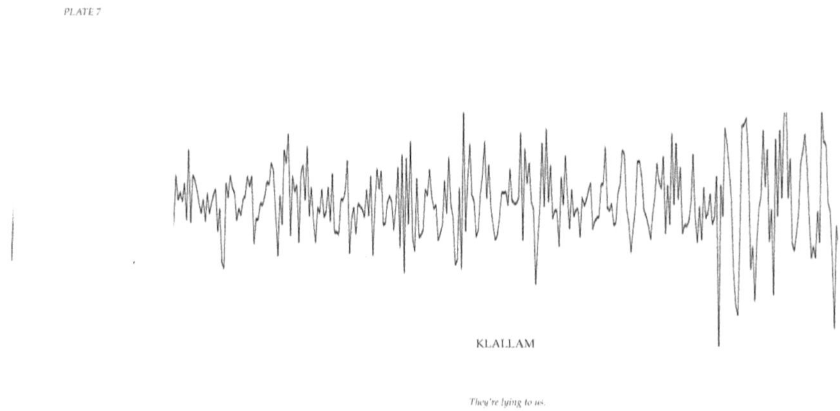

Figure 3.6 Susan Hiller, *The Last Silent Movie*, 2007. 25 etchings. Plate 7 Khallam, 'They are lying to us.' Courtesy of the artist.

all. Yet it evokes real silent movies, in its use of sub- and intertitles, the former translating the spoken utterances, by approximation or, on one occasion, not at all, the latter announcing the name and status of each language represented: for example, 'NGANASAN (nearly extinct)'; or 'BLACKFOOT (seriously endangered)'.[11] Extensive credits at the end list the archives from which each voice was sourced, give dates and locations and, where possible, name the speakers. The 'movie' breaks with a metaphorical silencing of extinction by rescuing these voices from the archives and by securing them an audience larger, different from and more diverse than archive users. A series of twenty-five etchings transcribe the sound waves produced by a selection of words from each of the collected sound clips.

The voices collected in *The Last Silent Movie* do not allow for the fact of their transmission to be left unnoticed or treated with indifference. They reach out to their audiences and touch them within the intersubjective space created by the work, even though this space is formed of distance rather than reciprocity. The phenomenological fabric in which the voice loops speaker and listener into a mutual proximity, be it intimately complicit or critical (Voegelin 2010, pp. 6–11), is here deliberately slashed by the indexical trace (linguistic extinction or threat thereof) of colonial crimes and postcolonial inequalities. *The Last Silent Movie* is both metaphorically and literally upsetting. First, it is composed out of the voices of the – doubly – dead, no longer living but also condemned to a cultural death, veiled in an obliterating silencing that is interrupted but not quite redressed by the work itself. Secondly, it effects affect – the work induces sadness for the dead or ageing speakers of dead or dying tongues, but only to immediately upset that too: one is not allowed to wallow in narcissistic melancholia, as this sadness is tinged with guilt, the implication of each viewer in the imperialist homogenization of global linguistic and thus cultural diversity, if not by action then by inactivity. In turn, the extensive credits at the end upset any affective response by revealing the institutional and more often than not anthropological archival sources of the work's materials, raising new questions around culpability and responsibility. Instead of any resolution between pressing political considerations and affective reactions, there is rather a wavering between the two, 'a constant oscillation', in the words of Jörg Heiser, 'between emptiness and weightiness, a kind of *psychoactive restlessness*' (Heiser 2007, p. 95, emphasis added).

In *Belshazzar's Feast: The Writing on Your Wall* (1983), a short film broadcast on Channel 4 and installed in galleries on TV monitors placed in spaces organized like living rooms, the television screen is taken up by a close-up of a burning fire, evoking the replacement of the hearth by the television set. The title refers to a biblical story from the book of Daniel about a feast in the middle of which a hand mysteriously appeared and wrote on the wall 'Mene, mene, tekel, upharsin'. According to the interpretation of the prophet Daniel, the only one capable of making out the writing's meaning, Belshazzar and his circle had been judged and found wanting for worshipping the false gods of gold and silver and would be punished. Daniel turned out to be correct and Belshazzar's kingdom was eventually destroyed, though what makes the story important to the work is obviously not its morality, but 'the distinction between literally reading … and interpreting … signs or marks' (Hiller 1996, p. 89).

On the soundtrack two voices can be heard: of a child, the artist's son, describing from memory Rembrandt's painting of Belshazzar's feast, and that of the artist herself singing or chanting in an improvised non-language, an example of verbal automatism that references 'speaking in tongues', or singing improvisation in jazz. The 'voices of the dead' experiments of Latvian scientist Konstantin Raudive are an important contextual reference for this work as well as other sound installations like *Élan*. Raudive believed that the voices of those long gone may still be detected if recordings of apparent silence are sufficiently amplified. The veracity of such claims is beside the point, although recording technology has made it possible – and ordinary – to listen to voices of people now deceased, without normally being aware of the uncanny quality of this auditory channel between the dead and the living. What matters most for Hiller is that nothing is always something, from another (or another's) perspective, simply hovering 'beneath or beyond recognition' and it is the job of the artist to make it visible or imaginable.[12] Raudive's experiments and the ambiguous psycho-cultural roles ascribed to the voice have therefore a bearing on Hiller's practice and world view that far exceeds the use of sound or the voice: they point to the haunted recesses of culture, where the repressed returns. The recorded voice does not merely possess an uncanny quality but becomes a cipher of the uncanny.

Belshazzar's Feast restores the possibility of reverie in front of the set, while acknowledging its multiple uses in everyday life. Hiller made this work after reading some newspaper articles about people seeing ghost images in TV static, after transmission was over. Its broadcasting on British television, into real living rooms, and its installation in mock living rooms stages a deliberate home invasion of the forgotten, repressed function of the hearth. This is an exemplary case of the uncanny as something which is not frightening in and of itself but only becomes so through its repression. By being discarded as unexplained and thus assumed inexplicable, illogical and therefore illegitimate, the 'insights' that come from sensing without understanding, interpretation without reading, become rejected and, as a result, take 'warped and twisted' forms (Hiller 1996, p. 91). Besides, the mock living rooms of *Belshazzar's Feast* make a mockery of domesticity and its associations with family, familiarity, comfort and security.

An earlier work by Hiller, *Monument* (1980–81), can be viewed as a companion piece to *The Last Silent Movie*, thanks to their shared focus on the interdependence between mortality and commemoration, as well as their use of voice recordings. Consisting of a fifteen-minute sound recording and a diamond-shaped formation of colour photographs of Victorian memorial plaques and one of faded graffiti that reads 'STRIVE TO BE YOUR OWN HERO', *Monument* interrogates the relationships and tensions between sentimentality and ideology, death and representation. A recording of the artist's voice, which, unlike the photographic installation, can only be accessed via headphones, one-on-one, and with each listener subsumed in the visual aspect of the work, reflects on transcience, mortality and its cultural compensations, the nature of heroism and its genderedness, the 'two modes of existence' of the commemorated subjects – 'in the body' and 'as a representation' – but also, crucially, draws attention to itself as the resonant imprint of a living – and thus also ageing and slowly dying – human being, reaching out of her time frame into the listener's. 'Are you still listening? This is my voice. Your presence, my absence. Your present, my past.

Our futures' (*Monument* soundtrack). In the words of media theorist Friedrich Kittler, who assigns primacy to the machine in the human machine interface, 'The realm of the dead is as extensive as the storage and transmission capabilities of a given culture' (Kittler 1999, p. 13). But rather than introducing death in the voice, recording technologies underline, repackage and mediate the death – some death – that is already intrinsic in it: 'Voice is neither dead nor alive: its status ... is that of a "living dead," of a spectral apparition which somehow survives its own death .... The life of a voice can be opposed to the dead letter of writing, but this life is the uncanny life of an "undead" monster' (Zizek 1997, p. 101). In recording, the voice has its intrinsic uncanniness simultaneously amplified and repressed, which Hiller's work captures and preserves, in all its vibrating, ambivalent ambiguity.

4

Squats and Evictions: The Uncanny as Unhomely

Saving Louise

Louise Bourgeois's *Femmes maisons*, that is, *Women Houses*, a series of four drawings on canvas produced concurrently between 1945 and 1947, depict hybrids of buildings and female nudes. All are faceless and headless, with torsos merging into or possibly consumed by the buildings, portrayed in varying degrees of stasis and distressed movement. Two are apparently armless but with gravity-defying clumps of hair, which could also be thick wafts of smoke. One is given disconcertingly spindly arms, which are conspicuously out of proportion to her curvaceously solid lower half. Another has three arms, all waving helplessly. In an ambitious but awkward article, Julie Nicoletta stages a confrontation between Bourgeois and Lacan on the basis of these enfleshed edifices and subsequent sculptural work, in which Bourgeois comes out on top over Lacan because she doesn't share his insistence on gender of not only individuals but also conscious and unconscious structures. For Nicoletta, Bourgeois gestures towards an overcoming of gender altogether, while Lacan appears cathected on a binary conception of it (2005). While some of Bourgeois's sculptures from the late 1960s and 1970s, such as *Sleep* (1967) and *Fillette* (1968), deliberately blur visual symbolizations of femininity and masculinity in form at least, *Femmes maisons* are not only firmly gendered but participate in the kind of sexual politics from which Bourgeois is known to have kept her distance, more often than not.[1] According to Phyllis Rosser, *Femmes maisons* capture a common, among feminists, 'feeling of entrapment' and anticipate 'the postwar condition of women who both created and were confined to the household' (1994, p. 61). In encouragement of biographical interpretations, which will here be sidestepped, Bourgeois commented on these works as follows:

> Cette petite main en l'air, semble dire: 'Venez à mon secours. Il y a quelque chose qui me fait mal, je souffre de cette situation. Ne m'oubliez pas, venez me

> chercher, parce que j'ai mal, j'ai le mal du pays.' Elle est partie dans un pays ou elle a besoin de reconstittuer, de collectionner et de serrer près d'elle une maison vide qu'elle a connue.
>
> This little raised hand seems to be saying: 'Come to my rescue. There is something hurting me, I'm suffering in this condition. Don't forget about me, come get me because I'm sick, I'm homesick.' She has gone to a place where she needs to rebuild, pull together and hold tight an empty house that she used to know.[2]

Viewed from a post-second-wave feminist perspective and with an awareness of feminist art from the 1970s, the meaning of *Women Houses* changes. From prisons of personal suffering and trauma, Bourgeois's uncanny hybrids turn into political indictments of the sexual division of labour, the cultural associations

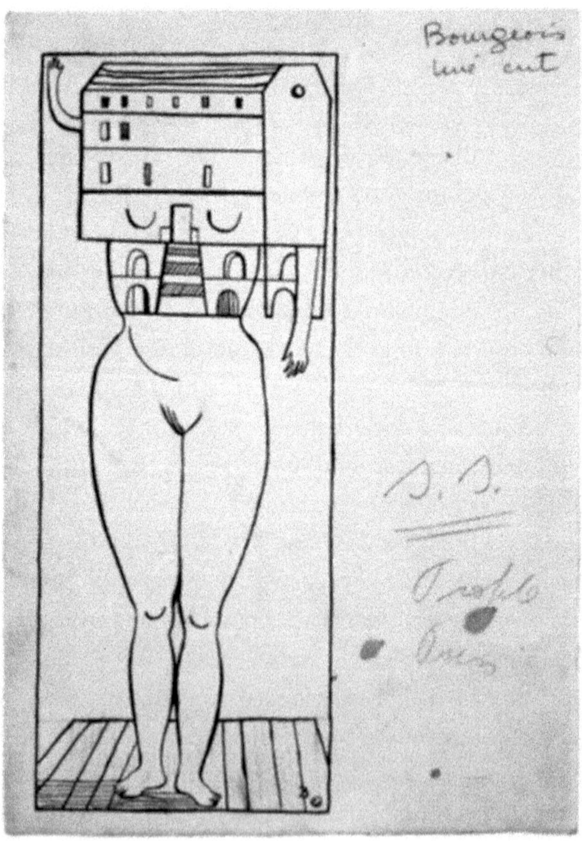

Figure 4.1 Louise Bourgeois, *Femme Maison*, 1946–47. Ink on linen. 36 × 14″; 91.4 × 35.6 cm. Private Collection; Photo: Christopher Burke. © The Easton Foundation/ Licensed by DACS, London.

between women and domesticity and the philosophical interweaving between femininity and dwelling. The call of the little waving hand appears to be finally and inventively answered by consciousness-raising and collaborative art projects, such as *Womanhouse* (1972), named after Bourgeois's four drawings (Nixon 2005, p. 77) and the *Women's Postal Art Event*, a.k.a. *Feministo* (1975–77). In response to the prisoner's homesickness, they don't offer a sounder, less-oppressive alternative dwelling (the 'empty house that she used to know') but shake her out of her nostalgia by demonstrating the inherent unhomeliness of (any) home, at least for women like her. Feminist homesickness cannot be treated in the home but only by breaking out of it and taking it down, at the very least as an ideological construct. If the stake is freedom, there will be no more playing house.

Although domesticity remains a feminist issue, recent feminist scholarship has sought to complicate the 'home' as a site of real and symbolic habitation, and even move away from it in a transnational turn, focusing instead on migration and the freedom or imperative to travel and stay mobile (Dimitrakaki 2013; McRobbie 2009; Meskimmon 2011). The impact of the global(izing) developments discussed by these scholars on both embodied subjectivity and labour practices (and, indeed, on their mutual implication, as Dimitrakaki demonstrates) is both beyond doubt and worthy of feminist analysis. However, in this chapter I am more interested in the ways in which responsibility for domestic maintenance and familial reproduction continues to fall overwhelmingly on women, and the manner in which this is spatially materialized in the home. In this sense, gendered domesticity itself travels: you are bound to take it with you; and the more it changes, the more it stays the same.

The next section examines some of the cultural and philosophical ways in which women and homes, femininity and domesticity have been tied together, to the former's detriment, examining the work of Emanuel Levinas in particular. I will then focus on two art projects, *Womanhouse* and, in far greater detail, *Feministo*, which address such problems by creating installations of treacherously domestic environments, thereby giving material form to a verbatim translation of the *Unheimliche* as unhomely.

Feminizing domesticity, domesticating the feminine

The impact of the long-standing mutual implication between women and the domestic sphere runs deep. Much has been written on the physical confinement of women in the home, their financial disempowerment and lack of independence due to the non-remuneration of domestic labour and the work of care, and the frustration of educational and professional aspirations through the assumption of women's destiny as wives and mothers, all of which have remained key feminist issues, both personal and political, debated in academia, in activism and the everyday. Idealized femininity has been ideologically shaped by the domestic sphere and its connotations, while the 'home' is cast as the personal project and reflection of the woman who keeps and runs it (even though she would historically be highly unlikely to own it).[3] Commenting on the ideology of the 'separate spheres', particularly in its ornate articulation by John Ruskin, in which man was assigned to the competitive and dangerous arena of business and politics and woman to the protected and protective domestic realm, Lynda Nead explains the degree of mutual implication between woman and domesticity:

> The purity of domestic life was maintained by the influence and attendance of the respectable woman. In this way the ideologies of the home and the feminine ideal reinforced each other; woman's moral and sexual purity guaranteed the home as a haven and a source of social stability, and, in turn, feminine purity itself was ensured through the shelter and protection of the domestic sanctuary. (Nead 1988, pp. 33–4)

These coupled ideals of femininity and domesticity, mirroring and bolstering each other, were obviously specific to their cultural and political context (Victorian England, in the above excerpt) and to the rising middle class, who did not only have the privilege of upholding such ideals but also the burden of inculcating them, by example and through 'good works', to the working classes. The home emerges as the mediator in an even more important coupling, in which a distorting reflection is at play: 'Women have served all these centuries as looking-glasses possessing the magic and delicious power of reflecting the figure of man as twice its natural size' (Woolf 1957, p. 35). A hovering, agreeable, soothing and auxiliary presence, 'the Angel in the House' effortlessly and 'naturally' expressed woman's calling of homemaker and guarantor of domesticity at once as 'labour of love'. Since this type of dedication requires a disavowed yet onerous amount of emotional labour and constitutes more than a full-time job, killing the Angel in the house – in self-defence – had to be among the principal obligations of any woman engaged in writing or other creative endeavours (Woolf 2012).

The domestic sphere as separate and specially gendered became possible through economic and social changes, such as the separation of the workplace from the family home, which were crucial but not exclusively responsible for its emergence. The mutual identification between idealized domesticity and idealized femininity can never be adequately explained through economic relations. In 'Bodies-Cities', Elizabeth Grosz reviews existing models for considering the relations between the body and the city and classifies them in two main strands: the causal, according to which the 'space' of the body produces and transforms that of the city to make it meet its needs and correspond to its evolution in time, and the representational, in which an isomorphism between the two is assumed. In this latter group of models, nature, in the form of and represented by the human body, is taken to be mirrored in architectured urban space. Grosz challenges both strands on account of the former's innate humanism and subordination of body to mind, and the latter's implied phallocentrism and conception of culture as the functionalized 'perfection' of nature (1995, pp. 105–6). She suggests instead a model that gives precedence to neither term but conceptualizes 'bodies-cities' 'as assemblages or collections of parts, capable of crossing the thresholds between substances to form linkages, machines, provisional and often temporary sub- or microgroupings' (Grosz 1995, p. 108). Whereas there may be some form of isomorphism between the two, this would not be a result of mirroring, but rather of a 'two-way linkage that could be defined as an *interface*.' This new conceptualization of their interrelation does not simply establish an openness and mutuality between the two terms, but also highlights their fundamental interdependence, if not osmotic inseparability. Predating Grosz in its original publication (1984), Rozsika Parker's conjunctive theorization of the feminine and the practice of domestic crafts as communicating vessels may be best understood as following the premise of the interface (2010, esp. pp. 4–6). Similarly, in this chapter the feminine and the domestic will be treated as an interface, entirely interdependent and perpetually (in)forming each other.

Before moving on to the artworks, I consider a philosophical model that casts femininity and existential at-home-ness in each other's image. This model isn't examined because of its influence but rather because it reflects, articulates and perpetuates long-established and already influential assumptions about the feminine/domestic interface. In *Totality and Infinity*, Emmanuel Levinas proposes two different kinds of otherness, in addition to and challenging the interiority of the 'I', resulting (as I will argue) in a gendered and hierarchical binary that feminizes enclosure by containing the feminine in a fundamentally secondary and auxiliary subjective position. For Levinas, who works within and against the phenomenological tradition,[4] the transcendence of the totality of interiority towards the infinity of exteriority is marked by the encounter with 'the face of the Other' [*Autrui*], the absolutely other who constitutes an

'I', a subject 'for itself' (1979, pp. 21–30). Hence infinity is not a void in which the subject claims boundless freedom but a site of responsibility. For Levinas, exteriority, namely the experience of the Other, has precedence over interiority and, as a result, the philosophy which finds freedom and power within totality gets replaced by another, that of the *ethical relation* between the 'I' and the Other (Levinas 1979, pp. 47–51). Even though 'I' and 'Other' are essentially distinct and hence are in the position to jointly embody the ethical dimension of alterity, they are notably also the same, since 'I' is 'Other' to the 'Other' who is 'I' to himself [*sic*]. In addition to the Other and the I, there are two other modes of alterity, amounting to three modes in total: an alterity which is 'formally', *not* radically other, such as food or other objects that lend themselves to use by the I/Other, and 'the other whose presence is discreetly an absence, with which is accomplished the primary hospitable welcome which describes the field of intimacy, … the Woman.' (Levinas 1979, p. 155) This last mode of otherness appears to lie somewhere in-between Other-ness proper and the same with regard to its relation to 'infinity', that is, vis-à-vis its authority to challenge the ipseity and self-containment of the 'I'. Appropriately enough, this discreetly absent (not quite) other features in two major aspects of Levinasian philosophy: his theory of the dwelling and his 'Phenomenology of Eros'. These two aspects have a lot in common as they each stand for a different degree of 'being-at-home-ness' or, in Irigaray's terms, of 'enveloping'. In both, Woman heals or relieves I/Other's nostalgia for a proper place of his own, which, in psychoanalytic terms would be described as the pre-Oedipal – the imaginary lack of division between self and the maternal. For Levinas, 'dwelling' is the condition of belongingness that (pre)conditions all human activity.

> Man abides in the world as having come to it from a private domain, from being at home with himself, to which at each moment he can retire. … Concretely speaking the dwelling is not situated in the objective world, but the objective world is situated by relation to my 'dwelling'. (Levinas 1979, pp. 152–3)

Although no direct correlation may be established between the Levinasian and psychoanalytic discourses, the function of the dwelling is reflected, if only in the reverse, in Freud's essay on the uncanny and, with a slightly different inflection, in Lacan's concept of extimacy (*éxtimité*). The dwelling, defined as the feeling of at-home-ness (*le chez-soi*), is a model for establishing a form of psychical translatability between the inside and the outside, ipseity and Otherness in Levinas; or between the imaginary (as site of the primary *jouissance*, that of wholeness or absence of distinction) and the barred subject in Lacan; or between the secret and its revelation; or between the repressed and its returns (as symptom, in dreams, and in analysis) in Freud. In the theorization of the uncanny and extimacy, the 'dwelling' as facilitator and guarantor of such a translatability is absent. Instead, extimacy and the uncanny affirm a fundamental *un*translatability on account of an obstinate and omnipresent, though not always immediately discernible, residue post-symbolization. In Levinas, a mechanism of equivalence that allows for translation is maintained by the dwelling, the dwelling-ness of which relies on femininity as 'mediator'. As has already been noted, the feminine plays a pivotal role in the uncanny too, as one of its embodied sites (the effects of castration on show) but also as the symptom of its own untranslatability in the language of psychoanalysis. The repressed that renders Freud's essay itself somewhat elusive and, arguably, uncanny is what his writer leaves out: the truth of/in fiction; the automated Olympia perceived as an unsettlingly familiar fiction of femaleness; literary writing; the precarious status of psychoanalysis itself. The promise of the return of the repressed is enacted through a return of repression (Wright 1998, p. 124).[5]

Mladen Dolar's interpretation of Lacanian extimacy explains and elaborates on his paradox: 'The extimate is simultaneously the intimate kernel and the foreign body.' Its forgotten – repressed – familiarity points in the direction of the Lacanian real, 'the dimension beyond the division into "psychic" and "real"' (Dolar 1991, p. 6); it does not merely stand for the uncharted but the unchartable. Jacques-Alain Miller concurs: in psychoanalysis, the most intimate coincides with what is radically Other and specifically what makes the Other other: 'In a certain way, this is what Lacan is commenting on when he speaks of the unconscious as discourse of the Other, of this Other who, more intimate than my intimacy, stirs me.' In other words, extimacy is occupied by the *objet petit a* (the *other* as opposed to the Other) (Miller 1988, p. 124). The untranslatable *objet petit a* (Lacan 1998, p. 282) sustains – the cause of – (man's) desire and hence stands for the central lack expressed in the (psychical) phenomenon of castration, the split, the bar in the barred Subject; consequently, it is also the object of the gaze (Lacan 1998, pp. 76–7), and remains implicit in visual display, which is always gendered feminine, whether it is performed by man or woman (Lacan 1982, p. 85); it designates the unsymbolizable remainder of and in the Real (Lacan 1998, p. 83). Although unsexed and unsexable in itself, the *objet petit a* bears a greater affiliation with woman, as she, for Lacan, is 'not whole' with respect to phallic *jouissance* (Lacan 1999, p. 7). There is something of her specifically female – feminine – *jouissance*, of which nothing can be said, in other words, an untranslatable remainder. Lacan takes pains to clarify that man and woman are equally (of) *objet a*,[6] but then again the connection between woman and *a* is not one of belongingness or overlap (however fractional): *a* is *closer* to woman than to man, because the former's *jouissance* exceeds the phallic, while she also supports the movement of the Lacanian desire, a movement of metaphorical substitution that is nevertheless only made possible by her metonymical attachment to the Other's cause of desire.

The Levinasian dwelling and psychoanalytic theorizations of the unhomely converge in the locus of this explicitly or implicitly gendered remainder, even though, in Levinas, Woman is perceived as a link, while for psychoanalysis femininity designates a fissure. In Levinas, Woman enables the I/Other to situate his dwelling and himself in relation to the world. In Lacanian psychoanalysis, the (feminine) fissure represented by the *objet petit a* brings the speaking/desiring subject into being. In both, the catalyst is partially but unmistakeably gendered. In both, therefore, male subjectivity, namely a however flawed at-home-ness in language and the economy of desire, is conditional upon the simultaneous deployment and exclusion of the feminine.

The Levinasian I/Other needs Woman to envelop himself in. This not-quite-Other is described as the '*tu*' of familiarity ('thou' in the English translation), and, unlike the formal '*vous*' of the face of the Other (the partner in the ethical relation), it/she is always already in a relationship of intimacy with the I who is being welcomed inside the dwelling.[7] The 'recollection' that takes place in the home refers to a welcome, itself concretized in the face of the welcoming other. Since the intimacy of recollection would be impossible in the face of the Other of transcendence and language, the other who welcomes is so discreet and familiar that its/her presence almost flickers into an absence. Between the welcoming and the welcomed, 'an understanding without words, an expression in secret' is established, which is both outside and beyond language (Levinas 1979, p. 155). The essentially silent plane that this couple draws on is no rudimentary or undeveloped system of communication, but rather one that 'is comprehensible and exercises its function of interiorisation only on the ground of the full human personality, which, however, in the woman, can be reserved so as to open up the dimension of interiority' (ibid.). This would of course be not the interiority of/for herself, but of/for the object of her affection ('*amitié*'), the I for-itself of man. Thus, thanks to her disinterested gift of reservation, Woman can truncate her subjectivity (via her non-language of intimacy) to shelter her Other (which is the male 'I'), transform a building into a dwelling (via her welcome, out of love) and keep her distance (in all gentleness and discretion); her raison d'être is to envelop an Other, even at the cost of remaining homeless herself.

In 'The Phenomenology of Eros', this idea of 'woman' is developed further though in much the same vein. 'In love transcendence goes both further and less far than language' (Levinas 1979, p. 256). In other words, it both reaches out for a subliminal, ecstatic, wordless model of semiosis, *and* falls short of full access to and competence in the symbolic. In 'eros', utterances are not infinite but unfinished, imperfect and incomplete. 'To love is to fear for another, to come to the assistance of his frailty. In this frailty as in the dawn rises the Loved, who is the Beloved (*l'Aimé qui est Aimée*),' and it is therefore her (not his) 'frailty' that is at issue. Levinas generally uses the passive form of the participle for the feminine ('*Aimée*') and the active for the masculine lover ('*Amant*'), which illustrates the fundamental asymmetry between the two. Besides fragility, a certain 'exorbitant ultramateriality' characterizes '*l' Aimée*', 'no nothingness – but what is not yet', which evokes clandestinity, absence of signification and a vague avant-garde promise (she *will* be, maybe). The crux of Levinasian femininity is to be discovered in 'the simultaneity or equivocation of this fragility and this weight of non-signifyingness, heavier than the weight of the formless real' (1979, pp. 256–7). The caress, the mode of intercourse par excellence between the *Amant* and the *Aimée*, the lover and his beloved, 'overwhelms the relation of the I with itself and with the non-I', and yet it has to be 'an *amorphous* non-I' who 'sweeps away the I into an absolute future where it escapes itself and loses its position as subject' (p. 259). The face of the Beloved comes short of betraying the secret of Eros. It expresses nothing but its refusal to express (p. 260).

Levinas's conceptions of the feminine (as not wholly other because not wholly *equivalent*), the home (as dwelling via and thanks to the feminine) and most importantly, their conjunction are hardly new or unique, despite their opaque and at times poetic eloquence. The unnerving resonances in the Levinasian welcoming '*tu*' of Ruskin's quintessentially Victorian explication of the separate spheres indicate how insidious and resistant to social change the ideological couple of woman-house is. In effect, both Ruskin and Levinas reiterate popular(ized) notions of both the home and femininity in modernity and hence reaffirm deep-rooted preconceptions about the 'essence' of the former and the 'nature' of the latter. It is therefore not surprising that Levinas has attracted a lot of attention in second wave and subsequent feminist thinking.[8] Irigaray's writings on Levinas evoke a pronounced ambivalence: on the one hand, in him she finds an ally in her revision of Heidegger but on the other, she is ultimately betrayed by the language of philosophy, in the edifice of which Levinas remains trapped (1993, pp. 185–217). Irigaray is left both homeless and imprisoned within a world view where the feminine is both instrumental and by definition liminal. Neither in

Heidegger nor in Levinas is there a position from which the female philosopher may articulate a specifically feminine discourse. The Levinasian universe is not merely unable to accommodate woman as anything other than gentle homeliness and silent intimacy, but it arguably perpetrates 'the ultimate violence' on the feminine (speaking) subject – should she, for a moment, break into the house of philosophy. Even in its ethical transfiguration, the dwelling is to woman what the home of modernity is to (male) phenomenologists, namely the site of extreme yet masked alienation. In the Western philosophical tradition, 'The space of philosophy is not just a domestic space, it is a space in which a certain idea about the domestic is sustained and protected.' As a result, 'By being placed outside, the other is … domesticated, kept inside. To be excluded is to be subjected to a certain domestic violence that is both organised and veiled by metaphysics' (Wigley 1993, p. 107). The Law of the house – as well as that of the language of philosophy – is essentially one that subordinates the feminine, since it is itself founded upon feminine subordination. Postmodernist philosophy, in spite of its rigorous questioning of metaphysics, perpetrates the same – double – crime against the feminine. In *Evictions: Art and Spatial Politics*, Rosalyn Deutsche explores how even theorists who unambiguously interrogate the discursive foundations of the Western philosophical traditions (or explore the history of such interrogations) are guilty of replicating and relying upon this fundamental exclusion: in 'Men in Space' (pp. 195–202), she reveals how 'the Jameson school of interdisciplinarity' consistently excludes the feminist problematic, while David Harvey's totalizing vision of society (1989) casts the feminine as a threat of loss of boundaries and hence carefully keeps it at bay ('Boys Town', pp. 203–44).

This lengthy investigation into the philosophical foundations of the woman-house ideological coupling was deemed as a necessary context for art practices that reflect on and protest against the home on feminist grounds. The next section focuses on examples of such art practices, which critique domesticity thematically, formally and in their processes: they rely on more or less loosely formed collectives that cut across nuclear family structures and suggest alternative living arrangements, to produce installations that debunk domestic ideals.

Womanhouse (1972) and the Women's Postal Art Event, a.k.a. Feministo (1975–77)[9]

'Home' becomes an issue when it is faced with external or internal forces that disrupt its established meanings as a site of security and belongingness. The interfaces of home and homeland, home and woman, not simply as concepts but in terms of the lived experience of exiles, the homeless, refugees, escapees from intimate partner violence are constantly being interrogated and contested in both theory and a range of practices, including visual art.[10] On the other hand, the canonized body of theory that identifies 'homelessness' as the condition of the subject in modernity partly confirms the character of 'home' as a safe – and safely self-evident – metaphorical structure: 'home' offers the stable centre against which the centrifugal subjectivities of modernity are conveniently demarcated.[11] Again, 'home' emerges from the ruins of a mythical 'at-homeness', ever-deferred to a premodern past which turns out to be closer to the pre-Oedipal imaginary.

For second-wave feminism, 'home' was recast as a site of crisis and violence in itself, by overhauling the concept of the domestic sphere to uncover its gendered cultural connotations as well as its innate and essentially sexist biases. The home was revealed as a privileged site because of its preconceived links with femininity, both metonymically and metaphorically: metonymically, because of woman's presumed belongingness to the domestic space and her indispensable role in its maintenance; metaphorically, because, as Irigaray has often argued, the domesticity of the house – its 'homeliness' – is modelled after the primordial nostalgia for the maternal body and is guaranteed by the presence of the woman in/of the house. Not only is this nostalgia implicitly gendered, but it also succeeds in subordinating the (m)Other, who forever strives to satisfy it, to a position of irredeemable, un-subjectifiable otherness. She is thus encumbered with the thankless task of playing hostess to man's 'homelessness' and, for this reason 'she lacks, notably, the power to fold back around the dwelling which she is. … Tradition places her within the home, sheltered in the home. But that home … encloses her, places her in *internal exile*' (Irigaray 1993, p. 65, emphasis in the original). In other words, the (expectation for) homely domesticity extinguishes the possibility of a feminine subject on both material and symbolic levels. Irigaray's observations reveal the psychoanalytical and philosophical workings behind the empirical truism that the unacknowledged drudgery of housework corrodes the housewife's 'sense of self'.[12] Woman is wholly consumed by her designation and service as 'homemaker': she morphs into 'home'.

The famous art project and exhibition *Womanhouse* (30 January – 28 February 1972) was the outcome of experimental feminist pedagogies implemented in the recently relocated Feminist Art Programme (FAP) at the California Institute of the Arts. It was based on an idea by art historian Paula Harper and took place under the leadership of FAP co-directors Judy Chicago and Miriam Schapiro (Gerhard 2013, pp. 41–2) and with the participation of twenty-six students and invited contributors.[13] *Womanhouse* consisted of an installation in an abandoned Hollywood house and a programme of performances, documented in detail in Chicago's book *Through the Flower* and in the 1974 film *Womanhouse* by Johanna Demetrakas. The choice of the project's location was predated and determined by the focus on the home in consciousness-raising discussions among the group, as a site of both personal and social significance and, crucially, where the personal is revealed to be political and vice versa. Domestic space was symbolically reclaimed and transformed into a psychic lab, where women's fears and fantasies were not only projected but given material form.

> The age-old female activity of homemaking was taken to fantasy proportions. *Womanhouse* became the repository of the daydreams women have as they wash, bake, cook, sew, clean and iron their lives away. (Chicago and Shapiro cited in Wilding 1977)

The mindless repetition, drudgery and frustrations of the homemaker were not merely vented but monumentalized. After all, most participants were students with little or no experience of keeping house, although they would have most likely watched their mothers and their mothers' peers play that role. More nightmare than daydream, *Womanhouse* awakened the domestic unconscious with unsettling outcomes. The walls of its *Nurturing Kitchen* by Vicki Hodgetts swell with round breast protrusions that mockingly undo the nurturing and comforting associations of the breast by rendering visible the assumed but normally unspoken interface between women's bodies and the homeliness of home. Robbin Schiff's *Nightmare Bathroom* considers vulnerabilities, some of which are gendered (e.g. 'the fear of being intruded upon'), and which are conveyed in the fragility of the figure in the bath, composed out of loose sand and slowly disintegrating as more and more visitors gave themselves permission to touch her. Other works were more ambivalent towards the intricate connections between women and homemaking: Faith Wilding's *Crocheted Environment* celebrates 'the primitive womb-shelters' built and maintained by women through the ages but also revels in 'the freedom of not being functional' (Wilding 1972). Some of the performances were 'maintenance pieces', dramatizing usually hidden and systemically denigrated activities in real time. As Wilding's powerful poem/performance *Waiting* also suggests, the *Womanhouse* installation and performances cannot be reduced to political protest (although that alone would have been valuable at the time) since they unpicked the psychosocial implications of the sexual division of labour, which were both widespread and profound: 'Isn't cleaning up all about hope? And doesn't the futile repetition of endless housework mean losing hope?' (Lippard 1976, p. 58)

Womanhouse has acquired iconic status for all the right and wrong reasons. It captured the confluence between art practice, consciousness-raising and pedagogy; it actively questioned the myth of the genius artist working in hallowed isolation in his private studio; it exemplified feminist strategies of DIY, making do, recycling and upcycling materials and reclaiming disused spaces; it pivoted on cross-generational exchange. Furthermore, *Womanhouse* can be viewed as a precursor of what has subsequently come to be known as institutional critique, thanks to its rule-breaking experimentation with university education and its hierarchical structures (A People Missing, 2013), and its distancing from the inherently institutionalized and overdetermined space of the gallery. Comparing the installation to other artistic explorations of domesticity and the home in the 1980s, Mira Schor suggests that the exaggeratedly (un)homely style of *Womanhouse*, with its cluttered rooms and penchant for ornament, marks

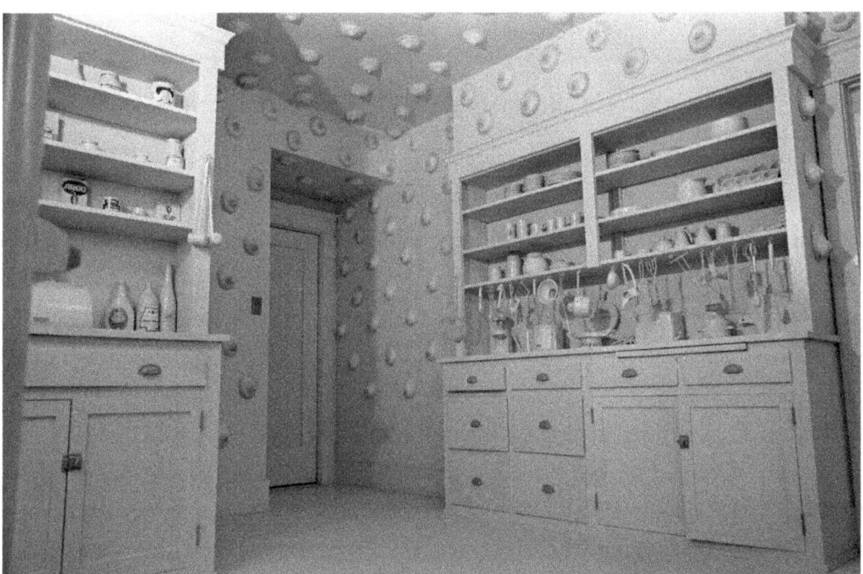

Figure 4.2 Robin, Weltsch, The Kitchen, installation view, *Womanhouse*, 1972. Courtesy of the California Institute of the Arts Institute Archive.

Figure 4.3 Faith Wilding, Crocheted Environment, installation view, *Womanhouse*, 1972. Courtesy of the artist.

a deliberate break with the white cube (1996, p. 196) as well as, I would add, a defiant resistance to the then dominant minimalist aesthetic. Yet *Womanhouse* was also plagued by the ambivalence and negativity it set out to explore. The working relationships between Chicago, Schapiro and the student-participants were often strained and resulted in at least one uprising, which Chicago reportedly took to heart (Gerhard 2013, pp. 43–7). Their chosen domestic and familial paradigm brought with it Oedipal baggage, which led Chicago to eventually accept that 'symbolically behead[ing] her was part of the process' (p. 46). In the late 1990s, Ulrike Müller published her correspondence with many of the students in the Feminist Art Programme, in which their post-graduation career (or lack thereof) in the art world is examined alongside the impact of their political and educational experiences as students on their lives in general. Most respondents express some ambivalence and a couple

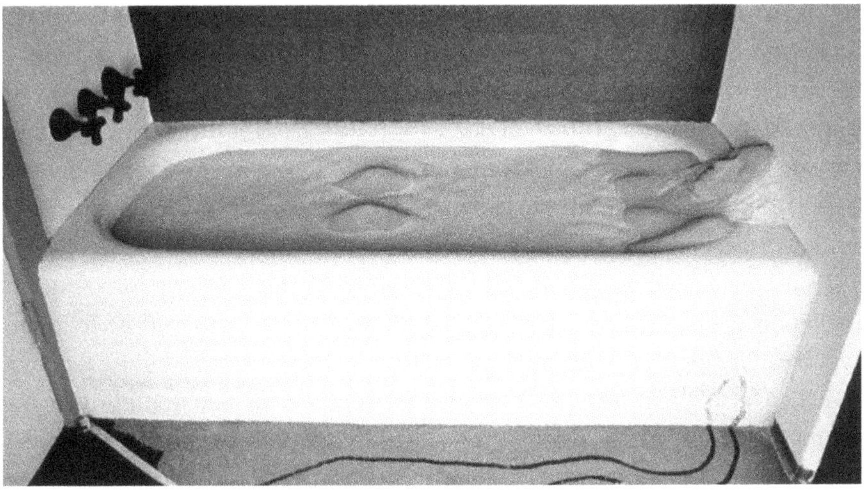

Figure 4.4 Robin Schiff, Nightmare Bathroom, *Womanhouse*, 1972. Courtesy of the California Institute of the Arts Institute Archive.

are open about their feelings of intense stress and rejection while working on *Womanhouse*; respondent C. G. characteristically notes: 'Put 30 women together and see what happens. A nightmare' (Müller 2015). Looking back, there is a real danger of reducing the subversive unhomeliness of *Womanhouse* to a feminist gothic confessional that perpetuates rather than challenges damaging gender stereotypes and casts strong women as harpies and harridans. Without intending to minimize anyone's experience, it is worth remembering the magnitude of the ambition and attendant risks of projects such as *Womanhouse*, not in art-world terms but on a sociopolitical and even philosophical level, involving 'a set of heterogeneous operations of the denaturalization of the relations between sex, gender, visuality and power' (A People is Missing, 2013).

A lesser known UK-based equivalent of *Womanhouse* is the international postal art event and travelling installation *Feministo: Portrait of the Artist as a Housewife* (1975–77), which, similarly, reveals and explores the inherent violence of the domestic sphere from gendered perspectives. First, the fake domestic environment of *Feministo*'s installations is haunted by a distinctly feminist discontent in the face of the sexual division of labour under patriarchy and its insidious psychical supports and implications. More significantly, *Feministo* stages a virtual eviction from woman-enabled domesticity as well as the comforting metaphorical self-evidence of home. The fake and palpably un-homely installation at the Institute of Contemporary Arts

(1977) *mimics* the domestic environment in the postcolonial sense of the word. *Feministo*'s fictional domesticity is *almost* the same as patriarchal domesticity – *but not quite* (cf. Bhabha 1994, pp. 85–92). In the gap opened up by their disparity, feminism articulates a critique of domesticity as a lived reality for women and a menace to the patriarchal ideal of domesticity. Borne in such gaps, mimicry is constitutive of the specifically feminist perspective from which domesticity is critiqued, derided and symbolically undone.

I will start by giving a short history of *Feministo* and a description of its last exhibition in the UK, the 1977 installation at the ICA. This will be followed by a consideration of women's work as 'labour of love' from Marxist feminist and then a feminist art/craft historical perspective, demonstrating how the naturalization of women's domestic work simultaneously guarantees a model of patriarchal femininity while also keeping women in their place, namely the home but also an unproductive (reproductive), non-aesthetic (decoratively 'creative') sphere of production. In *Feministo*, the employment of women's traditional craft skills, passed on from one generation to the next,[14] exemplifies the fundamental ambivalence of the installation in its entirety. Women's crafts are valued for their non-implication in the art world, thus allowing for a woman-specific, non-exclusive communication, but they also evoke the 'internal exile' of domestic femininity. Finally, parts of the installation will be examined in some detail, exploring *Feministo* as a multiple but consistently angry and humorous portrait of artists/housewives, and as a proposed escape route from their shared 'internal exile'.

Home truths: What is *Feministo*?

The postal art project that was later to be given the name 'Feministo' started off casually and in private in late 1974, between friends Kate Walker and Sally Gollop, after the latter moved house.[15] These two initiated a network of postal exchange of small artworks, most of which drew on traditional domestic craft techniques, while also thematizing the experience of domesticity in 1970s Britain from an explicitly dissident, mostly feminist perspective. In 1976, the accumulated works went on a touring exhibition (*Portrait of the Artist as a Young Woman*) that culminated in the installation *Portrait of the Artist as a Housewife* at the ICA (10 June – 20 July 1977).[16] Although *Feministo* initially consisted of a personal exchange of small (and thus cheap and easy to post) artworks which originally served the purpose of keeping the line of communication open between friends, it was gradually politicized and expanded to include more women of different ages and backgrounds. Not all of the participants knew each other, some had received fine art training (or were students at the time) and some not, and their perceptions of the women's movement and feminism also varied widely.

Feministo's transformation from a private way of keeping in touch to a postal art project began at the 1975 conference 'Women in Art History' in London, when members of the Birmingham Women Artists' Group heard Kate Walker speak:

> She was frustrated by some long-winded discussion and she said suddenly, 'Look, aren't there any housewives here who want to make some art, and who are fed up with all this fine art business? Aren't there any of you making things at home that you'd like to show each other?'. (Richardson and Davidson 1987, pp. 37 and 39)

Su Richardson's account of the events places the project on the cultural and political map, at the intersection of a developing feminist rethinking of the discipline of art history (listening to Griselda Pollock speak at the conference was also immensely influential), emergent feminist art practices, and the will to establish more and wider networks of exchange and debate, of which consciousness-raising groups are a prominent but not singular example. *Feministo* itself has been likened to a consciousness-raising group due to its character as a free women's forum and the themes explored under its auspices: the domestic, housewifery, ambivalent attitudes to children and partners, frustration with the art world and disabling prejudices against women's creativity. Through the format of postal correspondence, participants sought to establish correspondences on a one-to-one basis, but also to accommodate disagreements and explore ambivalence. From the conference of 1975 to the ICA installation of 1977, the number of participants fluctuated considerably from a dozen to about thirty. The age of the participants (from their late teens to their eighties) varied as much as their background (struggling artists, full-time housewives) and aspirations, especially as regards the possible role of the personal in the public sphere. When the first exhibition of the accumulated three hundred works was held in Manchester in 1976, Sally Gollop decided not to have her works shown, as she considered the postal exchange a strictly personal affair (Walker 2000).

Since the first show at North-West Arts in Manchester, most exhibitions, both in the UK and abroad, were installations curated by the participants themselves. As Kate Walker confirms, every show presented a central methodological and political problem: 'how to place effectively these expressions of domestic isolation and frustration – this anger against the prevailing male "artocracy" – within the white-walled neutral spaces intended for a very different kind of art' (Walker 1980, p. 34). At the ICA exhibition, which had by far the most elaborate installation display, the problem was solved by 'building a house pastiche which broke the space up into intimate rooms' (ibid.). Among these rooms were a bedroom and a kitchen, but also a 'memory room' and, disturbingly, a 'rape room', over the entrance of which hung a blinding light, alluding to interrogation and torture.

After the ICA show, the installation went on a final international tour including Australia. Not all of the works made it back, some having been stolen and others fallen apart in transit. Those that were returned to their creators were either destroyed or kept as personal memorabilia, that is to say reclaimed as something more, and less, or in any case, other than an artwork (Ross 2000b). The over one hundred slides kept at the Women's Art Library/MAKE (Special Collections, Goldsmiths, University of London) are mainly from the ICA installation and were donated by Walker and Richardson separately.[17] The fate of the individual works is no sign of negligence, since it serves to reinforce the character of the event as a process and a dialogue – an exchange of ideas rather than objects, or perhaps ideas translated into small artworks. It is not just a disregard for ownership (Ross in Parker and Pollock 1987, p. 211) that the disappearance of the works conveys, but it also reveals the fundamental function of the event as an intervention in domestic and art politics, in the historical context of the late 1970s Britain.

Postal exchange constitutes a critical aspect of *Feministo*, not least because it highlights its eclectic relationship to 'mail art' and other anti-art movements such as Fluxus and Dada. 'Mama', the name of a Birmingham women artists' collective that got involved in *Feministo*, puns on Dada and, like Dada artists, the *Feministo* group missed no opportunity to express its disregard of, and even contempt for, *fine* art aesthetics. In an appropriately irreverent and playful manifesto by Kate Walker, a table comparing 'Art MANifest' to 'Arts Feminist-O!' the 'status' of the latter category is described as follows: 'Art is like cooking. Art is like childbirth. Art is like breathing. Our art is ancient magic. Art is *solidarity*. Our artwork is together even when we are apart. Ours is ordinary + useful magic. We don't boast.' The extent to which this feminist manifesto (or: *Feministo*) was fuelled by the desire to come together and communicate is thrown into relief by the following explanatory note attached to the table in MAMA's centrefold:

> This statement was not designed as such, but as a letter to comfort my friend Catherine Nicholson because she was thinking that what she does is not 'proper art'. I read it aloud at a meeting of the Women Artists in Scunthorpe and it

> seemed generally appropriate to the exhibition so we included it. (Walker in MAMA Collective 1977)

A letter about and against 'proper art' is thus transformed into an improper and unplanned manifesto. Purposeful defiance of boundaries and definitions has serendipitous results, as works and ideas are shared in meetings and through the post to be heeded, reinterpreted and, like many of the materials used in the creation of the artworks, reused. By virtue of both its international postal character and the domestic mimicry of its installations, *Feministo* cancels out the connection between home and hometown/-land[18] by articulating the demand for a new, otherly community in the post, the non-place between two addresses and in a gallery masqueraded as a home, thus also wilfully eroding definitions and boundaries of both 'home' and 'gallery' alike (cf. Parker 2010, p. 209).

Evicting homeliness: 'Labour of love' versus feminist (art)work

Women's work has been a feminist issue since the emergence of the second wave. But although women's work, even forty years ago, covered a wide range of occupations, paid (however unfairly) and unpaid, the Women's Liberation Movement focused as much on equal pay and access to heavily gendered trades and professions as on domestic work, by definition unpaid. The 'wages for housework' campaign, fought on many fronts and with disparate agendas, highlighted the economic oddity and social injustice of the unpaid domestic labour of women (and some men), but fundamentally failed to address the forged contiguity and correlation between domesticity and femininity. The common starting point of many feminist analyses (for and against wages for housework) is the misconception that women's work in the home does not constitute 'productive labour' in the terms of traditional political economy.[19] Serendipitously, these analyses succeed in unmasking the fundamental gender-blindness of Marxist frameworks, but only do so by falling short of their stated goal of critiquing and rectifying the assumption that raising children and keeping house is a womanly 'labour of love' and thus, by definition, beyond remuneration. Despite locating the problem in the assumption that 'it will always be women who do housework and look after children' (Malos 1980, p. 7), in their overwhelming majority, Marxist feminist critiques approached women and/in the home as forming a *relation* to be examined, whereas it is actually the lack of relation – namely, their virtual overlap – that is guilty of perpetuating the predicament of the separate spheres of the (presumably two) sexes.

Where Marxist economic analysis fails, feminist art history succeeds. It is by overhauling the hierarchical distinction between art and craft that the covert yet effective implication of femininity and domesticity starts to surface. In *Old Mistresses*, Rozsika Parker and Griselda Pollock unravel the fabric that holds together needlework and femininity, while simultaneously looking into the similarly gendered distinction between amateurship and professionalism in the crafts. Since the Middle Ages, a series of cultural and economic developments resulted in a split between professional and amateur craftwork, reflected in their physical separation in space – the former confined to the workshop and the latter to the home. This was not a neat split along gender lines, since the majority of paid craftwork was still done by working-class or disadvantaged middle-class women (Parker 2010, p. 5). What the split made possible, however, is the classification of *all* of women's craftwork in the home as an amateurish feminine pastime – a labour of love and thus not labour proper. By the 1750s, women's needlework had already been so far removed from any notion of paid labour that it served as 'proof of gentility, providing concrete evidence that a man was able to support a leisured woman' (Parker and Pollock 1981, p. 61). Paradoxically, its role as a gage of class and financial position is no indication that this already feminized and homebound occupation was ever limited to wealthy households. In most cases, women's needlework as well as other forms of craftwork had both decorative and utilitarian functions, often allowing for considerable savings in the household budget (ibid., p. 63). *Old Mistresses* explores the historical developments surrounding the ever-diminished status of women's craft not as an explanation for it, but, on the contrary, in order to demonstrate how biased and arbitrary the demotion of women's craft was. Parker and Pollock emphasize the lack of causality between the professionalization of needlework and the surreptitious emergence of hierarchical binaries such as craft – art, amateurship – professionalism and thus highlight the ideological nature of such binaries. In *The Subversive Stitch*, Parker takes this investigation further by framing the history of women's embroidery as a symbol of and a means of inculcating and maintaining the ideal of femininity. The iconography of embroidery patterns and the domestic context in which women embroidered since the seventeenth century contributed to the creation of a feminine stereotype, whereas the widespread practice of embroidery from an early age served to naturalize this stereotype: 'Embroidery and femininity were entirely fused, and the connection was deemed to be natural. Women embroidered because they were naturally feminine and were feminine because they naturally embroidered' (Parker 2010, p. 11). The naturalized and naturalizing role of embroidery precludes any recognition of women's craftwork as either an aesthetic or an economic commodity. Therefore, its ideological role fulfils at least three functions: it casts women as non-productive labourers; it keeps them labouring, in the appropriate – domestic – settings; it ensures that their labour will not be bestowed with any but decorative value at best, befitting their femininity. For these reasons, embroidery and, by extension, women's domestic craftwork exposes the support of the separate spheres of the sexes as ideological while, at the same time, demonstrating how women's work is depleted of both economic and aesthetic value by being cast as a 'labour of love', namely a natural expression of the femininity that it embodies. As in the case of woman and home, woman and women's crafts merge into a model of patriarchal femininity which women's crafts help form, maintain and propagate. Women are held captive by the idea(l) and expectations of their housewifely *amateur*ship, just as they are reduced to the psychical and ideological founding block of domesticity (Wigley 1993, p. 134–6).

In the works of *Feministo*, the use of women's craft techniques may not be exclusive but it is emblematic. The rejection of women's art by the majority of the art world was not one-sided, as the most vocal of the participants (including Philippa Goodall, Monica Ross and Kate Walker) explicitly condemned the gender and class biases of galleries and the discipline of art history. *Feministo* was originally conceptualized as an anti-art project in the sense of Dada anti-art (Walker 2000), but was also grounded on the belief that the division of production into the sanctity of fine art and the quotidian profanity of craft is inherently sexist. The participants opted for used, recycled materials that were assembled on kitchen tables not simply out of necessity but as a political choice, as part of an ecological, anti-technological and inclusive model of creativity and communication.[20] Su Richardson notes, moreover, that many women were already competent in skills such as crocheting and that 'men don't know enough about it to pass comment' (Richardson and Davidson 1987, p. 41). Tainted though it may be by patriarchal projections, the exclusively female tradition of women's domestic crafts provides a platform other than and parallel to the Women's Liberation Movement for an intergenerational dialogue.[21] As Philippa Goodall succinctly put it, *Feministo* 'both celebrated the area of domestic creativity and "woman's world" and exposed it for its paucity' (Goodall 1987, p. 213). The project owes its unsettling quality to the ambivalence of this double focus: comfort and exile, the homely and the uncanny are both simultaneously present in each of the works and the installation as a whole.

Tricia Davis's *Something Nasty in the Bottom Drawer* is exemplary of the psychical workings of the *Feministo* exhibitions, from the perspective of both its makers-curators and spectators. An assemblage of ready-mades consisting of the black-and-white photograph of a woman with downcast eyes and a piece of jewellery, the work evokes mourning for a female loved one, lost intimacy and, possibly, frustrated aspirations. Its implied nostalgia, however, redefines 'homesickness' as the fundamental condition of woman *at home*. Domesticity, familiarity and familiality are all evoked but, at the same time, they are prefixed by the 'un-' of repression (Freud 1919, p. 368) by virtue of the work's title. In Davis's work, the relics of somebody close who is now gone become the painful reminder of their absence – 'something nasty' – and are discovered tellingly 'in the bottom drawer' – where one keeps what is best kept secret (Schelling cited in Freud 1919, p. 345). Analogically, *Feministo* reveals home truths by uncovering the discontent that has been veiled for so long under the sheath of 'natural' femininity. By uncanny-ing both house and 'housewife' and unearthing the semiotic oppression and repression inherent in such terms, a new, anti-domestic feminist model of femininity is proposed. The fact that this act of uncanny-ing is perpetrated within the symbolic space of domesticity by women only serves to exacerbate its menace (Johnson 1987, pp. 153–4): suddenly and retroactively, the angel in the house turns into the madwoman in the attic.

Feminist(o) matters: This portrait which is not one

In her essay 'This Sex Which Is Not One', Irigaray (1985b) argues that, due to a fundamental asymmetry between the two sexes, in which the masculine sets the standards, the feminine does not in fact qualify as a 'proper' sex at all. The female sexual organs represent the scandal of vacuum, nothing-to-be-seen, whereas female sexuality is always at least double: suspended between nothingness and an unorthodox plurality, the feminine, in patriarchy, is not – it is always already elsewhere. The French term 'propre' evokes propriety as well as cleanliness and property. *Feministo*'s installations operate in a virtual realm of impropriety in this wider sense: not only do they portray a stereotypical example ('housewife') of the improper gender (not quite one because more than one), but they also suggest a rejection of 'proper' housekeeping (cleanliness) and 'proper' art (in terms of aesthetics, media or the status of its maker) in a 'proper' gallery (taxonomical clarity) alike. Moreover, the exchange of the works through the post prior to their exhibition makes ownership ambiguous (Ross 1987, p. 211), as does the makeshift labelling of the works at the ICA installation with almost unreadable tags hanging from a string.

Figure 4.5 A Portrait of the Artist as a Housewife, c.1977. Black-and-white publicity poster, 21 × 29.5 (A4). *Feministo: Portrait of the Artist as a Housewife*, Women's Art Library/MAKE, London.

There is yet another, all too obvious sense in which this is not a proper portrait. Whereas some figurative representations of female bodies are scattered throughout the ICA installation, they far from dominate the format of the individual works. More importantly, the 'portrait as a housewife' consists of the installation as a whole and is conveyed in the form of the viewing experience of a visitor walking through the metamorphosed ICA. 'Housewife' is therefore represented in spatial terms, in the shape of a dystopian home. The metaphor of the body that envelops becomes literal and invades a space – an art gallery – where it ostensibly does not belong. This portrait is no less than an enactment of a culturally overdetermined crime against property: a squat. Tellingly, the South London Women's Centre at 14 Radnor Terrace in Lambeth, which housed the similarly (un)domestic installation *A Woman's Place* in 1975, was an actual squat.[22] Gender identities are manipulated and revised by means of invading and misusing spaces onto which they had been mapped: the squat in the gallery, which mimics the invasion of the domestic sphere by feminist discontent, evicts patriarchal subjectivity from its privilege in the 'Empire of the Self-Same' (Cixous and Clément 1986, pp. 63–132).

In the installation at 14 Radnor Terrace, Kate Walker described the different rooms of the transformed space 'as images of mental states' (cited in Parker 1987, p. 200). *Feministo* follows this format to the letter, by altering the ambience of domestic rooms (kitchen, bedroom) and adding new ones, such as the 'memory room' and the 'rape room'. Approaching the rape room, a visitor would have to wince by reflex, but also in anticipation of the horrors displayed inside: Kate Walker's *Rape Cup and Saucer*, an obvious homage to Meret Oppenheim's *Fur Cup and Saucer*, is lined with newspaper clippings reporting incidents of sexual assault. The suggested juxtaposition of the two works amounts to an indictment to the sexual politics of fetishism, alluded to by the use of fur by Oppenheim on the concave surface of an object firmly associated with homeliness. The use of traditional women's craft techniques makes some of the works into traces as well as icons of housewifery. In the 'kitchen', Su Richardson's *Burnt Breakfast*, a slightly overdone, woollen full English with burnt egg and bacon, not only references the housewifely occupation of cooking the family meals, but is simultaneously an indexical sign of another womanly skill, crocheting. Yet cooking and crocheting cancel each other out, making this *Breakfast* into a mockery of more than one aspect of housewifely duties. More subtly, it is the black edging around the egg and alongside the burnt sausage that mark the cook's ambivalence, suggesting neglect, resentment or a mix of both. Richardson's crocheted sandwiches do not make packed lunches but eloquent statements about motherhood and domesticity, showing a dry and punning sense of humour. The deceptively beautiful *Butterfly Sandwich* does not satisfy hunger but gives whomever eats it butterflies instead; hold the butter and it turns into a revolting *Fly (and Tongue)* sarnie. The intense ambivalence of smothering between two crocheted slices of bread the face of a baby doll, a pivotal ideological instrument in the inculcation of motherly femininity in little girls (*Babyface Sandwich*), tips over into gagging abjection in the *Dirty Nappy Sandwich*. Boxes of chocolates, the perfect romantic gift, are found to contain bite-size amputated limbs – lips or labia, some with teeth (*Keep Smiling Chocs* by Kate Walker) or female body parts, including severed sexual organs (Walker, *Black Magic Bodies*). Fetishism is indicted again for the commodification of the female body beautiful, whereas the allusion to sexual violence is still discernible. Also on the kitchen table,

Figure 4.6 Su Richardson, *Burnt Breakfast* and *Packed Lunch*, 1975–76, crochet and mixed media. *Feministo: Portrait of the Artist as a Housewife*. Photograph by Susan Richardson, 2010. © Susan Richardson. All Rights Reserved, DACS 2015.

Figure 4.7 Kate Walker, *Keep Smiling Chocs*, c.1975–77, mixed media in chocolate box, *Feministo: Portrait of the Artist as a Housewife*. Photograph by Michael Ann Mullen. Courtesy of the artist's estate and Michael Ann Mullen.

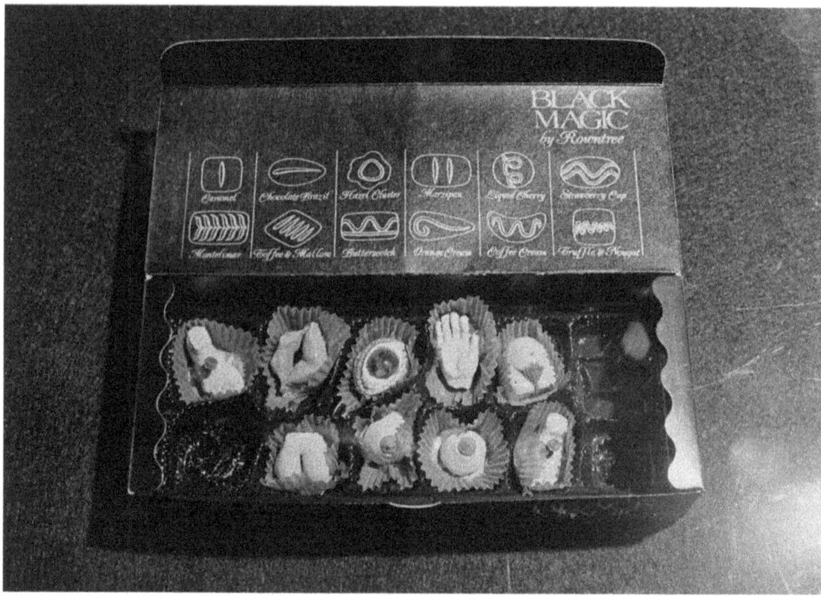

Figure 4.8 Kate Walker, *Black Magic Bodies*, c.1975–77, mixed media in chocolate box, *Feministo: Portrait of the Artist as a Housewife*. Photograph by Michael Ann Mullen. Courtesy of the artist's estate and Michael Ann Mullen.

there is a raw-looking papier mâché nude resting on a bed of paper lettuce and cucumber slices. Through its pose, Catherine Nicholson's *Salad with Woman* evokes Orientalist odalisques, while also presenting a 'domesticated' version of Manet's *Luncheon on the Grass*, rendered simultaneously banal and violent. The metaphor of the female body as something to be consumed is literalized to harrowing effect. Her *Packed Meat in the Fridge*, 'limbless bodies encased, like battery-bred poultry, in plastic shrouds', also literalizes the sexist expression 'meat market' with a directness so grotesque that prompted the Women's Free Art Association to reject one of Nicholson's paintings as 'unsuitable', unpalatable even by certain feminist standards (Walker in MAMA 1977, p. 39).

The disturbing effects of the ICA installation are documented in the reactions of many of its spectators. 'Miserable bitches', 'bitter and twisted' are only a couple of the printable comments entered in the visitors' book (cited in Parker 1987, p. 209). 'Pornographic' and 'tatty' apparently refer to the aesthetic quality of the material, pronouncing it 'out of place' in (and contaminating of) the culturally invested space of the gallery. The Northwest Arts Association, which housed the first *Feministo* installation, reacted to its content by putting up notices reading 'Unsuitable for Children', which was ironic, as most of the works were made at home and many in the presence of young children.

Ritualized squats and symbolic evictions are valuable strategies in feminism's constant battle against the most pervasive and insidious of structures, such as 'home' and the spaces of art, which are revealed to be complexly gendered and imbued in the politics of power. Most of *Feministo*'s material traces (the works) have now been erased: 'The intent not the object was the issue, the process of making art works as communication rather than the production of commodities' (Ross 2000a, p. 5). And yet it is precisely its precarious, 'flickering' quality that ensures this project's continuing relevance. Suspended between memory and the (art) history books, *Feministo* is in the privileged position of being both personal and context-specific as well as emblematic of second-wave poetics and politics. This wilfully improper imitation of dwelling remains appropriately homeless, partially dematerialized, in memory, a legend to some and now, in some small way, embroiled in an argument between feminism, art, philosophy and psychoanalysis.

5

Dinner Parties: Eating Out, Coming Together

Setting the scene

In *Looking at the Overlooked: Four Essays on Still Life Painting* (1990), Norman Bryson turns to the uncanny in an attempt to explain the contradictory thoughts and ambivalent feelings of the (male) painter of still life: 'In the case of the male what must be repressed and discarded if gender identity is to be secured, are the ties with the world of nourishment and creaturely dependence that centre on the mother' (p. 170). Bryson writes of the 'seductiveness' and 'mystique' of the mother's body (p. 172), which he conflates with her surroundings. His understanding of repression leaves a lot to be desired, since to conflate repression with the act of discarding is psychoanalytically unsound, unless discarding is meant as an allusion to the abject, the jettisoned not-quite-object, which, for Kristeva, represents the more radical and physical manifestation of the uncanny (1982, p. 2 and pp. 5–6). In terms of heteronormative male socialization, Bryson is not wrong to underline the expectation of separation from the sphere of influence of the mother. What is both interesting and troubling about his argument is the assumption of a 'public – private' dichotomy that is firmly and permanently gendered. Sue Rowley interrogates the persistence of this dichotomy and its implications for art practice informed by feminism. She argues that a more 'nuanced, flexible and open-ended conceptual framework' (1994, p. 225) is necessary for appreciating feminist practice in its full political potential as opposed to a form of confession or art therapy. The public and the private are neither directly opposed nor completely separate: if the personal is indeed political, domesticity needs to be considered as a microcosm of widespread ideological operations, a lab for world-making. Furthermore, the artists and implied viewers in the context of this book neither are nor are they assumed to be male, so Bryson's narrative of mystique, seductiveness and abjection is necessarily revised and complicated through the ambivalence, pleasures, complicity and conflicts of the mother–daughter plot.[1]

The double thematic focus of this chapter on dinner parties and the kitchens that make them possible requires some explanation. After all, kitchens and dinner parties belong to different orders: one is a space, the other an activity, which would, as a rule, take place in a different, less intimate and informal space. Both kitchens and dinner parties are culturally charged and invested with feminist potential. Both are historically gendered, in opposite ways. In visual culture, dinner parties have more often than not been dominated by important figures who are, more often than not, male. Their encounters and conversations matter enough to be facilitated through the sharing of food and commemorated in visual representations. As this chapter examines, the subversive potential of feminist revisions of the dinner party scene is demonstrated in Mary Beth Edelson's poster remake of the Last Supper as a meal shared among living American women artists, which has been met with a surprising amount of controversy. Unlike dinner parties, kitchens and the people who work in them normally stay out of sight, off stage, even deemed ob-scene (Ferris 2002, p. 187). It is not merely kitchens and dinner parties that are feminist issues but so is the ideological gulf that separates them. Judy Chicago has often described her monumental installation *The Dinner Party* as 'a reinterpretation of the Last Supper from the point of view of those who've done the cooking throughout history' (Chicago 2015). Bobby Baker's perverse kitchen 'actions' are made from the point of view of not merely a cook but of a hostess attentive to her guests. Caryl Churchill's 1982 play *Top Girls* brings the scene of a lavish women-only dinner party at a restaurant together with a more fraught and intimate scene between two sisters in a kitchen, as two interdependent sides of the struggle of and within women's movements. Blurring the boundaries between dining rooms and kitchens, dinner parties and syncopated conversations and silences behind the scenes challenges the spatial separation between the public and the private and, more radically, the pervasive hierarchies between history and stories. Last but not least, a contemporary invocation of the goddess Kali as (more than one) housewives in an early painting by Sutapa Biswas blends the sacred and the profane, as Kali has always done. In Biswas's painting, Kali becomes a disturbingly familiar feminist avenger whose powers include time travel.

Too much?

A recent pedagogical experiment threw into relief the fine line between the uncanny as aesthetic experience and the uncanny as pure discomfort that inhibits and interrupts any process as dispassionate and detached as the phrase 'aesthetic experience' suggests. In a change of pace from normal course delivery, I decided to screen the video versions of two performances by Bobby Baker, *Kitchen Show* (1991) and *How to Live* (2004) in a first-year undergraduate class in visual culture for fine art students. As well as personally admiring Bobby Baker and her work, I also knew that, unlike other favourite artists of mine, she has wide appeal and the gift of engaging diverse audiences, including those not otherwise familiar or comfortable with performance art informed by feminism. I expected that the superficially light-hearted tone would come across as both inviting and, eventually, as the performance unfolded, humorously subversive. I thought, in all honesty, that this would be a soft introduction to feminist performance. I had also for a moment considered Chantal Akerman's *Jeanne Dielman, 23 Quai du Commerce, 1080 Bruxelles* (1975) but rejected it due to its length (just over 200 minutes) and its potentially alienating real-time rhythm, rather than its violent ending. Akerman's film will not be discussed in this book either, even though it is almost too perfect an exploration of the uncanny inflected by feminism. *Jeanne Dielman* simply and flawlessly 'reveals as strange' 'what is familiar and domestic' (Margulies 2009). All I have to offer the reader is my recommendation to watch it.

After a deliberately short prologue that provided some factual information about Bobby Baker and her work, and quotes aimed at whetting the viewers' appetite rather than pre-empting analysis, the screening began. My small student audience squirmed in their seats. They were female, young (i.e. straight from foundation courses, not 'mature students'), a mix of British and foreign, none of them white English. I could see them tacitly regret turning up to this non-compulsory screening, not out of boredom but embarrassment. They were also genuinely spooked. Once the screening ended, I asked them what they thought. 'I don't know' 'That was awkward.' 'Was this meant to be funny?' 'I really felt bad for her.' I reminded them that this was a scripted, well-rehearsed performance they just watched, *by* a seasoned artist, not a documentary *about* a disturbed and fragile middle-aged woman. 'I know, but …' 'She made me sad.' 'I felt embarrassed for her.' Could it be that we had stumbled on the limit at which artwork that deals with and in discomfort simply becomes too uncomfortable to fully engage with? Had we somehow reached the horizon of the uncanny, where unhomely affect overwhelms any capacity to reflect on the return of the repressed?

According to Rosemary Betterton, Bobby Baker's performances subvert codes of gender through planted failures, deformities and parodic repetitions, therefore anticipating Judith Butler's formulation of the performativity of gender (2014, p. 154). The twenty-minute video of *The Kitchen Show* was a performance first presented as part of the London International Festival of Theatre (LIFT) in Bobby Baker's own domestic kitchen in 1991, lasting approximately seventy minutes. Subtitled 'One Dozen Kitchen Actions Made Public', both the video and the performance consist of thirteen 'actions' (a baker's – generous – dozen) accompanied by an equal number of 'marks', which Baker has compared to a public showing of stigmata (Baker 2007, p. 54). The actions are those of a housewife and dutiful, middle-class hostess, and include stirring milk and sugar into hot drinks for guests, with the mark of bandaging her hand in an ideal shape for holding a teaspoon, resting a spoon on top of a pan on the stove, at a friend's recommendation, with the mark of fixing a wooden spoon into her hair, and indulging in little 'taste sensations' to keep herself stimulated while cooking, with the accompanying mark of putting on bright red lipstick. Griselda Pollock examines the transgressive character of the actions and marks, noting that hair in food and food in hair is taboo and a sign of an abjectly failing performance of domesticity (2007b, p. 181), while action no. seven, which produces the mark of 'lipstick applied to make the mouth a cherry' (p. 182), recalls and revises the Freudian narrative of the little girl seeing her mother's body and, immediately and in shocked disappointment, realizing that it is lacking. In action no. seven, Baker shares an embarrassing incident from her childhood in order to redeem it: as a little girl, she had accidentally walked into a breastfeeding mother, a friend of her own, and at catching a glimpse of the cherry-red nipple she thought that some lipstick may have been applied to it. According to Pollock, Baker hereby reverses and fills up the projected idea of lack with a sensual fullness:

> [She] invents another startled girl-child encountering what is much more interesting and strange about the adult female – the breast, a fullness, a redness, a capacity to sustain life out of the body itself that precisely poses the singularity of woman not as closer to nature, but as a more complex site of human subjectivity as it lives its psychic and symbolic realities in and through a body. (2007b, pp. 182–3)

The final action, no. 13, involves Baker using a cake stand as a pedestal, on which she revolves slowly so that all the marks (gardening knee pads, margarine on cheeks, wooden spoon in hair, pillow stuffed under her overall, pear in breast pocket, bin bag worn like a cape, cutlery worn around neck like a pendant, J-cloths stuffed in the back of her shoes to look like Mercury's winged sandals) can be witnessed at leisure and committed to the memory of the audience.

Lesley Ferris has likened this final action and mark, which would usually come with musical accompaniment on the piano, to a 'tongue-in-cheek reconfiguration of the Pygmalion myth', whereby Baker presents herself 'defaced, soiled, and stained by the traces of her kitchen work', as far removed from any male fantasy of idealized female beauty as possible (2002, p. 201). Yet, rather than jokey abjection, I think that a compromised, ambiguous and ambivalent redemption is at stake in Baker's performances, to echo the subtitle of a book of and on her work, *Redeeming Features of Daily Life*. Baker, Marina Warner suggests, 'works with what is concealed in the domestic and the homely and the banal and exposes its complexity and its conflicts with humour and imagination and reefs of pain' (2007, p. 100). She 'has turned her perception of her own vulnerabilities and folly and anger both as herself and as a woman into a brave show, a new way of fooling' (p. 107). Humour makes her truth-telling palatable, often literally so. I decided (or, rather, hope) that the missing ingredient in the encounter between my students and *The Kitchen Show* is time and a setting other than the classroom, where they would feel freer to laugh.

The kitchen resonates in second-wave feminism thanks to its cultural baggage as a 'woman's place' par excellence, but also as an emergent reclaimed space, an alternative studio in which the nature and purpose of women's labour can be redefined. Kitchens became makeshift studios for artists who didn't have any and who also lacked the time free from other duties to work with no distractions, outside the home. Much earlier and in a different historical context, Hannah Höch's famous collage, *Cut with the Kitchen Knife: Dada Through the Last Weimar Beer-Belly Cultural Epoch of Germany* (1919–20) prefigures, both in its title and its choice of media and composition, the urgency, domestic DIY aesthetic and violence bubbling under the surface (Lavin 1995), which characterize much second-wave feminist art practice that addresses domesticity. In Maud Lavin's monograph on Höch's photomontages, 'a disturbing tension between pleasure and anger, confidence and anxiety', namely an emotionally charged ambiguity, develops into an uncomfortable and discomforting ambivalence (1995). More than any other room in the domestic imaginary, the kitchen is the site of passing on the burdens of patriarchal femininity from mother to daughter. It is where idealized domesticity is supposed to be performed most evidently, with all the ambivalence that this inspires. In the planning stages of the installation *Womanhouse*, Miriam Schapiro, one of the two teachers on the CalArts Feminist Art Programme, suggested to the participating students a consciousness-raising session on kitchens 'as a psychological war zone between themselves and their mothers over the giving and receiving of food' (Gerhard 2013, p. 51). In *Powers of Horror*, Kristeva considers the skin forming on top of hot milk as it cools down as an emblematic material manifestation of abjection and a common gagging trigger, not only because that skin forms a slimy barrier between liquid and the atmosphere and is itself composed of a viscous, indefinable in-betweenness (neither liquid nor solid), but primarily because milk, in this situation, signifies parental desire (1982, pp. 2–3). In the offer of nourishment, the parent (Kristeva writes mother and father, not specifying which) threatens the autonomy of her/his offspring, against which the latter revolts in both senses of the word, by rebelling and/or throwing up. It is significant that such familial psychodramas unfold in kitchens and dining rooms (provided these are separate), infecting them with their troubled affect. Upon reflection on the consciousness-raising process about kitchens, Schapiro noted that, predictably, the students adopted the perspective of daughters while she that of the mother. The resulting kitchen in *Womanhouse*, painted a cloying pink, mapped out that ambivalence but went further to evoke the violence of that barely sublimated warzone.

> We had a consciousness-raising session on kitchens. Some people saw kitchens as fulsome, warm, nurturing. Others saw kitchens as dangerous with hot stoves and sharp knives ('Viciousness in the kitchen – the potatoes hiss'). (Hodgetts 1972)

In the complex video performance *Semiotics of the Kitchen* (1975), Martha Rosler interrogates gender performativity within and in reference to the kitchen as an already overdetermined, contested and fraught cultural site. The work suggests that femininity, domesticity and the kind of repetitive, invisible, 'labour of love' that ties them together are inextricably intertwined. Standing in front of a table on which nineteen kitchen implements are laid out, Rosler picks them up one by one, in alphabetical order, names them matter-of-factly, and then demonstrates their function in an awkward and comically exaggerated manner. The kitchen of *Semiotics* is also 'exaggerated' and awkward, made to look more like a TV studio (Davis 2007, p. 219) to underline its idealizing and ideological function. Like the white cube of the gallery, the kitchen shapes the meaning of what it encompasses, including the female domestic worker.

> *Semiotics* is a performance about the performativity of gender constructed through the sign-system of maintenance labour, and suggests that through such repetitive performance woman self-inflicts her oppression through the lack of counter-performative actions. However, *Semiotics* implies that such a counter is possible. (Davis 2007, p. 210)

The possibility of a counter-performance is more than implied: it is enacted in the final six letters of the alphabet, which aren't represented by objects but gesturally spelt out by the increasingly stiff and violent movements of the artist's body who 'like a psychotic half-time cheerleader spell[s] out the team's name' (Davis 2007, p. 221). The outsized knives used in the final few demonstrations, which climax in a Zorro-esque slashing in the air of the last letter of the alphabet, signal to the viewer that all of the implements used look vaguely retro. Davis notes that no explanation for their outdatedness has been offered (p. 216), so I would like to propose a few different possibilities. The obsoleteness of the kitchen tools transports the viewer not to their own kitchen but the kitchens of their childhood, and probably not their lived kitchens but the TV kitchens to which their (fore) mothers would be expected to aspire, the very same kitchens that were the focus of the *Womanhouse* consciousness-raising sessions. What is more, the old-fashioned kitchen implements evoke the time of the stereotypical 1950s housewife who was Betty Friedan's reference in *The Feminine Mystique*, and was also spoofed in Ira Levin's satirical thriller *The Stepford Wives*, first published in 1972. On a practical level, the less automated kitchen tools enhance the escalating violence of the performance, which perhaps couldn't have been as effectively conveyed by the relatively technologically advanced gadgets of the mid-1970s.

There are multiple layers of uncanniness in *Semiotics of the Kitchen*. First and most obvious is the threat of unexpected violence towards the end, as the culmination of an exaggeratedly neutral and deadpan demonstration of 'semiotics'. Secondly, the uncanny emerges between the unsettling incongruity of the stylized domestic setting, which already looks hollow and staged like a TV studio, and the threat of violence: like *Womanhouse* and the installations of the Women's Postal Art Event, *Semiotics* translates the *unheimliche* verbatim as unhomely. Thirdly, familiar cooking implements (although slightly out of date) are defamiliarized: the viewer is encouraged to see them in a new light and consider possible uses unintended by the designer, improper, violent and criminal. Fourthly, the pinafore-clad artist exhibits a strange rigidity, more befitting to an automaton rather than a human being, reminiscent in this respect of Olympia in Hoffmann's 'The Sandman'. Fifthly, hauling the high-theory domain of semiotics into the kitchen transgresses the sexual division of labour and cross-contaminates the sacred of critical analysis with a housewifely profane.[2] More than anything else, *Semiotics of the Kitchen* messes with the performance of a certain kind of domesticated femininity in a subtle yet profound way. It replays the performance of femininity but only to show it failing and portray (this) femininity in the process of being untamed. Its answer to the question that long troubled Freud 'What does woman want?' is implied rather than fully articulated but remains deeply unsettling for that very reason. Her knives aren't for cutting steak.

Dinner parties: Coming together

The all-women dinner party resonates as a trope not only with second wave but more recent feminisms too. The first chapter in Jennifer Baumgardner and Amy Richards's *Manifesta*, hailed as the feminist manifesto for generation X by Naomi Wolf (2010, blurb), is titled 'The Dinner Party' and shows just how influential the biblical motif of the Last Supper continues to be. What if, the authors ask, all the female characters in the Bible had come together over a meal? The suggested answer is that, exchanging information, stories and thoughts, and gaining strength from each other would have allowed them to question their status as scapegoats or, at best, marginalized helpers (2010, pp. 12–13). An all-female get-together has negative connotations precisely because of the untapped potential of women's congregations: they are viewed with suspicion, as consciousness-raising groups at least if not witches' covens (p. 13). Judy Chicago's *Dinner Party* gets an obligatory mention, drawing attention to the provocative anachronism of the named dinner guests (p. 14). The chapter culminates in the description of a dinner party that the authors organized in 1999, partly illustrated by a textual collage of snippets of conversations. Reading this from the perspective of a Southern European immigrant to the UK fifteen years after it took place, I can't help noticing its specificity, not just American but profoundly first-world urban and specifically New Yorker, and also the common background of all guests and their hosts in terms of class and professional position (most appear to be career writers). This is not to necessarily criticize *Manifesta* but to reflect on the specificity of its authorship and intended primary readership and also on the limits of feminist identification. Witnessing a convivial dinner party as an outsider does not have the same benevolent, empowering and bonding effects as it does on its guests.

Caryl Churchill's play *Top Girls*, first staged in 1982, is also highly historically, culturally and politically specific, but its specificity is deliberately foregrounded. The play opens with a very formal dinner party in a London restaurant in the early eighties to celebrate the host's promotion, but whose female guests from across the globe include both historical and fictional characters and span many centuries. Although I don't plan to discuss any particular performances of the play, its structure makes a powerful argument for the feminist connections between dinner parties and kitchens. Rather than a celebration of female accomplishments or a cathartic sharing of oppression and personal trauma, the dinner party of the first act may have elements of both but is not exactly the cross-cultural consciousness-raising session one might hope for. The guests, including explorer Isabella Bird, Pope Joan, Dull Gret (Dulle Griet), a figure from Flemish folklore and the subject of a painting by Pieter Brueghel the Elder, don't converse as much as compulsively deliver their ghostly monologues, often interrupting and talking over each other. Their adventures both transgress and affirm the limitations of their gendered and social positions in their respective social settings. Gret, who is represented as a middle-aged peasant housewife in armour leading other women into hell to fight devils, tellingly compares hell to her village (Act I; Churchill 2008, p. 27), suggesting an unexpected continuity in each character's struggle from their family homes to the new faraway places that they've reached through courage, aspiration and chance. In the second act, Marlene, the successful host of the dinner party is shown at work, in the employment agency 'Top Girls' where she was just promoted to managing director. The second scene of act two is a domestic one, in which Marlene's sister Joyce clashes with her teenage daughter Angie, who shares her thoughts and frustrations with a younger friend, including her suspicion that Marlene might be her real mother. The third and final scene of the second act brings Marlene's high-flying metropolitan world of work and her sister's messy small-town domesticity together, when Angie, eager to spend time in the company of her glamorous aunt (whom she suspects to be her mother), pays Marlene an unexpected and, as it turns out, unwelcome visit. The third act takes place a year earlier in Joyce's kitchen, where the disproportionately shared cost of Marlene's success becomes clear, and Angie's suspicion that she is really Marlene's daughter is confirmed to the audience, though not to Angie herself. In Churchill's play no redemption is on offer: families aren't reconciled, social inequalities are affirmed, ambition is paid for by those left – literally – holding the baby and caring for the elderly. Even the dinner party of Marlene's own 'top girls' from across history and the collective imagination is tainted by its own awkwardness and, retrospectively, by the bitterness of the final act. The trajectory from the lavish restaurant to the kitchen of the put-upon sister of the career woman unravels the promise of the Thatcherite version of the capitalist dream of the early 1980s and shows that opportunities for individual success for women at the expense of others – quite literally, in this case, their own sisters – are but a hollow imitation of feminist objectives. Although Joyce's kitchen is not where the meal for Marlene's restaurant guests was prepared, it still marks out the unseen/obscene site in which it was indirectly made possible. It should have remained hidden but was brought to light in this haunting and timely play, as a warning against the diminishment of feminist politics and practice to a celebration of exceptional women.

Judy Chicago's (in)famous *Dinner Party* benefits from sharing no such doubts. Seeing it first-hand in its now permanent installation as the centrepiece of the Elizabeth A. Sackler Center for Feminist Art at the Brooklyn Museum, I found it both overwhelmingly beautiful and inspiring in the best sense possible, that is, not vaguely empowering but a potent trigger for thinking, again, about the place of women in history, including the history of art. The drive behind *The Dinner Party* is not as much aesthetic as it is cultural and pedagogical. Chicago's principal aim 'to make history' (Gerhard 2013, p. 75) should be understood as literally as possible: Chicago led what was originally envisaged as a research project to discover and recover the names and stories of women who have had a decisive impact on their times and beyond from across the globe, most of whom have been confined to the margins of history. Chicago's commitment to pedagogy is evident throughout her career, from her days as a teacher at the CalArts Feminist Art Programme, to the development of *The Dinner Party* curriculum project for K-12 (primary and secondary) art education, to her latest book *Institutional Time: A Critique of Studio Art Education*. Whatever its shortcomings and 'for all its lack of radical credentials, *The Dinner Party* performed a radical task', that of reaching an impressively large and diverse audience (Gerhard 2013, p. 16). It is one of a handful of works whose place in the canon of art informed by second-wave feminism is completely assured and 'Chicago's is the name that is most likely to come to mind for writers, curators and teachers who wish to include an example of how feminist thinking has influenced art practice' (Robinson 2015, p. 173). Crucially, the reputation and popularity of *The Dinner Party* and Chicago's own name recognition are almost entirely the result of the artist's own personal efforts, flying in the face of a more or less consistent dismissal of both the artist and her art by prevalent critics and institutions. Judy Chicago exemplifies the entrepreneurial streak in feminism like no other.

The Dinner Party employs a variety of craft media, including embroidery, ceramics and china painting, to challenge the division between art and craft and expose its gendered nature. It names and symbolically represents 1,038

Figure 5.1 Judy Chicago, *The Dinner Party*, 1974–79, installation view. © Judy Chicago. ARS, NY and DACS, London 2015.

women from various historical periods and the collective imagination (e.g. the Primordial Goddess), thirty-nine of whom are honoured with a place setting at a large triangular table, including a painted ceramic plate, embroidered runner, a chalice, napkin and utensils; the rest have their names written in gold paint on the 'heritage floor' tiles that fill the middle of the triangle (Brooklyn Museum 2015). The work also includes six woven entry panels, seven hand-painted heritage panels that tell of the lives of the women on the heritage floor and acknowledgement panels that name and depict the 129 members of the creative and administrative team with black-and-white photographs, giving details of each member's occupation, residence, specific role and length of involvement in the project. One of the most immediately noticeable and eventually controversial aspects of the work, which has consistently inspired strong and polarized feelings since its first exhibition in 1979 (Jones 1996, pp. 84–95), is its use of 'central-core imagery', worshipful allusions 'to female genitalia as icons – as strong, clean, well made, and whole as the masculine totems to which we are accustomed' (Rose 2001, p. 576). 'Central-core imagery' locates the commonality of the symbolically assembled diners in the body and attempts to revisit and redress sexual difference as no longer the site of oppression but an opportunity for positive intervention (Jones 1996, p. 22). Chicago's imagery was arrived at after much experimentation and a process that she describes as 'peeling back', through

Figure 5.2 Judy Chicago, Kali place setting from *The Dinner Party*, 1974–79. © Judy Chicago. ARS, NY and DACS, London 2015.

which a fusion of vulvar shapes and butterfly motifs (regarded as an emblem of resurrection) emerged. As Amelia Jones's exemplary exhibition *Sexual Politics: Judy Chicago's Dinner Party in Feminist Art History* suggests, Chicago and many of her contemporaries used the form of the vulva as 'a metaphor for an assertive female identity' (Chicago 1996, p. 6): female experience rather than eroticism was the main issue.

> There's lots of vagina in our work, but it is not about vaginas. Rather, we are inventing a new form of language radiating a female power which cannot be conveyed in any other way this time. … These images are universal, for they are about being a human body in the world … a holy body: which knows, thinks, pains, remembers, works, imagines, dreams, yearns, aspires, and which may not be violated. (Faith Wilding cited in Jones 1996, p. 13)

Figure 5.3 Judy Chicago, Georgia O'Keeffe place setting from *The Dinner Party*, 1974–79. © Judy Chicago. ARS, NY and DACS, London 2015.

This insistence on metaphor and form isn't shared across the board in art informed by feminism, and the exhibition *Sexual Politics* includes examples of practice where a vagina is most definitely a vagina: for instance, Tee Corinne's drawings in *The Cunt Coloring Book*, 1975, make no attempt to abstract or metaphorize the collection of the decidedly individual vulvas represented, nor downplay their erotic potential, even though the work was originally conceived as a sex education manual addressed to both adults and children. All the same, it appears that 'vagina' rather than vaginas dominate the agenda of Chicago's *Dinner Party* and the exhibition *Sexual Politics* in its majority. This privileging of 'vagina' is reminiscent of the psychoanalytic insistence on the metaphorical status of the phallus, which feminism ironically tried to challenge by exposing its asymmetrical and privileged association to masculinity. Chicago and Wilding are strategic in their preference for 'vagina', since it comes the closest to being analogous to the phallus and, in this sense, only it can compete with it for the coveted place of privileged signifier.[3] 'Central-core imagery' seeks to redress this asymmetry that supports patriarchy in the symbolic economy and thus forms 'part of that broader, cultural and ontological threat' to phallocentrism that theorists including Luce Irigaray identify (Robinson 2006, p. 164). The censorship of Susanne Santoro's artist's book *Towards New Expression* by the Arts Council of Great Britain, as it was then called, attests to the threat that such visual experiments pose (ibid.). Santoro's case is particularly interesting not only because it has been famously contrasted by Rozsika Parker to Allen Jones's book *Projects*, whose more obvious 'obscenity' was presumably balanced by what was deemed to be its artistic excellence (Parker cited in Robinson 2006, p. 164), but also because it appears to combine and juxtapose photographic and potentially erotic representations of women's vulvas with a collection of corresponding natural forms (shells, flowers) and details from canonical works of art (ancient statues; old masters including Cranach and Raphael). More than the beginnings of 'a syntax appropriate to women' (Robinson 2006, p. 163), Santoro laid the foundations of a dictionary suspended between a heretofore censored, just emergent visual language and the marginalia of well-established visual cultures. Her quest was for a visual cunt vernacular (to evoke Tracey Emin's C. V.), as a response and antidote to the omnipresence of the graffitied phalluses she found in Italian cities.

The visual representation of the female sexual organs has long been a feminist issue, in efforts to challenge improbable, contradictory, yet still damaging misconceptions around them and female sexuality in general, ranging from shame to the assumption of absence, namely that there is 'nothing' 'there', no organ and, by extension, no specifically female sexuality, even though Freud recognizes the role of the clitoris but only in either immature or aberrant female sexualities (1925). There is no better demonstration of the concurrent discursive power and ineptitude of phallocentrism, or rather phalloculologocentrism,[4] than the absurd idea that there is 'nothing to see' between women's legs: the absence of a penis is interpreted as absence pure and simple. Freud's deeply flawed and revealing theory of fetishism is both symptomatic of and complicit in the perception of female external sexual organs as 'missing', as well as the perpetuation of their taboo status. Worse than absence, they are interpreted as the result of a primordial castration, on the level of phantasy. In his *New Introductory Lectures on Psychoanalysis*, Freud goes as far as to speculate that plaiting and weaving, which he considers to be one of the very few strictly female contributions to civilization, are motivated by female shame and modelled after 'the growth at maturity of the pubic hair that conceals the genitals' (1933, p. 166). It is the taint of castration even more than misrecognized nothingness that breeds shame; shame is subsequently branded as a typically female trait and even elevated it into the feminine ideal of modesty. Shame, which has been curiously ignored by psychoanalysis (Pines 2008), 'lies precisely in the fold of the ethics and politics of sexuality' (Pollock 2008, p. 126).

Despite his departure from and attempted correction of many biological slippages in Freud's work, Lacan retains the phallus as the master signifier, the organizing principle of the symbolic, that is, the sum of all systems of signification, cultural codes and the Law. Despite painstakingly detaching sexual difference from biological essentialism, Lacan fails to shake off the gender asymmetry that plagues Freudian psychoanalysis. Lacan's provocative statement that 'Woman' does not exist suggests that there is always something that does or can escape representational economies, symbolic and imaginary, and he locates this potential on the side of femininity. French feminist theorists have explored and exploited this condition, arriving at it from fundamentally psychoanalytic although certainly not (orthodox) Lacanian let alone Freudian angles, as discussed in the chapter 'The Feminist Uncanny'. The promise of an avant-garde escape, however, also points to a gap in current regimes of representation. As regards sexuality, Freud famously assumed that there was one libido and that it was masculine, while Lacan also insisted in describing sexual *jouissance* as phallic; again, he makes a special dispensation for another kind of *jouissance*, woman's, which excitingly but also conveniently remains outside the realm of representation (1999).

A discussion on pornography in the pages of the journal *Screen* over the late seventies and early eighties (anthologized in Screen 1992, pp. 129–220) brings together a range of arguments around the significance and possible significations of representations of female genitalia, which had only recently begun to be included in mainstream adult magazines such as *Penthouse*. While the field of vision was clearly identified as a platform for debating and challenging the invisibility of female sexual organs and of female sexuality in Freudian psychoanalysis, the feminist implications of their then-increased and ever-increasing visibility in both art informed by feminism and different genres classified as pornographic were much more difficult to determine. For Griselda Pollock, any radical potential of 'vaginal imagery' in art informed by feminism is ultimately compromised by the growing prevalence of the same in 'big selling sex magazines' (1992, p. 141), noting that context must always be acknowledged and that analysis of specific images is incomplete and possibly misleading without also an awareness of the historical processes, market circulation and representational codes by which they are produced and interpreted. For others, any genre, even so-called pornography, potentially provides nearly as many opportunities for reimagining the operations of sexual difference as art does (e.g. Pajaczkowska 1992 and mostly Sterne 1992). These texts are fascinating in their breathtaking theoretical complexity, and also serve as a timely reminder of what a hot feminist issue pornography was at the time, and with what conceptual sophistication it was approached from different camps. I am not really interested in pornography nor its definitions but rather, more specifically and simultaneously much more broadly, the possibility and permission to represent female genitals and its implications. In the ongoing and understandably tense dialogue with Freud, feminist artists and thinkers have claimed the right to representation of what they supposedly lacked with defiance, although there is little consensus on exactly what should be represented and how. As usual, this fight for representation takes place in the composite and diverse field of visual culture, straddling art practice, design and the diverse economy of now also digital visual signs.

On the cover of Germaine Greer's *The Whole Woman* (1999), described as a sequel to *The Female Eunuch*, a flat brass object is set against an undulating shiny red surface vaguely alluding to the interior of a biological form. *The Female Eunuch*, although not a psychoanalytically informed book per se, is based on the Freudian idea of the castration complex and of woman as always already castrated, although the female (as) eunuch dates back at least to Aristotle (Taylor 2002, pp. 114–15). The object on the cover of *The Whole Woman* is circular with an opening at the bottom and two protrusions on either side, representing a uterus, cervix and fallopian tubes. The cover design is attributed to Jonathan Ring, who, on his website, archives this image under 'concepts' with no further explanation (Ring 2015). The cover was reportedly chosen over a photograph of Greer herself biting the head off a Barbie doll, as the more affirmative option.[5] Greer's choice to have femininity represented through the *internal* female reproductive organs needs to be read in the context of her now well-documented transphobia, already evident in *The Whole Woman*, specifically in the chapter 'Pantomime Dames', and very publicly noted since (for a summary see Lyons 2015). However, I don't think that the quest for a visual vernacular for women's genitalia, as an antidote and counterbalance to the omnipresence of the eminently representable and reproducible phallus, is inherently exclusive or discriminatory of people who identify as non-binary and/or transgender. On the contrary, it has the potential to pave the way for a multiplicity of representation of embodied gendered identifications, by challenging phallic monism.

More interestingly, artist Sophia Wallace's project *Cliteracy* (since 2012; ongoing) was conceived as a response to the paradox of the simultaneous oversexualization of women and a widespread illiteracy about female sexualities. Wallace builds on recent scientific research on the clitoris which was discovered to be a much more expansive organ than originally thought, since what is externally visible turned out to be only the 'tip of the iceberg' (Wallace 2015). Among the works produced for the *Cliteracy* project is street art in gold spray paint using a clitoris stencil, and a golden sculpture of a clitoris, on display from 25 February to 11 March 2015, in the library of Sewanee, The University of the South in Tennessee. 'Sewanee's Women's Center has promoted the event on social media with hashtags such as #SolidGoldClit and #yeaSEWANEEScliterate' (Schallhorn 2015). Although the smooth and shiny surfaces of Wallace's statue appear, to me, removed from the embodied realities of having and benefiting from a clitoris, the act of giving form and even monumentalizing an ignored, misunderstood and maligned organ holds much feminist promise.

The struggle over the representation of female genitalia was therefore fought on many fronts: against the presumption of nothingness; against the discourse of castration, with its implications of taboo and shame; against the feared and actual appropriations of female genitalia by the porn industry; and against the absence of a tradition of representation, which, however limited, would provide formal templates for their visual representation and combat their imposed invisibility.[6] This latter front explains why the rediscovery of ancient fertility figures like Sheela-na-gigs in Ireland and Britain and Baubos, found in Egypt, Greece and Asia Minor has been significant. In terms of the uncanny, the figure of the Baubo, an older woman who, according to Greek mythology, exposed herself to goddess Demeter to cheer her up when her daughter Persephone was abducted by Hades, rewrites the psychoanalytic script that always places woman on the side of the uncanny and challenges the casting of her body as the site of love and death (for man): 'Baubo's exhibitionism is interpreted as a potential alternative to the castrating display of the medusa: Baubo's display is to another woman and its effect is to provoke laughter and to end grief and mourning' (Peter Wollen cited in Kaplan 2002; see also Siopis 2008, pp. 144–7). The image of the vengeful, already castrated castratix, terrifying in herself, yet reassuringly familiar insofar as she abides by the assumption that she is indeed castrated rather than whole, is replaced by that of a grinning matron, lifting up her skirts to comfort another woman, a grief-stricken mother, with her bawdy outrageousness.

Although participating in these efforts for representation and clearly embedded in sexual politics, *The Dinner Party* stays away from sex. The development of *Dinner Party* curricula for primary and secondary education confirms its sanitization, particularly in the context of contemporary US public schooling. However, I think that the distinction between 'vagina' and vaginas isn't as solid as Chicago's work and Wilding's text suggest, especially when one considers different audience perspectives. Unless the work is approached historically and in full awareness of its context in feminist art practice, would the contemporary viewer see 'central-core imagery' and a struggle against the invisibility of women's (always embodied) experience, or rather glistening, idealized and vaguely appetizing vaginas on a plate? The clear potential for a lesbian reading of *The Dinner Party* has been noted by Laura Cottingham, who imagines what would happen if the thirty-nine invited guests were to come to Chicago's *Dinner Party* and take their places at the table. Some of them are self-identified lesbians, 'others, such as Emily Dickinson, Virginia Woolf and Georgia O'Keeffe, would arrive surrounded by a lesbian aura; and others might be silently lesbian' but all would 'participate in a lesbian gesture' as they take their seats and proceed to eat from the plates (1996, p. 210). This intriguing scene is not quite developed into a lesbian reading of *The Dinner Party* but rather becomes the trigger for an important discussion about the overlaps between feminist and lesbian perspectives and practices in art, theory and politics.[7] Were she to develop it further, Cottingham would have to account for the obvious twist that the guests wouldn't be eating each other but themselves, in symbolic effigy, pushing female narcissism to literal extremes.

It is not necessary to imagine the resurrection of the dinner party guests in order to contemplate eating (from) these beautiful plates. Of all the exhibits in the Elizabeth A. Sackler Center, *The Dinner Party* is possibly the most seductively tactile. As I slowly paused in front of each place setting in November 2008, I glanced at the visitors around me, all women that day, and wondered if they, like me, were more than usually tempted to touch the plates, even sit down to dine. I thought about the potential of *The Dinner Party*, never 'consumated' by its ghostly guests but visited and enjoyed by thousands around the world since 1979, as a feminist and female homosocial, if not lesbian, alternative to the most famous dinner party template in psychoanalytic writing, Freud's originary parricide in *Totem and Taboo,* and the totem meals that allegedly commemorate it. Here is how Freud presented his hypothesis, which by his own admission 'has such a monstrous air' (2001, p. 165, n. 1):

> One day the brothers who had been driven out came together, killed and devoured their father and so made an end of the patriarchal horde. United, they had the courage to do and succeeded in doing what would have been impossible

> for them individually. (Some cultural advance, perhaps, command over some new weapon, had given them a sense of superior strength.) Cannibal savages as they were, it goes without saying that they devoured their victim as well as killing him. The violent primal father had doubtless been the feared and envied model of each one of the company of brothers: and in the act of devouring him they accomplished their identification with him, and each one of them acquired a portion of his strength. The totem meal, which is perhaps mankind's earliest festival, would thus be a repetition and a commemoration of this memorable and criminal deed, which was the beginning of so many things – of social organization, of moral restrictions and of religion. (pp. 164–5)

Rather than the violent killing and consumption of the father's flesh, *The Dinner Party* suggests the possibility of a spectral communion with the primal mothers, who aren't feared and envied but celebrated and honoured, as most of them were not in their lifetimes. Self-identifying feminists would not cannibalize them but show them their appreciation and share in their strength by giving something back. Our primal mothers would finally be 'allowed to come, and so to come alive' (Carter 1979, p. 128). In her breathtakingly brave and at the time unpopular interpretation of the writings of Marquis de Sade, Angela Carter looks for and finds the limit of the arch-libertine: it appears that the only thing that remains out of bounds for Sade, that stays unthinkable, is the mother's orgasm. In *Philosophy in the Boudoir* (1795), which culminates in a young girl's violent sexual assault upon her mother, the victim faints, so that she would 'no longer co-exist with even the possibility of pleasure' (Carter 1979, p. 129).

> Were Madame de Mistival to have come … pleasure would have asserted itself triumphantly over pain and the necessity of the existence of repression as a sexual stimulant would have ceased to exist. There would arise the possibility of a world in which the concept of taboo is meaningless and pornography itself would cease to exist. (ibid., pp. 131–2)

In the feminist totem meal taboo evaporates. Its uncanniness emanates from turning Freud's 'monstrous' hypothesis into something altogether more benign but also much more surprising. Ultimately, the fascination that *The Dinner Party* undeniably exerts is not only thanks to its sensual beauty nor its ambition but its ambiguity. Is it a restaging of 'the Last Supper as a first supper, a religious ritual for and about women' (Gerhard 2013, p. 142) or an invitation to a trans-generational oral orgy in which the living feast on the dead to make them come (alive)? Even more startlingly, could it be both?[8]

The next section continues with feminist reprisals of religious visual motifs but also returns to the more familiarly uncanny theme of beheadings.

Off with their heads

Mary Beth Edelson has played an integral role in the New York feminist art scene as a founding member of A.I.R., the first all-women co-operative art gallery, and the *Heresies* Collective. According to Laura Cottingham, Edelson's art practice is best approached in terms of 'narrative reconstruction: to rewrite the codes of fine art's terms and distribution; to re-script the story to include women's experience within the context of both historical and cultural experience' (2002). In the conceptual art project *22 Others*, which came out of a Jungian seminar in which she participated (Aleci 2002), Edelson invited proposals from individuals for work for her to produce, thereby challenging the assumption of the autonomous artist operating in a state of self-imposed and treasured isolation. Artist Ed McGowin suggested that she made a work critical of organized religion. In response, Edelson chose a black-and-white reproduction of Leonardo Da Vinci's *Last Supper* (1498) as a starting point. By replacing the heads of Jesus and his disciples with photographs of living women artists based in the United States, and adding a collaged border of sixty-nine more artists, Edelson produced a poster that was to become celebrated and controversial almost in equal measure.

> My intentions in publishing this poster [were] to identify and commemorate women artists, who were getting little recognition at the time, by presenting them as the grand subject – while spoofing the patriarchy for cutting women out of positions of power and authority. (Edelson cited in Mark 2007, p. 232)

It is not only the reworking of a masterpiece, nor the interference with a religious scene that are transgressive in Edelson's poster. Every single element of her seemingly matter-of-fact, descriptive title *Some Living American Women Artists* deals a blow to the cultural sanctity and privilege assumed in both Da Vinci's original itself and more so through its reception since the late fifteenth century, and its elevation to the highest ranks of the Western art historical canon. In response to the twelve chosen disciples who sat on either side of Jesus Christ, Edelson proposes *some* women artists: she has described their selection as 'fairly arbitrary', not motivated by personal association or political choices but rather 'focused on diversity of race and artistic mediums' (Edelson 2015). All assembled artists were *living* at the time, still working and struggling against their marginalization in the art world, rather than benefiting from a stereotypical posthumous art historical canonization or, in its absence, a feminist mythologization. They were either *American or US-based*, international and of the new world, in pronounced contrast to the (very) old world location of the imaginary last supper and the actual location of Da Vinci's fresco in the Convent of Santa Maria delle Grazie near Milan. They were *women*, simultaneously idealized and debased in many organized religions and still excluded from priesthood in Catholicism. And last but not least, they were all free-thinking, risk-taking *artists*, no one's disciples, portrayed by Edelson as enjoying a lively conversation. Edelson has since often used the device of modifying highly recognizable works by old masters, replacing the faces with those of women in the arts. In *Bringing Home the Evolution* (1976), her transformation of the painting *Bringing Home the Dead King Charles XII* (1878) by Gustaf Cederström, she shows a procession of women artists and critics led by Louise Bourgeois, a feminist anti-racist 'peace walk', gleefully disposing of the corpse of patriarchy (Linda Theung in Mark 2007, p. 232). Despite their apparent simplicity of concept and technique, such appropriations provoke double takes on the part of the viewer and create dangerous hybrids between the familiar and unfamiliar, the established and the unlikely, the past and the opening of future possibilities.

The controversy and censorship attempts to which *Some Living American Women Artists* has given rise attest to its subversive power. In 1995, it became the target of eight faculty members at Franklin and Marshall College, where a copy of the print hung in the Women's Centre. Denouncing it as 'sacrilegious', the eight tried and failed to compel the Women's Centre to take the poster down, then called for the censure of its executive board and finally went to the American press with their complaint against 'the perceived intolerance and liberal secularism of the feminist community' (Aleci 2002). When, in 2000, the original paste-up for the poster was included in an exhibition of Edelson's work at the art museum of Franklin and Marshall College, controversy broke out anew. During a heated exchange at a forum sponsored by the Women's Centre, a critic of Edelson's work described it as an act of defacement, akin to 'putting a pig's head over the picture of Martin Luther King Jr.'. This extreme assertion and its abject analogy led Linda Aleci to the conclusion that 'it is indeed the entity Woman – embodied in the faces of actual women – that continues to be regarded with horror' (2002).

While Edelson's poster participates in a highly symbolic act of uncanny-ing world-making, in which Da Vinci's fresco is not merely defamiliarized but also infected by those whom the Catholic establishment has striven to exclude (and also, occasionally, to demonize), I find myself in a conundrum. The controversies described above clearly support the work's reading as an example of the feminist uncanny but also makes me wonder if describing *Some Living American Women Artists* in terms of the uncanny does not come uncomfortably close to the arguments, or rather knee-jerk reactions, of its detractors. Edelson, after all, is keen to point out that despite this negative publicity, the work was featured in a publication of the Episcopal Church and has been purchased by some churches to display on their premises (Edelson 2015). On the other hand, I can't help but notice some telling details in the discourses surrounding this work, which are highlighted by the context of this chapter, with its dangerous kitchens and sharp knives. In an elaboration of the thought and technical processes used to make work, Edelson reveals that the heads of Jesus and his disciples weren't merely covered but *removed* before pasting in the heads of women artists:

> By cutting out the male heads ... sacred territory was invaded ... the story of Eve, denying ordination to women as priests, rabbis, mullas (in Islam) and general control over their bodies and sexuality, limitations that are not inflicted on men. (Edelson 2015)

Figure 5.4 Mary Beth Edelson, *Some Living American Women Artists/Last Supper*, 1972. Cut-and-pasted gelatin silver prints with crayon and transfer type on printed paper with typewriting on cut-and-taped paper, 28.25 × 43" (71.8 × 109.2 cm). The Museum of Modern Art, New York. Courtesy of the artist.

Like de-occulation in his reading of 'The Sandman' in 'The "Uncanny"', Freud insisted that decapitation is a 'symbolic substitute' for castration (1918, p. 281), without supporting citations but relying on an assumption of shared 'common knowledge' between himself and his readership. This analogy would render *Some Living American Women Artists* and the rest of Edelson's collaged appropriated posters *technically* uncanny, in the narrow and largely misguided Freudian sense. Knowing Edelson's penchant for appropriations with both obvious and subtle twists, I would suggest that the work's exemplary Freudian uncanniness cannot be entirely accidental. This collaged poster is as much an example of the feminist uncanny as a sophisticated comment on it.

Femininity, the sacred and – righteous – violence also dominate an early work by Indian-born British artist Sutapa Biswas. Through its title, *Housewives with Steakknives* (1985) is embedded in second-wave feminist domestic politics. Yet, visually, it both adheres to and aggressively departs from the familiar iconography of artistic representations of unhomely domesticities. It is a self-portrait of the artist as goddess Kali, of whom her grandmother was a devotee (Miller et al. 1989, p. 47), of magnificent proportions (275 × 244 cms) to match Kali's divine status with a larger-than-life stature, but also to make trouble: for her all-important degree show at the University of Leeds, Biswas was assigned too small a space by her tutors so decided to make a painting that wouldn't fit in it (2014b). 'Scale is important; to be confronted with very large pictures alters the spectator's own sense of importance in relation to the figured presences in the images' (Pollock 2004, p. 28). The painting now belongs to the collection of Bradford City Museums and Art Galleries, where it hangs at an angle, with the top coming off the wall, so that Kali towers above every visitor. This position activates the image and also highlights its lack of fixity (Biswas 2014a), literally and metaphorically, within and between mythology, (art) history, personal and collective memory. Both the artist (2014a) and Griselda Pollock (2004, p. 28) have commented on the white background of the figure, which references Robert Rauschenberg's *White Paintings*: against that, Kali, whose name means black, appears all the more starkly, as an imposing presence not only in the painting but also in the institutionalized space of the white cube.

This incarnation of Kali/Biswas is thoroughly contemporary. 'Dressed in the colours of anarchy, red and black, this heroic goddess battles with the evils of capitalism, racism and patriarchy' (Miller 1989, p. 47). Her dark, grimacing face is framed by tousled, wild hair; around her neck she wears the traditional garland of human – male – heads, which have ostensibly been collected in the geopolitical North and, three of them at least, in the twentieth century. Biswas has argued that the heads are meant to be archetypes rather than identifiable historical figures, although their identity was widely speculated upon when the work was made. According to the curators of the *Images of Women* exhibition (1989), Adolf Hitler can be discerned on the right and opposite him Leon Trotsky. Below Trotsky is the head of a familiar representation of a rather frail Satan or perhaps a paganist troll, with pointed ears and nose, while Pollock suggests that the biggest head belongs to Conservative Prime Minister Edward Heath, 1970–74 (1989, p. 6). Biswas does not directly contest these identifications but instead argues for the flexibility of the heads as icons of white patriarchal power. The heaviest head on the garland, Biswas explains, is inspired by the equally elastic archetype of the art collector, borrowed from South African artist Gavin Jantjes, whose work Biswas had seen in the Mappin Art Gallery in Sheffield and with whom she shared a common colonial history (2014a). The significance of the collector is informed by Biswas's first-hand witnessing, on a trip to India, of 'missing sections' in temples and ancient buildings, and the discovery, upon her return to London, that similar antiquities were being openly traded through the most prestigious auction houses (2014a). I have long been baffled by the identification of top-left, monocle-wearing face on the garland as Trotsky's. Having trawled the web for pictures of Trotsky from youth to maturity, I have not been able to find any in which he wears a monocle or in any case bears any substantial resemblance to Biswas's painting. I am led to believe, however, that this seemingly erroneous identification reveals something of the critical context of the painting's original reception around the time of its making and the tensions to which it was assumed to be pointing. To have Trotsky's head alongside Hitler's and that of a conservative Prime Minister who passed laws to curb immigration from the Commonwealth smacks of an indictment of the British Left, with which British feminisms have had a long-standing, troubled, but also at times quasi-symbiotic relationship. It remains unclear to what degree this indictment was made in the work itself or assumed to have been made in its interpretations, but either way it has now been folded into the history of *Housewives with Steakknives*.

Kali's face and two sets of arms (one of arms and one of truncated, muscular forearms branching out directly from her ribcage) are locked into significant symbolic gestures, at least three of which may be identified as traditional *mudras* (ritual gestures). On the level of pictorial representation and beyond any mystical significations that they may possess, Kali's gesturing pairs of arms are a means of condensation, of fitting disparate scenes (and stories) into a single frame.

Considering the *mudras* strictly as a representational device introduces the viewer into the poetics of the painting, which is accumulative and conjunctive, fostering encounters of varying degrees of unlikelihood. Kali is sticking out her tongue to show humility at having sinned (*paap*) (Biswas 2014a), while her henna-tinted palm turned towards the viewer, a conventional gesture signifying peace and protection, is balanced out by her blood-stained machete. On the side of the machete, her lower forearm grasps the head of a Caucasian white-haired male with bushy black eyebrows, who, as Biswas points out, may or may not have been decapitated and bears a noticeable resemblance to Leonid Brezhnev, president of the USSR (1964–82), but stands, more generally, for an archetype of tyrannical world leaders. On the other side, Kali holds a red flower, as a symbol of peace, and a small red and black flag, consisting of two panels.

Kali's collaged flag is a key to the meaning of *Housewives with Steakknives.* The curators of *Images of Women* (1989) identify each panel as a rendition of the Apocryphal story of the slaughter of Assyrian General Holofernes by Judith, a young Jewish heroine who offered herself to him as sexual hostage while her people were under siege by his army. The left panel is attributed to Artemisia Gentileschi and the right to Elisabetta Sirani (Miller et al. 1989, p. 47). The juxtaposition of the two paintings alludes to the feminist art historical landmark *Old Mistresses: Women, Art and Ideology*, where different versions of this biblical theme by the same artists appear side by side, already forming a virtual banner (Parker and Pollock 1981, p. 24). Upon closer inspection, it turns out that both images are from paintings by Gentileschi on this theme, the one on the left, *Judith Slaying Holofernes* (c. 1620), showing Judith aided by a young female assistant in the act of cutting into her captor's neck, and the right, *Judith and her Maidservant with the Head of Holofernes* (c. 1625), portraying the two women after the act, attempting to clean up the crime scene. According to Griselda Pollock, the xeroxed reproductions out of which the flag is composed 'function as a metonymic sign for Western feminist art history', in which, unlike Kali's mythological universe, binary oppositions are still dominant: Judith is celebrated as exceptional only because of the assumption of femininity's passivity, an assumption which, in (white) feminism, is amplified and then projected onto Asian women (Pollock 2004, p. 25).

> In opposition to these false and essentialist categories, the precepts of Hindu culture reflect the ascendancy of ambivalence. Thus, the Western notion of 'femininity' as essentially fragile and passive is contested by the ambivalent status of the goddess Kali, who is at once both the goddess of war and peace. …

> Thus, Biswas implies, there is an element of the real in the mythologisation of 'femininity', and equally, an element of myth in the reality of black womanhood. (Tawadros 1989, p. 145)

Both Elisabetta Sirani and Artemisia Gentileschi painted themselves at work, sensing perhaps the disbelief and unwillingness of the generations to come to give them due recognition. Biswas also paints herself at work, though not in the act of painting but as an agent of revision and intervention in art history. At the same time as being a protest against the Eurocentrism of Biswas's art education (Pollock 1989, p. 6), *Housewives with Steakknives* forms allegiances across geographical, racial and, most radically, chronological boundaries. Not only does the painting establish a genealogy of painting women but it also participates in the overhaul of the politics of history-writing and positions itself among the work of feminists as diverse as Adrienne Rich (1993) and Dale Spender (1985), as well as, of course, the authors of *Old Mistresses,* which the flag references.

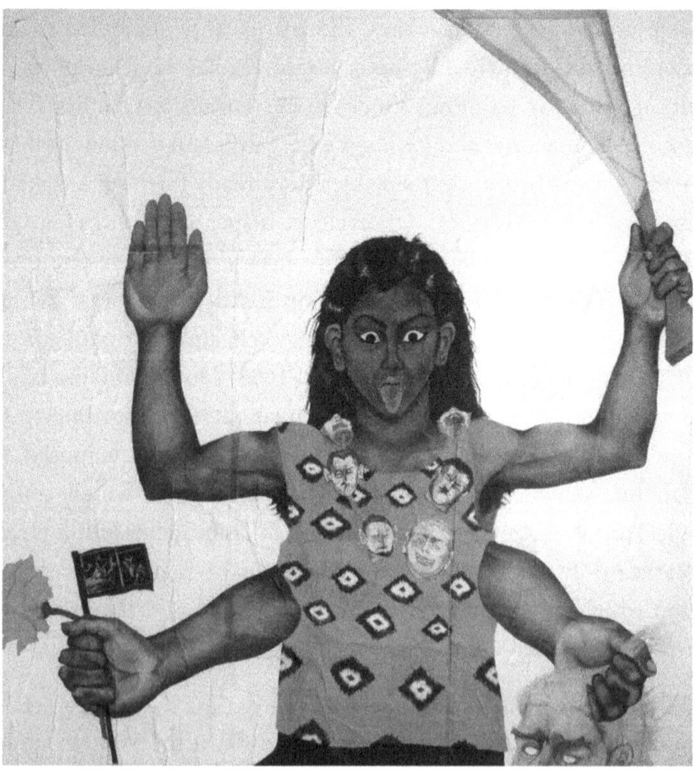

Figure 5.5 Sutapa Biswas, *Housewives with Steakknives*, 1985. Oil, acrylic and pastel on paper and canvas. Collection of Bradford Museums and Galleries.

In *Differencing the Canon*, Griselda Pollock warns against the dangers of the heroization of women artists such as Gentileschi. Biography and history should not be conflated, since they are not of equal value to feminism and feminist art history; or rather, biography has to be informed by history in order for it to be of any use to art history (1999a, pp. 103–8). For the second wave, however, biography, autobiography (particularly the auto/biographies of cultural producers) and the urgent task of history-writing merge into one. In an impoverished tradition such as that of women artists and writers (even though its destitution is not due to lack of achievement but censorship and suppression), biographical scraps and autobiographical traces are often cherished, recycled and put to new uses. The three-fold alliance between history, biography and autobiography helped create a network of producers and audiences of immeasurable political importance. What is more, this alliance is symptomatic of the consistency with which feminist writers and artists write or portray themselves through a persistent retracing of matrilineal family trees.[9] I would go so far as to argue that Biswas's Kali, made in the image of herself and metonymically invoking her grandmother, operates as a collector of biographies and autobiographies and as a feminist historian.

Figure 5.6 Sutapa Biswas, *Housewives with Steakknives*, 1985. Flag detail. Photograph by Sabine Reyer. Courtesy of Sabine Reyer. http://neu.sabinereyer.de/wp-content/uploads/2011/10/sutape-biswas-3.jpg

In *Housewives with Steakknives*, Kali's traditional nudity is not covered through modesty, but because her clothing functions as a sign. Among the belongings of her late grandmother Biswas found an image of Kali wearing exactly the same tunic as in the painting (Roth 1995, p. 37). The pattern had remained imprinted on her memory and unconsciously resurfaced in *Housewives* and much of her work of this period. Thus, the cloth pattern not only places Kali in Biswas's oeuvre and family history, but also clues us into the shared origins of Kali, Biswas and the other women featuring in her work[10]: 'Housewives, mothers, friends emerge like goddesses, mythic and monumental, from the banal, urban and domestic landscapes of contemporary Britain' (Rochdale Art Gallery 1986). Like the pattern, Kali plays the role of a connective tissue between different stories, mortals and immortals, the dead and the living, protection and bloody revenge. She brings together a Hindu goddess, a Jewish heroine (Judith), the artist, her grandmother, housewives with steak knives (or rather machetes) and a dead Italian mistress of her art through the double session of representation – portraying and looking out for her all at once.

Gayatri Spivak describes Kali as a 'child-mother who … is also a moral and affective monitor' (Spivak 1992, p. 183), which once again highlights this entity's extreme ambiguity. Although described as one of the aspects or manifestations of the supreme goddess Devi, Kali, the Black One, is most definitely *not* one. Despite her popularity, she has always remained in the fringes of Indian society and is intimately associated with the mystical Tantric tradition.[11] Kali's 'proper' place is the battlefield strewn with corpses or the cremation ground, although she is also worshipped as a local deity in the rural South. By virtue of her traditional dwelling, Kali is also the goddess of cyclical time, the mistress of destruction and thus also rebirth. According to the most complete version of her myth in the fifth-/sixth-century epic poem *Devi-mahatmya*, Durga, another manifestation of Devi, comes to the rescue of the gods when they are threatened by the demons Canda and Munda, whom her husband Shiva has accidentally dreamt into being. Durga's rage at the indignation of the approaching demons gives birth to Kali from her brow. She has matted hair, is adorned with a garland of human heads, wears a tiger's skin (although in some accounts she is completely naked) and is armed with a sword and noose. There is a great variety of myths associated with Kali's creation and exploits, including the tradition of the dance contest between husband and wife, which are not, however, essential to the present discussion. Suffice it to note that the leitmotiv in most accounts is that Kali is born out of defensive rage and the desire to protect her own, but all too often gets (literally) intoxicated by her newly found power. Kali defeats the demons whom she is summoned to kill, but gets drunk on their blood and threatens the world with total destruction. It is imperative to note Kali's history of service in racial and ethnic conflict. She has been associated with Bengali nationalism, particularly at the time of the 1905 partition:

> The Mother [Kali] asks for sacrificial offerings. What does Mother want? ... She wants many white *Asuras* [demons]. The Mother is thirsting after the blood of the *Feringhees* [foreigners] who have bled her profusely. (From the nationalist Bengali journal *Yagantar*, quoted in Kinsley 1975, p. 127).

Cynthia Ann Humes charts the transformation of Kali in the British colonial imagination, reflecting on the progress of and resistances to the annexation and governance of territories by the British. The colonial treatment of Kali was inevitably inflected by British oppressive and repressive attitudes to gender and sexuality at home:

> Women were either saintly and untainted by sex or decidedly otherwise. British women (at least of the proper class) came to occupy the first niche, and Asian women the latter. As woman out of control, Kali symbolised the disorder and panic the British themselves felt when they found to their chagrin that South Asians were hitting back. (Humes 2003, p. 164)

In other words, Kali came to symbolize a specifically Indian 'heart of darkness' for the colonizers and, on the other hand, a site of anti-colonial resistance for her native followers; crucially, Kali also occupied the intersection between imperialism and Western patriarchal ideas about femininity. Conversely, the associations of Kali with feminine power have not gone unnoticed nor have they remained unexploited in women's movements. For example, Kali for Women, a New Delhi-based publisher established in 1984, since split into two imprints, Zubaan and Women Unlimited, focused on feminist activist and academic writing in various languages of the Indian subcontinent as well as English, with the aim of promoting female empowerment from specifically third-world feminist perspectives (Spinifex Press 2015). More recently, poet, writer and activist Meena Kandasamy, evoked Kali as an inspirational and deadly source of womanly power, avenging the victims of rape and domestic violence and leading a women's revolt against misogyny in both the public and private sphere (Bhatia 2012).

The uncanniness of *Housewives with Steakknives* is obvious insofar as it illustrates not merely severed heads but also, specifically, references the beheading of Holofernes by Judith. In 'The Taboo of Virginity' (1918), Freud uses this story in its dramatic adaptation by Christian Hebbel (1841) to support his tenuous argument that 'defloration … unleashes an archaic reaction of hostility' by the woman to the man responsible (p. 282). Judith's 'uncanny wedding night', a disturbing Freudian euphemism for her rape, stages the realization of a common fantasy of female revenge with a beheading, 'well known to us as a symbolic substitute for castrating' (p. 281). Moreover, Kali and psychoanalysis may turn out to be closer than they appear. Mystical practices associated with Kali present unexpected similarities with psychoanalytic practice, insofar as they both engage in 'an exercise in excess, a ritualised confrontation with both universal and culturally constituted anxieties about death, sexuality, pollution, and the dissolution of the socialised self' (Kripal 2003, p. 196). Biswas's Kali (Biswas as Kali) avenges Judith's 'uncanny wedding night' by unleashing more (symbolic) violence on (male) heads (of state, or at least of oppressive and dangerous ideologies). Among the targets of this Kali, however, are feminist and feminist art historical assumptions, including the justified yet problematic elevation of Artemisia Gentileschi to a feminist heroine, and the still operative structural opposition between masculinity and femininity, assertiveness and passivity, anger and peace. Since destruction and regeneration are no longer opposites but forever intertwined in a sacred dialectic, any cut invites a suture, any loss is also a promise of rebirth, self-reflective resistance and continuous change.

6

Family Albums: World-Making as Compensation

Between snapshot and document

British photographer, organizer and writer Jo Spence (1934–92) started her artistic career as a high street studio photographer, accepting commissions for weddings, family portraits, as well as modelling and actors' portfolios. This experience gave her an insight into the conventions of photographing families and became the starting point of a life-long reflection, founded in practice, into the ideological and psychosocial role of the family portrait and, by extension, the family album. She observes that in all the years she ran a studio (1967–74), she was never asked for a 'father and child' portrait (1988, p. 30); on a collection of portraits of alternately angelic and cutely mischievous infants and young children, she retrospectively comments: 'These are not real but imaginary children, conjured out of the skills of the photographer, in collusion with parents' (p. 31). She came to the realization that the family albums to which she was contributing the glossiest, most professionally made parts, constituted a fairly uniform genre governed by strict conventions and didn't so much document as visually constructed an idealized version of assumed landmarks in the lives of individuals and/in their families. The family album performed 'a structuring operation on memory' in ways that also instituted 'the very mechanisms of forgetting' (Evans 2005, p. 42). Looking back at her own family albums, Spence found no record of her poor health, her problems at school or the trauma of her broken marriage. Beyond the personal, a dimension systematically obfuscated by the genre of family album photos was the realities of working-class lives: 'I realised I had to reject the whole of my learned photographic practice because it had made me visually represent others in ways not necessarily in their class interests in order to earn a living as a photographer' (Spence 1988, p. 83). In a business card that she made in the course of her collaboration with Rosy Martin in 1986, she is photographically portrayed as a tired fairy godmother; the text reads: 'JO SPENCE PHOTOGRAPHER/AVAILABLE FOR DIVORCES, FUNERALS, ILLNESS, SOCIAL INJUSTICE, SCENES OF DOMESTIC VIOLENCE, EXPLORATION OF SEXUALITY AND ANY JOYFUL EVENTS' (Spence 1995, frontispiece). As a specific evocation of the politics of 'reading' the visual as text, semiologically, Spence's work on and with family albums exemplifies genre-fuck (cf. Barnard 1994, esp. p. 266), not only for subverting the familiar conventions of a genre, but for raising consciousness in herself, her collaborators, viewers and readers of the politics of representation within and beyond genre restrictions, of photography as an ideological apparatus and of identity as a process – and, always, a work in progress.

This strategic subversion of the conventions of the family album resulted in a visual autobiography that was first exhibited as *Beyond the Family Album*, part of *Three Perspectives on Photography* at the Hayward gallery in 1979. Spence scrutinizes a selection of photographs of herself since infancy in lengthy commentaries and begins to experiment with alternative representational conventions in a documentary mode, as a transformative addendum to the family album. The cover includes what is probably the first professional photographic portrait of Spence at eight and a half months, naked on her tummy, on the Woodford high street photographer's white frilly bed, the perfect prop for baby's first photo; and a recreation, 'five hundred and twenty-eight months later', in exactly the same pose but facing the other way, in a noticeably different, middle-aged body, on a black sofa – a satirical mirror image (Spence 1988, p. 84). One of the final panels consists of a collection of contemporary print advertising addressed at women and portraying idealized notions of femininity. This work, which Spence found 'totally alienating' to show in a major art gallery with little opportunity for direct audience engagement (1988, p. 83), is a clear precursor to later investigations into phototherapy, principally those in close collaboration with fellow artist Rosy Martin. Heavily informed by psychoanalysis, radical and feminist psychotherapy,[1] feminist activism, media and cultural studies and critical pedagogy, Spence and Martin's version of phototherapy consists of a 'reframing technique' that develops into 'a kind of internal permission-giving … to change, to re-view, to let go, to move on' (Spence 1988, p. 172). Spence and Martin were each other's photographers/therapists; photographs were chosen from the family album for their capacity to condense and screen intensely negative emotional reactions and were then recreated as a challenge to the fixity of truth of the photographic image, but new photographs were also staged as pertinent, originally repressed components in the exploded family album. In restaging photographs of her parents at different ages and stages in life, Spence attempted to work through her feelings towards them but also, symbolically, to give birth to herself and start anew, baggage-free. The metaphor of rebirth is again found to be particularly resonant (cf. Clément and Cixous 1986). This new beginning means no clean slate but rather marks a commitment to painful process rather than catharctic products, continuous exploration and a restorative restlessness. As a 'newly born woman', Spence aspires to be 'her own parent' (Spence 1988, p. 181) and momentarily becomes it through phototherapy, by humorously literalizing the social expectation and psychoanalytical principle of assimilating and thus identifying with her first love objects, mum and dad. Suspended between an exorcism and an emergent empathy, I find the recreations of informal parental

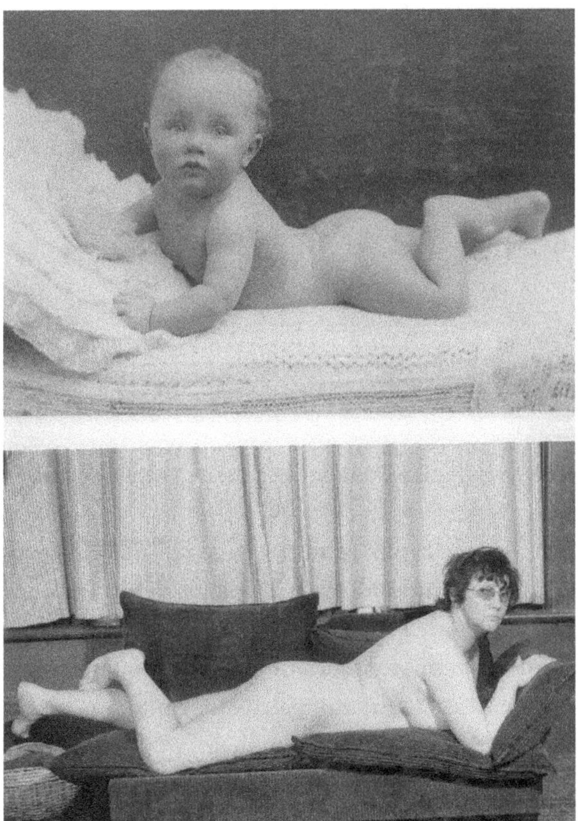

Figure 6.1 Jo Spence, 'Eight and a half months (High street photographer – Woodford) & Five hundred and twenty-eight months later', *The Family Album 1939–79*, 1979. © Estate of Jo Spence. Courtesy of Richard Saltoun Gallery.

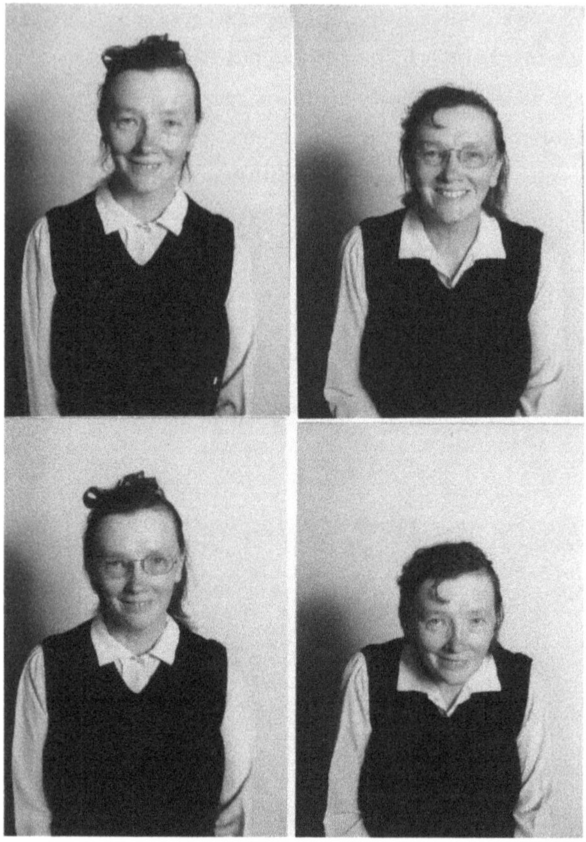

Figure 6.2 Jo Spence, Phototherapy Sessions with Rosy Martin: Transformations, c.1984, 'Picturing my dead parents'. © Estate of Jo Spence. Courtesy of Richard Saltoun Gallery.

portraits particularly poignant, as they condense the ambivalence that informs phototherapy as a whole.

Jo Spence and Rosy Martin's reconstructions of the family portrait can be read as evocations of the uncanny in the field of vision, as they work with 'what is disavowed and forgotten … to produce a *counter*-memory of the everyday' (Evans 2005, p. 70). Even more interestingly, they compulsively pick at the fissure between the familiar and the familial, making it wider, impossible to ignore and also impossible to mend. Their strength lies not in their aesthetics (which wilfully trump bourgeois propriety with a proto-punk kitsch) nor in their conceptual context, but somewhere in-between, insofar as, once encountered, they cannot be unseen: they haunt every family album subsequently viewed, even in its contemporary scattered and obsessively shared digital transformations.

Although keeping family albums is arguably a dying practice in domestic material culture, such albums still occupy an important place in the collective imagination; their creeping obsolescence may even contribute to their idealization. And although most people no longer keep them, many of my peers have had and will have the experience of inheriting the photo albums of older family members and possibly also of fighting over these irreplaceable documents of family history with siblings and other relatives. Regarding artistic explorations of the uncanny more broadly, there is a valuable lesson in Jo Spence and Rosy Martin's body of work and its unfailingly deadpan sense of humour. Rather than diluting the uncanny or making it more palatable, humour, this smoother, controlled and more welcome return of the repressed, may help defend against the danger of the uncanny slipping into the ridiculous.

Jo Spence and Rosy Martin's influential genre-fuck, in which the family album is terminally contaminated by a multifaceted, practice-led critique of the family as structure and its psychosocial implications, becomes a reference point in Griselda Pollock's interpretation of the subversive and deconstructive uses of the family snap in feminist conceptualist work of the 1970s (Pollock 1998, p. 223, n. 59). Tracing the impact of Brechtian poetics, Pollock considers the disidentificatory tendencies in post-structuralist criticism and feminist art practices, through which the viewer's passive identification with representations would be transformed into an active engagement towards the production of meaning and the recognition of representation as shaping – rather than reflecting – social realities. In such practices, 'Distanciation is not a style or aesthetic gambit but an erosion of the dominant structures of cultural consumption' (Pollock 1988, p. 163). Feminist artistic interrogations of femininity from this perspective often steered away from the representation of women as visual signs, to discourage any direct identification but also recognizing that, in both popular visual culture and the history of art alike, 'the visible object par excellence is the image of woman' (p. 181). The challenge of evading images of women is particularly heightened in contexts in which there is a rich tradition of their visual representation and also where the 'subject matter' evoked in the art work is intensely emotive. For example, Mary Kelly's *Post-Partum Document* did not only fill in a gap in Lacanian psychoanalysis by inventing a representational system for a specifically maternal fetishism, but also broke with the virtual repertoire of idealized portrayals of motherhood in the Madonna-and-child traditions. *The Only Woman* (1984–85) by Marie Yates stands as the counterpoint of *The Post-Partum Document* in some ways, as it deals with the separation from the mother through death, from the perspective of the adult-mourning daughter (Pollock 1988, p. 181).

The family album is once again used as raw materials, although the work adopts formats that sometimes replicate and sometimes distance themselves – and the viewer – from the familiar familial associations of collections of family snaps. *The Only Woman* consists of three sections, loosely corresponding to 'stages' of grieving as laid out by Freud in 'Mourning and Melancholia'. Thus, Part I, 'Rage', is made out of four photographs blown up to poster size and criss-crossed by ribbons of text that is reminiscent of newspaper headlines in both its graphic design and the style of its content. Part II, 'Pain', is composed of smaller panels that require physically, as well as affectively, a more intimate look, and include a collection of objects, including notably the dead mother's glasses, which allude

Figure 6.3 Marie Yates, *The Only Woman*, 1985. Section 1. Rage, 4 panels (detail). Photograph by the artist. Courtesy of the artist.

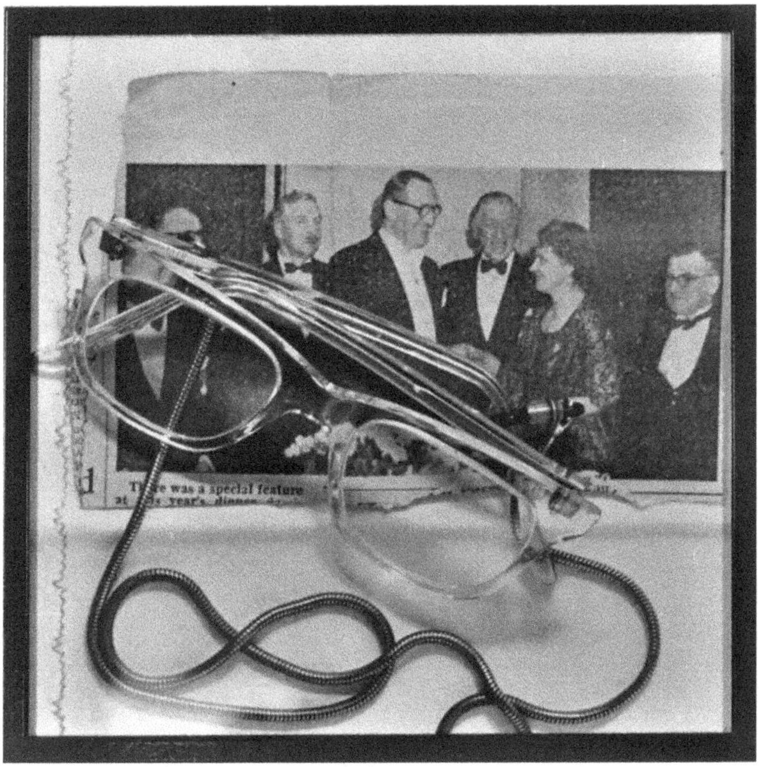

Figure 6.4 Marie Yates, *The Only Woman*, 1985. Section 2. Pain, 10 panels (detail). Photograph by the artist. Courtesy of the artist.

to looking as well as perspective, but also to psychoanalytic reflections on object loss and the importance of (actual) objects in the process of overcoming it. Such an act of overcoming is suggested in Part III, 'Gaze', in which the intimate look of the previous section is interrupted by a virtual zooming out, whereby the artist becomes aware of also being looked at, gradually (and only metaphorically) becoming part of the picture, caught in the act of looking and working through her mother's effects and her own grief (cf. Yates 2015). Like parenting and being parented, even in its deepest psychical implications, mourning is unavoidably a public event, visualized here politically and elliptically, through fragments of photographs and stories that don't quite come together into any whole, and which for this reason maintain a richer evocative potential. Made during the historic British miners' strike of 1984–85, the work does not so much deny the affect of mourning but scatters it beyond the personal into social and cultural histories, reminding the viewer that the latter are also punctuated by trauma which cannot be straightforwardly represented but may – and must – be

Figure 6.5 Marie Yates, *The Only Woman*, 1985. Section 3. Gaze, 6 panels. Photograph by the artist. Courtesy of the artist.

recognized.[2] The miners' strike and its forceful quashing by Prime Minister Margaret Thatcher in 1985 has been widely perceived as a watershed moment – comparable to a death in its finality, a death which is still being mourned – of a collective working-class way of life. The poetic faux headlines in 'Rage' address issues of class in tandem with gender and familial relations, alluding to a private as a well as national trauma:

> CONFRONTING REJECTED/FATHER EVERY PICKET.//DYING UNEXPECTEDLY ON WRONG SIDE.
>
> MEN PUT HER IN/THE GROUND FAR FROM/DISPOSSESSED NORTH
>
> WANTED MORE/NOT TO BE WORKING CLASS//AND TO BE LOVED
>
> PROMISE OF/HER DAUGHTER AN ARTIST//BITTERNESS/REFUSAL OF RESOLUTION[3]

Family albums are transformed into historical documents not despite but thanks to their capacity for making absence, mourning and melancholia visible, or at least for drawing attention to their fragile, fragmentary yet indelible traces. Concomitantly, history is found to be lacking, not only because of its marginalization of women and other minorities (defined not by their relative numbers but by their access to power)[4] but due to the systemic difficulties in accommodating the psychopolitically reconfigured family album as a document of historical significance. If, as Hannah Arendt points out, the distinction between the private and the public rests on a deeper division between 'things that should be hidden and things that should be known' (1998, p. 72), then inserting the family album into history is tantamount to the profoundly uncanny gesture of airing dirty laundry (Evans 2005, p. 52), bringing to light what should have remained hidden. Moreover, the family album as an object of analysis and a medium of phototherapy becomes a conduit of repressed memories, thoughts and emotions. As Jo Spence had often remarked, this visual unmaking of identity exposes a lot of shame, 'a form of internalised self-oppression which blinds us and prohibits us' (Spence cited in Evans 2005, p. 51). '[Rosy Martin and I] also travelled the path of our own heterosexualisation and class social mobility, with all the pleasure, pain and humiliation this involved' (Spence 1995, p. 185). As a marginal and domestic visual form, the family album lends itself to exploration of marginalized subjectivities, exposing 'the overlap between history and fantasy, using popular entertainment, reading official histories between the lines and against the grain' (Holland 1991, p. 9). As long as family snaps in their customary collections are found to participate in subject formation, the family album becomes not only a means of deconstructing subjectivities that are found to be oppressive but also a platform for experimentation towards the emergence of new possibilities across – and criss-crossing – the public/private divide.

The contents of the family album are troublesome to confront and assimilate not only for history but on a personal level first and foremost. Despite having long drawn on her family's photo albums as a source for her painting practice, artist and *Heresies* Collective co-founder May Stevens stumbled when she came across a snapshot of her mother in late life, crippled by sexism, classism, 'male authority and poverty-and-ignorance' (Stevens cited in Tickner 1996, p. 22). This snapshot, initially 'too terrible to deal with'[5] was a turning point in Stevens's practice and the uses of family photographs as materials. A double-page spread in the first issue of *Heresies* in 1977 (pp. 28–9) responded to this new magazine's identity as 'socialist-feminist' and combining art and politics, while also giving the artist the challenge to experiment with assimilating an unbearable photograph into her practice (ibid.). Stevens's defeated mother Alice, and writer, philosopher and revolutionary Rosa Luxemburg became the double focus of this spread that would eventually evolve into the series *Rosa Alice: Ordinary/Extraordinary* (1977) and artist's book (1980) of scriptovisual photomontages that combine photographs, private and public, and textual excerpts from the lives of these very different women. The ingredients of the work are simultaneously aesthetically beautiful, at least for the artist, and have 'an old library flavour, of something musty and archaeological, dug out of a damp cellar' (Tickner 1996, p. 27). The first names of the artist's mother and Luxemburg aren't separated by a slash in the work's title, to discourage any simplistic alignment between each woman's life and either 'ordinary' or 'extraordinary', since each is both, 'and one point of the comparison is to fracture such terms, especially in regard to women' (p. 23).

From a contemporary perspective, *Rosa Alice* would be classified as a work that addresses the archive and its silences, an emergent genre that is inherently uncanny, for dwelling on and amplifying the unrepresented and asking uncomfortable questions about its status, for mimicking the often treacherous promises of the archive for order, taxonomy and knowledge, and for devolving data collection into hoarding obsession (Enwezor 2008). Lisa Tickner discovers in *Rosa Alice: Ordinary/Extraordinary* a vernacular update of the hallowed genre of history painting, from which women had been systematically excluded (Nochlin 1989), for its use of allegorical and (fragmented) narrative devices and its reflection on recent history while also asking 'whose history?' (1996, p. 23). The use of collage underlines the incoherence of the collected and juxtaposed photographs and texts, 'held in tension' in a kind of bricolage, 'drawing on whatever is to hand' with a DIY sensibility but also recycling objects and images as signifiers (ibid., p. 27). In this pieced together family story/history, in words and pictures, the known, the unknown and the unknowable flicker, emerge and recede in ways that don't challenge everyday experience and 'ordinary' consciousness but rather aim to replicate it as closely as possible, making it visible. 'That form is the truest form that I can think of, or that I know of .... And it does come out of the Women's Movement,' Stevens remarks (p. 26). The ambition of such formal experimentations shouldn't be missed, especially as they are articulated in recognizably avant-garde terms: 'A redefinition of art, at least as violent in its breaking up of received ideas as the birth of abstraction, is going on. These artists ... have things to say that demand these ways of saying and ways they are still working toward' (from an exhibition proposal, Stevens cited in Tickner 1996, p. 26).

Ultimately, the work does not 'reveal' the life histories of either Alice Stevens or Rosa Luxemburg, despite – at the very least – piquing the viewer's curiosity for the apparently known, the unknown and their surprising relationship, which is closer and more intricate than ordinarily assumed. If Jo Spence and Rosy Martin's phototherapy work discussed earlier in the chapter was interpreted with little attention to healing, I am tempted to read May Stevens's *Rosa Alice: Ordinary/Extraordinary* in the opposite direction, as a collage-therapy of sorts. Starting as an assimilation of an unbearable photograph of an elderly and infirm mother, the work proceeds through pronounced daughterly ambivalence: 'I think the whole thing was an attempt to validate my mother's life and its failure. … In some way I was trying to get some distance on my mother, and to bring Rosa closer' (Stevens cited in Tickner 1996, p. 29). Albeit not quite redemptive, *Rosa Alice* brings this ambivalence to the surface allowing the viewer, including the artist as viewer of her own work, to finally contemplate if not confront it. Extraordinarily, the uncanniness of the work, which, at first glance, brings the

Figure 6.6 May Stevens, *Rosa Alice: Ordinary/Extraordinary*, 1977, collage and mixed media. Courtesy of RYAN LEE, New York.

unbearable image to light in an almost exemplary fashion, begins to be unmade. What is revealed is not merely 'the mutual interdependence … of public and private tyranny' (Tickner 1996, p. 21) but the *productivity* of the ambivalence[6] which fuelled the work's making and which, in itself, may be uncomfortable to live with and difficult to admit. This ambivalence permeates and enlivens *Rosa Alice: Ordinary/Extraordinary*, producing a third term, yet an other, from the scraps of the two revenants evoked in the work's materials: 'Rosa Alice', or 'Alice Rosa', both ordinary and extraordinary, 'an articulation of difference contained within the fantasy of origin and identity' (Bhabha 1994, p. 67), exceeds the regime of her own representation by emerging as both so much more and somehow less than the sum of her many broken parts. There is no repressed left to make its return, nothing's lacking because everything is shown to be incomplete. In their exaggerated, Xeroxed chiaroscuro graininess, the result of copying copies many times over, Rosa, Alice and Rosa Alice (dis)appear together across their lifetimes and the multiple occasions of their viewing, as children, young adults, on the verge of death (Alice) and as decomposing corpse (Rosa). While the ghosts of real and chosen mothers remain forever ungraspable, they are also restored to an ambiguous posterity, safely tucked in-between layers of memories, projections and reproductions, at once iconic and persistently enigmatic.

The artist and/as model: 'You're primitive but very pretty' (unravelling modernism)[7]

The French Collection (1991–97)[8] by African American artist Faith Ringgold is a series of twelve 'story quilts' in two parts, consisting of paintings on already quilted canvases, with strips of hand-written text along the top and bottom border. They are framed by colourful scraps of fabric pieced together in the traditional manner of African American quilting with a sack backing, but are also a reference to Tibetan tankas, portable religious paintings on cloth, a format with which Ringgold experimented since seeing a Tibetan art exhibit in Amsterdam in 1972. Ringgold explains that she was tired of dragging stretched canvases up and down narrow stairways, while tankas are made to be light and mobile. The new format ushered in a new phase in Ringgold's oeuvre, during which she explored different media, themes and styles, including soft sculptures, masks and costumes that were used in individual and public participation performances but also displayed in their own right, and most notably the 'story quilts': subsequent projects include a story quilt series on jazz, its theme and format bringing together the two undervalued African American artistic traditions (Mainardi 1982 and Grudin 1990). The shift to cloth and stitching also marked the beginning of a collaboration between the artist and her mother, Willi Posey, fashion designer and dress maker, for whom Ringgold had modelled and MC-ed at her fashion shows in her twenties (Wallace 1998).

The French Collection is an investigation into the colour and sex of the Parisian art scene at the turn of the twentieth century from the point of view of the excluded while also, significantly, interweaving its own revised narrative of modernism with the personal and domestic history of its protagonist. It is the result of substantial research into and critical analysis of the racial and sexual politics of European art, framed as the autobiographical narrative of a fictional character and possibly the artist's alter ego, Willia Marie Simone, who travelled from Atlanta, Georgia to Paris to be an artist. In frustration of her ambitions, Willia Marie finds herself getting married immediately upon arrival (tries to escape but soon has children), is simultaneously delighted and exasperated at her encounters with the Modernist masters for whom she models out of necessity, takes over her husband's café after his death and manages to get some painting done too. *The French Collection* pays homage to historical figures through portraits, including writers and artists, political activists and feminist intellectuals, but also highlights the suppression of a female African American heritage. The driving question behind the series is: How can one be a serious artist in the absence of a tradition that recognizes her as one? Or, more pertinently: How can one be an artist when she has historically been misrecognized, ignored or misconstrued as anything but? (cf. Roth 1998, p. 53). Very pretty, but primitive, as her fellow painters insist on calling Willia Marie, even after she delivers her artist's manifesto (II:11 Le Café des Artistes); valued as a model for the European primitivist/Modernist master, but not as an artist in her own right (I:7 Picasso's Studio). Thus, *The French Collection* simultaneously gives a historical and critical account of exclusion and undertakes the work of reparation in fiction and in visual representation. In a slide presentation at the conference 'A Visual Arts Encounter: African Americans in Europe' in 1994, Ringgold comments on the incongruous and usually anachronistic encounters staged in the story quilts, by saying, 'What I'm doing here is rewriting history.' This ambitious project unfolds as a critique of certain types of the artist-model transaction and an attempt to reimagine and revise it as a means of effecting wide-ranging cultural and political changes. Following and adding to Carol Duncan's analysis (1989), the artist-model dyad is here taken as the blueprint of the patriarchal and racist underpinnings of 'fine art' as the most succinct figuration of a 'heterosexual active-passive division of labour' (Mulvey 2009, pp. 19–20). But unlike Duncan (1989) and similarly to Frances Borzello (2010), Ringgold also looks into the possibilities of resistance within the artist-model schema. *The French Collection* may be viewed and read as a portfolio of conventional, unexpected and subversive artist-model transactions that may be imperfectly categorized into five partially overlapping types:

1. the concrete and symbolic manifestation of a power relationship shaped by race, gender and socio-economic conditions; this is the kind of artist – model transaction that has most concerned feminist art history and visual theory so far (e.g. I:7 Picasso's Studio);
2. the humorous yet aggressive inversion of this relationship, which appears in the quilts as a visual pun (also I:7 Picasso's Studio);
3. a respectful and celebratory tribute to the model. This is more than a portrait, for two reasons: it is always informed by a close personal relationship and a dialogue and is always supplemented with a commentary on the aesthetic and political implications of beauty (of people and of art), modelling, and the act of painting (e.g. II:10 Jo Baker's Birthday);
4. a visual and narrative exploration of familial relationships. Writer and academic Michele Wallace, who is also the artist's daughter, reads parts of *The French Collection* as a virtual family album, which is all the more real because its fictional format allows for a freer and more accurate articulation of the complexity and ambivalence of family bonds (Wallace 1998) (e.g. the very first and final quilts, I:1 Dancing at the Louvre and II:12 Moroccan Holiday, which frame the whole series);
5. an illicit act of plagiarism, the appropriation and eclectic assimilation of objects, signs and texts without proper acknowledgement. There is a specific example of this type in I:7 Picasso's Studio, where the African masks decorating the studio walls are recognized as the models for the faces of two of the Demoiselles. However, this fifth type infuses the whole of the *French Collection*, as it lays bare the fundamentally colonialist character of Modernism's primitivism.

All five types are sometimes internal to the narrative representational domain of Ringgold's re-envisaged Paris, as well as always being external to it. In other words, Ringgold the artist represents her chosen models and the artist-model transaction by portraying her alter ego Willia Marie Simone modelling or in the act of painting others. Thus all types are further complicated by the fact that many of the story quilts are also self-portraits of sorts, so far as Willia Marie is a stand-in in Ringgold's attempt to rewrite history through story-telling in painted quilts.

The French Collection story quilts

Dancing at the Louvre (I:1) is the first of the series and belongs to the family album category. The incongruity of the situation is clear and, at first sight, whimsical: without having read the text a viewer could easily mistake this for an irreverent exorcism of the museum's civilizing rituals, to paraphrase Carol Duncan. Yet, as both Moira Roth (1998) and Thalia Gouma-Peterson (1998) note, the accompanying text sheds a new light or rather a shadow over the colourful image, prompting a double take. A recently widowed Willia Marie welcomes her sister and nieces to Paris, only to be interrogated by her sister Marcia about having sent her own children back to Aunt Melissa in Georgia. Marcia's children grate on Willia Marie's nerves – one can almost hear the racket from their dress shoes on the hardwood floor – but at the same time she's guilt-ridden. Looking and not looking are directly and multiply addressed: the youngest of Marcia's children keeps her eyes firmly shut in an ecstasy that has little to do with the paintings in the gallery. Willia Marie is prevented from looking at the paintings as she wants to do, having her contemplation disrupted by unruly children who break the conventions of appropriate gallery behaviour but also by the Madonna-and-child paintings hung in this composite Louvre gallery, all of which idealize the maternal function and remind her of the children she's left behind (Wallace 1998, p. 21). In *The Picnic at Giverny* (I:3), Willia Marie is shown in the act of painting a group portrait. The quilt alludes both pictorially and in the text to at least two famous paintings: Monet's *Nymphéas*, which is copied in Willia Marie's canvas and in the background, representing the actual landscape of Willia Marie's France; and Manet's scandalous juxtaposition of a recognizable nude model and clothed men *Dejeuner sur l'herbe*, which is reversed with a vengeance. A frail, old and naked Picasso, blushing with shame, is placed in the presence of a number of important – clothed – women. This is the visual equivalent of a pun like 'Old Mistresses' (Parker and Pollock 1981), poignant precisely thanks to its absurdity: certain terms, like certain conventions of vision, looking and being looked at, fail to translate across gender lines. Willia Marie pays tribute to

Ringgold's contemporaries and friends, who have both inspired and supported Ringgold in her career, including feminist art historians Moira Roth and Thalia Gouma-Peterson and her daughter writer and academic Michelle Wallace. *The Sunflowers Quilting Bee at Arles* (I:4) counterbalances and complements *The Picnic at Giverny*: it transports the viewer to a different landscape of modernism, it at least trebles 'sunflowers' as a sign (the scene is set in a sunflower field; Van Gogh is shown carrying a vase of flowers, in preparation for painting a still life, as Willia Marie explains; the women are finishing a sunflower quilt), and marginalizes another master. The quilting bee consists of black women leaders and activists from across the eighteenth, nineteenth and twentieth centuries and all walks of life, having arrived at Arles to lend their support to a homesick Willia Marie at Aunt Melissa's request; they include Mme C. J. Walker, who patented a key improvement on the hot comb and became the first American-born millionaires as a result, Rosa Parks and Sojourner Truth. Van Gogh is turned away from the bee because he reminds Harriet Tubman, instigator of the Underground Railroad, of a Dutch slaver who assaulted her and her family.

The first instance of Willia Marie modelling is represented in *Matisse's Model* (I:5) against a flat background made out of Matisse's cut outs, in the stylized odalisque pose, musing on the impossibility of love, the rejection of her dark skin by black boys in Atlanta and the fascination it holds for some Europeans. 'I love playing the beautiful woman,' she admits, but 'what would HE think if I took out my glasses and started to read … Tolstoy's *War and Peace* or Richard Wright's *Black Boy*?'[9] Yet Willia Marie knows the conventions of posing because she is herself a painter and doesn't move. She is aware that in spite the superficial inactivity of all those reclining nudes, their attraction lies in their power to evoke erotic fantasies beyond the frame. A nude too tired to be 'waiting for love' would be not nude at all, she concludes, which is a shame because women resting after a long day's labour are also beautiful. For Willia Marie, posing as a model instead of painting is clearly a source of frustration but also a rare opportunity to day dream and analyse her own life, as well as the racial and sexual politics of her transhistorical context, as Picasso's Studio (I:7) demonstrates most poignantly. Frozen in an awkward combination of the reclining nude and the upright *Venus Anadyomene* pose – to indicate perhaps that what is at stake here is no less than the entire repertory of the female nude, vertical and horizontal – a bored Willia Marie continues her investigation into the sexual politics of visual representation and expands into postcolonial considerations. Picasso's other models, his collection of African masks, break their silence and beckon her from the wall; they know and she knows cubism's debt to them, even though Ringgold's Picasso denies it. The sex workers from the euphemistically named *Demoiselles d'Avignon* behind her, whisper encouraging words and remind her that, even if she fails as an artist, she will always have her beautiful body to sell: 'That's been going on since Adam and Eve.' Willia Marie plucks up at this sobering thought and becomes even more determined to succeed as an artist.

This hallucinatory or magic realist scene is undoubtedly informed by art historical debates around primitivism and not least by the famous 1984 exhibition of *'Primitivism' in 20th c. Art* at the Museum of Modern Art, where the *Demoiselles* was a centrepiece, juxtaposed with a wide variety of African masks and statuary. In his opening essay to the 2-vol. catalogue, chief curator William Rubin discusses Picasso's relationship with the so-called *art nègre* in a vocabulary that disavows any possible equity of value or qualitative similarities between cubism and its sources. Rubin repeats Picasso's assertion that the 'African sculptures that hang around … my studio are more witnesses than models'. Although Rubin consents that they were actually both, he describes Picasso's collection of over one hundred objects as 'mediocre or worse'. That Picasso held on to this material 'with fetishistic devotion throughout his life', only underscores their role as other than art, material signs whose meanings are assigned out of context and according to their collector's personal (as opposed to professional-artistic) interests (Rubin 1984, p. 17). Even Patricia Leighten's interpretation of *Les Demoiselles* as anti-colonial propaganda (2001) does not deny the abstractive and – in spirit – colonial mission that was Modernism's primitivism: to mourn and resuscitate the lost savagery of the Western world through the magical powers of looted and misunderstood artefacts.

The penultimate quilt of *The French Collection*, *Le Café des Artistes* (II:11), portrays the largest congregation of the series, consisting of black-and-white artists, writers and intellectuals from different chronological periods, including Faith Ringgold as herself, in the presence of Willia Marie. This doubling of the artist's self-portrait – one realistic and the other of a fictional alter ego – opens up a time lag between the time of Modernism and that of its postcolonial reinterpretation. While the last quilt has Willia Marie confronting her now-adult daughter and her past guilt for having sent her back to America (*Moroccan Holiday*, II:12) this one shows her negotiating her place among the clientele of the café, which she inherited from her late husband. The ambiguous position of the hostess, not quite belonging because she is the enabler and guarantor of belongingness, evokes the writings of Luce Irigaray (1993) on woman's internal exile (cf. Chapter 4). Willia Marie no longer tolerates her marginality and issues 'The Colored Woman's Manifesto of Art and Politics', shown on her lap in the painted quilt. She is disappointed though not exactly surprised by the comments of her listeners: 'You are primitive but very pretty'; 'You should learn French cooking. It will help you to blend your couleurs' and the counter-response: 'No she is a natural with couleur. Very primitive.' And, finally and most devastatingly, a promise that sends her right back to *Picasso's Studio*: 'You will come to my studio Madame Willia Marie. I will … teach you to paint like a master. But first you will model for me my African maiden! Earth Mama! Queen of the Nile!'

The most unexpected aspect of Faith Ringgold's world-making project is its bravely persistent sobriety. In addition to haunting Modernism with its disavowed non-European sources, models, collaborators and, ultimately, fellow artists, it is itself haunted by the racisms and sexisms it seeks to dismantle. Uncannily, Willia Marie Simone's France turns out to be the same as Picasso and Matisse's: fascinating and frustrating, vibrant but divisive, diverse as long as everyone knows their place, primitivist and therefore also racist, despite some opportunities for inclusion. Nevertheless, the new worlds made in *The French Collection* are not without their compensations, although these are small and often hidden, as the next section suggests.

Coda: Picasso's age

Bald, out of shape and with an ashen complexion, Picasso at work in *Picasso's Studio* (I:7) looks even more uncomfortable and out of place than in his comic nakedness in *The Picnic at Giverny* (I: 3). His advanced age is a historical inaccuracy, which cannot be accidental. In the convoluted chronology of *The French Collection*, the event represented in *Picasso's Studio* cannot postdate by much Willia Marie's arrival in Paris in 1920, when Picasso would be barely in his forties, an age in which, as we know from photographic documents, he still retained most of his hair and youthful posture. The anachronism may be read as a joke, but is also a key to the interpretation of *Picasso's Studio* and the whole of *The French Collection*.

On the one hand, this is a humorous symbolic punishment for one of the most allegedly virile and stylish of modernism's masters. Not only is he squeezed to the side of the canvas, appearing almost as an afterthought, but his nervous expression mirrors the blank canvas in front of him, resistant to his impotent brush. His ageing body must be interpreted in reference to a Ringgoldian sign system, in which youth and beauty are unashamedly admired and praised in the texts of the story quilts as well as in the artist's statements. On the other hand, Picasso's age presents a different view of the Modernist master and, by extension, of the meanings of European modernism. In his later years, Picasso had evolved from the poverty-stricken anarchist and risk-taking agent of the avant-garde to a revered icon of modernism, part of the establishment, a millionaire and jet-setting celebrity. In spite of having acquired so much cultural, social and economic capital, this mature Picasso is well past his peak. One thing that most theorists of the avant-garde agree on is that 'when a specific avant-garde that has had its day, insists on repeating the promises it cannot now keep, it transforms itself … into its own opposite' (Poggioli cited in Gibson 1998, p. 67). This carefully planted anachronism opens up a time lag between the Picasso of the 1920s and the ageing master, between European primitivism and an African American female modernism that never happened, but whose representation in *The French Collection* revises and challenges the Modernism that did.[10] It is precisely this disjunction that both makes Ringgold's intervention possible and makes up its content. *The French Collection* infects history with fiction, power with impotence and vice versa, to demonstrate that the past, like the present, is always provisional and contested, constantly reimagined as it gets reimaged.

World (un)making

Zoe Leonard's *Fae Richards Photo Archive* (1993–96),[11] a series of seventy-eight black-and-white photographs, four colour photographs and a six-page notebook of typed text, was originally created for Cheryl Dunye's film *The Watermelon Woman* (1996), the director's first feature-length film. Labelled a 'dunyementary', Dunye's unique spin on the mockumentary injected with a self-deprecating mix of autobiography and fictional story-telling, *The Watermelon Woman* follows Cheryl, a character very close to – and played by – Cheryl Dunye herself, in her efforts to make a documentary about the life and career of a forgotten African American Hollywood actress and singer from the 1930s, Fae 'The Watermelon Woman' Richards, who never actually existed outside Leonard and Dunye's practice. In the course of her research, which includes an interview with celebrity feminist academic Camille Paglia playing herself, Cheryl learns about the degrading racially stereotyped characters that Richards was forced to play, her involvement in the civil rights movement in later life, and also discovers that Richards was a closeted lesbian in a secret relationship with a white female director. Considered independently from the film, *The Fae Richards Photo Archive* lacks its light-hearted tone, although it also underlines a dimension intrinsic in Dunye's feature. As Dunye straightforwardly puts it in words that resonate with the poetics of Ringgold's *French Collection*: '*The Watermelon Woman* came from the real lack of any information about the lesbian and film history of African-American women. Since it wasn't happening, I invented it' (cited in Birmingham City University Art and Design Archives 2015). This 'fake' archive is not merely made up but it is called upon to make up – to compensate – for lacunae in real archives. Cheryl's motivation to research the life and work of Fae Richards is at once personal and political, professional and social, cultural and existential. She is looking for confirmation that people like her, female, gay and black, had existed and had been involved in film-making before her, that happiness and success were and are possible despite (continuing) sexism, racism and homophobia. Ironically, Cheryl's documentary aspirations cause friction in her day-to-day life, with both her new (white) love interest and her colleagues at the video rental business where she works.

The indexical aspect of the (analogue) photographic sign, namely its identity as a direct imprint of the subject of visual representation, amplifies the artifice of this *Archive*, which otherwise mimics very closely the look and feel of a historical document, while also highlighting the artifice of photography as a medium with a long and varied history of its own. Props, clothing and make-up are true to the chronological periods portrayed, while a vintage typewriter was used to type the captions to the visual documentation. As well as the life of a fictional character, *The Fae Richards Photo Archive* also charts different photographic uses and genres and their development through the twentieth century, from film production shots to photobooth pictures, from glamorous promotional portraits to intimate family snapshots (Zapperi 2013, p. 30). Furthermore, this *Archive* more than most draws attention to the intersection of document and desire, which is at play in the interface of any archive with any user. Leonard's collection of simulated photographic documents casts archives as spaces of encounter between the past represented by its contents and the desire of the user/viewer/researcher to make sense of these contents, to apprehend, comprehend and even recognize herself in them. Fruitfully anachronistic, serendipitously distorted and elliptical, the gaze of the archive user, in the/her present, does more than see: it 'fix[es] the past of the image, to make it exist' (Zapperi 2013, p. 25, drawing on Griselda Pollock and Walter Benjamin). Made-up archives that make up for the absences in real ones play a key role in the feminist, queer, and queer feminist world-making project insofar as they materialize, in collaboration with their user-allies 'a virtual social world', not quite '*unrealizable* as community or identity', as Berlant and Warner suggest (1998, p. 558, emphasis added), but rather perpetually in the process of becoming, shifting, being rethought and reimagined. The opposition between the real and the artificial is recast as a dialectic between the already and the not yet realized.

What makes the *Fae Richards Photo Archive* uncanny is not its participation in world-making, but its intervention in established narratives of film, sexuality and the personal and public lives of African Americans. The archival materialization of 'the real lack of any information' that Dunye points out is tantamount to an indictment. Moreover, once the *Archive* has been made, whether 'fake' or authentic, a (real) archive or an artwork in the shape of an archive, it is there, an indelible mark of the return of the stories of the oppressed, which had heretofore been repressed. In this sense, the *Archive* exemplifies what Abigail Solomon-Godeau has described as a 'tactical deployment of haunting' (2006, p. 373), which mines 'the collective unconscious and its historical determinations' (p. 378). Such hauntings, which may be welcome or unwelcome by different audiences, are pivotal in the aesthetic, ethical and political meanings and uses of these works:

> Being haunted draws us affectively, sometimes against our will, and always a bit magically, into the structure of feeling of a reality we come to experience, not as cold knowledge, but as a transformative recognition. (Gordon 1997, p. 8)

While Zoe Leonard's *Archive* partakes in an intersectional queer feminist world-making, Maud Sulter's work on and with the repressed (hi)stories of the oppressed has sometimes adopted the opposite tactic of world-*un*making. Scots-Ghanaian poet, curator, cultural historian and artist Sulter (1960–2008) has used photography 'as evidence, not of visibility, but invisibility' (Mother Tongue 2014, p. 1). During her residency at Tate Liverpool in 1991, Sulter undertook extensive research in the representation of work by women artists in national collections of historic and modern British art. The installation *Hysteria* (Ikon Gallery, Birmingham 1991), consisting of a series of photographic works centred around a slab of marble, was a loose, symbolic recreation of the life of African-American sculptor Edmonia Lewis. Lewis left America for Rome, where she had a successful career as a sculptor for most of her life, about which little is still known. When Sulter made *Hysteria*, the circumstances around Lewis's death, including its exact date and location, were enveloped in mystery, since it wasn't until 2011 when Lewis scholar Marilyn Richardson confirmed that the artist died in London in 1907 (2011). In *Hysteria*, Sulter plays the role of Lewis as she retreats from history into unconfirmed sightings (including, allegedly, the last one by the lawyer Frederick Douglass, whose recreated portrait with his wife is included in Sulter's installation) and eventually into nothingness. Lubaina Himid suggests that the work is 'about disappearing in an uncanny way' (cited in Mother Tongue 2014, p. 8), while Deborah Cherry, drawing on and modifying Mieke Bal's concept of 'hysterics' or 'hysterical poetics' (1991, pp. 63–4), proposes a reading in which the retrieval and recreation of that which has been edited out becomes possible, but only by skewering expectations of reading, viewing and interpretation (Cherry 1998, p. 21). 'Hysterics' allow the categories of the literal and the figural to stereoscopically shift in the difficult process of the recovery of the repressed from documentary scraps and silences that speak volumes. There is more than a little irony in the discovery by curatorial team Mother Tongue, formed by Tiffany Boyle and Jessica Carden, that Maud Sulter herself has been more or less written out of the narrative of the 'Glasgow Miracle', despite having been born in Glasgow and having spent much of her career there. In addition to noting the ethnic whiteness of the artists associated with the 'Glasgow Miracle' (a whiteness which is assumed and thus never commented on), a series of interviews with Glasgow art notables confirms that hardly anyone appears to remember meeting or speaking with Sulter in the late 1980s or 1990s (Mother Tongue 2013). Unwittingly, Sulter appears to have become enmeshed in the disappearing acts of black women artists that her work visualized, documented and indicted, although the continuing writing and curating of Deborah Cherry and Lubaina Himid, among others, has been challenging this invisibility.[12]

Maud Sulter's long-term research into Jeanne Duval, a.k.a. Jeanne Lemer or Lemaire, an actress, performer and, most famously, the life partner and 'muse' of Charles Baudelaire, resulted in a range of works, including essays, at least two series of photographic portraits (*La chevelure*, 2002 and *Les bijoux*, 2002), and at least two series of collages (*Duval et Dumas*, 1993, and *Jeanne: A Melodrama*, 1994–2002).[13] For Sulter, Duval, who was of mixed race and described as a 'mulatto', the granddaughter of a slave from Guinea who ended up in a brothel in Nantes, is simultaneously a trace of continued black presence in Europe and a symbol of its systematic marginalization and even imposed disappearance. 'Jeanne Duval', the partly emptied out name of a woman whose history is fragmented and obscured is both 'the sign of difference' (Cherry 2013a, p. 149) and the focus of much feminist and postcolonial analysis. According to Griselda Pollock, the figure of Duval has long been the victim of eminently uncanny alignments 'with the key images of night and death, hence of imaginary blackness: the prostitute and the vampire' (1999a, p. 296). Still, it was Duval's reputation as muse that struck Sulter as a particularly insidious kind of marginalization, both gendered and racialized, of which she had also had personal experience. The artist's reflection on the figure of the muse dates at least as far back as *Zabat* (1989), a series of nine Cibachrome photographic portraits of black women artists, musicians, writers and strategists, including Alice Walker, Lubaina Himid and Sulter herself, cast as the Greek muses and sumptuously framed in gold. In *Zabat*, the nine muses, traditionally and unquestioningly represented as white women, are figured as black women who act as models but also are (or should be) recognizable as cultural producers in their own right, and should therefore be considered as collaborators in the production of the work (cf. Cherry in Sulter 2003, pp. 51–2).

Sulter's research into Duval's elusive biography helped her articulate the predicament of 'musedom' and to map a whole range of different roles, from unacknowledged collaborator (as in the case of the African masks and, of course, Willia Marie as model, in Ringgold's *Picasso's Studio*), to complete silencing through sexual objectification. Sulter's personal experience appears to cover much of this range. She recalls the 'lewd drawings' that Peter Edwards had made in preparation for his final portrait of her (1988) for an exhibition of poets' portraits at the National Portrait Gallery. Considering the 'pedestrian nature' of the official portrait, Sulter was surprised to discover that, in the drawings, she was represented as: 'Wait for it – Jeanne Duval, Baudelaire's Black muse naked with legs akimbo. Stripped of the identity [of] poet reframed as sexualised muse in one easy brushstroke' (2003, p. 14). Taking ownership of this uncomfortable identification of herself as Jeanne in order to subvert it and, in the process, to enrich and complicate existing assumptions about Duval, Sulter re-figured herself as Duval but not 'as an active muse and artist, but in a funk of post musedom' (2003, p. 15) Having discovered that Duval sold her jewellery and possibly also her hair to keep herself and Baudelaire, who earned very little money in his lifetime (ibid.), Sulter made two series of portraits of herself as Duval – or, just as plausibly, of Jeanne Duval played by Maud Sulter – named after two poems by Baudelaire, *Les bijoux* and *La chevelure*, in which the French poet exalts, exoticizes and fetishizes the beauty and sexual allure of his mate. In these portraits, Duval/Sulter equivocally emerges from or disappears into a velvety black background. While, quite literally, showing us the money,

Duval/Sulter oscillates between a jaded performance of seduction, indifference and discomfort, tugging at her necklaces or equally decorative hair around her exposed neck.

Both the birth date and the exact date and circumstances of Jeanne Duval's death remain unknown, which is, according to Sulter, symptomatic of a wholesale obfuscation of her life story: 'Each text refuses to allow her to step out of Baudelaire's shadow and the murky haze of post slavery. She seems disavowed, becoming by default a miscegenistic spectacle, less than whole' (Sulter 2003, p. 21). Duval's imposed disappearance is sometimes counterbalanced (and sometimes made visible) in a series of representations by her contemporaries. She was probably photographed many times by Félix Nadar, with whom she is said to have been involved before her relationship with Baudelaire, although she is not identified by name in any of them (Sulter 2003; Margantin 2013). She was painted by Manet as *Jeanne Duval (Baudelaire's Mistress Reclining)*, 1862. She was included in Gustave Courbet's magnum opus *The Painter's Studio: A Real Allegory Determining Seven Years of My Life as an Artist* (1855), right next to Baudelaire, but was subsequently removed at Baudelaire's insistence after a falling out. Their relationship was restored but not the painting, in which her rubbed out frame may still be discerned in the right light. Although magnificent

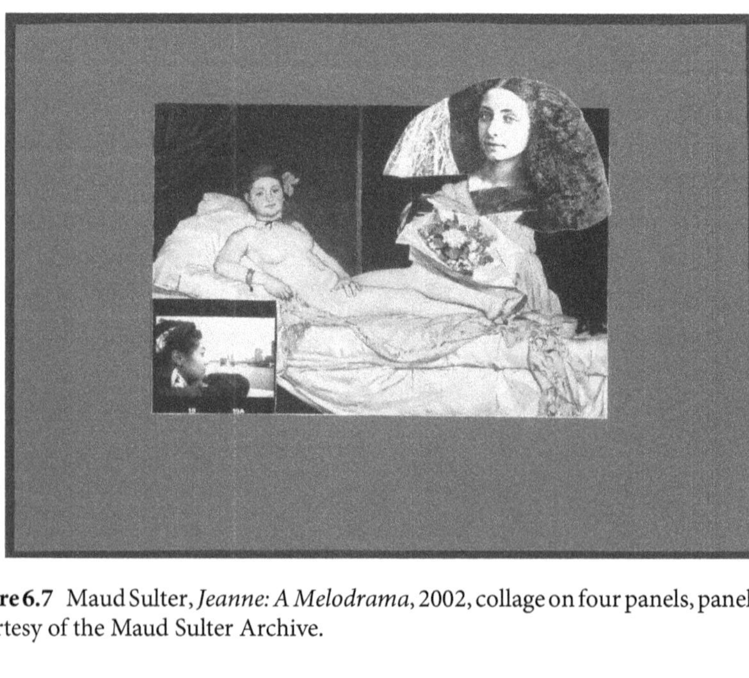

Figure 6.7 Maud Sulter, *Jeanne: A Melodrama*, 2002, collage on four panels, panel 1 of 4. Courtesy of the Maud Sulter Archive.

Figure 6.8 Maud Sulter, *Jeanne: A Melodrama*, 2002, collage on four panels, panel 2 of 4. Courtesy of the Maud Sulter Archive.

in her presence and charisma by all accounts, Duval's life story has been subsumed in and by Baudelaire's. Viewed this way, her existence is important but fundamentally ancillary: love object in life and, more famously, in poetry; 'muse'; editor and archivist to one of the most important poets in the French language; and financial provider to the same.[14]

Jeanne: A Melodrama I-IV, a series of four collages framed in red, dramatize and – only partially – repair Duval's disappearance. Sulter cuts out the female figure from Nadar's portrait *Jeune modèle* (*Unknown Woman*), which she has identified as Duval, and inserts her in the visual culture of 19th c. imperial Europe. The first of the collages casts Duval in the role of Laure, the barely visible African servant of Manet's *Olympia*: Duval is now not only clearly visible but bigger than her mistress, dominating over the reclining white nude and at the same time indifferent to it. Across from Duval, in the bottom left corner, there is a photograph of Sulter in Paris, looking out what seems to be a train window into the distance, across the Seine but also, in this new context, bearing witness to this restaged scene. The second collage inserts Nadar's Duval into a sideshow, evoking Jeanne's career on stage: her torso impassively performs on a swing, while her lower half, to which the MC points deadpan, is replaced with a decisively non-phallic, doleful peg. In the third, Duval is on a theatre stage as Pierrot, the sad clown, taking a comically exaggerated step with another stock character in hot pursuit, donning a Benin mask, 'a conjunction that acts as a reminder, once again, of the contacts between Africa and Europe' (Cherry 2013a, p. 155). The last collage consists of a black-and-white reproduction of Courbet's *The Painter's Studio*, in which Duval's only faintest shadow remains. A blown-up copy of Nadar's Duval emerges from the right, ten times larger than the figures in Courbet's painting, her face touching Baudelaire's who, oblivious, is bent over a book. Another black-and-white photograph is inserted on the right side, propping up both the present and the absent Duval: it is of a 1878 statue of Africa by Eugène Delaplanche and Antoine Durenne as a voluptuous, bare-breasted young woman holding a basket of fruit to underline her own youthful fertility and, more so, that of the continent that she allegorically represents. The location of the statue at the Musée d'Orsay is significant, as it is also there that Courbet's painting, the ultimate document of Duval's disappearance, resides. Signs of empire, intersectional layers of masquerade, erasure and emergence congregate in these four ominously tinted frames, not quite cohering into a story, let alone history, finally putting Duval into the picture but only in ways that draw attention to her non-belonging. Duval's comically large head plays peekaboo with the viewer, even though it would be hard to miss. Nevertheless, Jeanne Duval never becomes the butt of this bitter joke; rather, it is the endeavour of giving her her dues that gets contaminated with the upsetting suspicion that it may all be in vain.

It is not immediately obvious why both Sulter's collage series and her exhibition on Jeanne Duval at the Scottish National Portrait Gallery, Edinburgh, 2003, are subtitled 'A Melodrama'. Cherry (2013a, pp. 150–1) points to Duval's career on the Parisian stage and involvement in popular entertainment. The genre was popular in the nineteenth-century theatre and is characterized by its sentimentality and

> an improbable plot that concerns the vicissitudes suffered by the virtuous at the hands of the villainous but ends happily with virtue triumphant. Featuring stock characters such as the noble hero, the long-suffering heroine, and the cold-blooded villain, the melodrama focusses not on character development but on sensational incidents and spectacular staging. ('Melodrama' 2015)

It would be tempting to imagine Jeanne as a victim, a temptation that Sulter does not really entertain although she does picture it in her collages, as a way of convincing the viewer of its implausibility. As in the case of Edmonia Lewis in *Hysteria* (1991), the last sighting of a woman who has been partially erased from history acquires legendary status and get inflected by the sentimentality of both the original witnesses and those who pass the story on. Duval was reportedly last seen by her old lover Nadar, 'hobbling off into the sunset on crutches' (Sulter 2003, p. 24) after a stroke, at the epicentre of a dramatically changing city at the time of the Paris Commune. The exhibition *Jeanne Duval: A Melodrama* closes with a short text by Sulter titled after the muse of eloquence and epic poetry 'Calliope', who was represented by the artist herself in *Zabat*. Written in the first-person singular, Calliope, Sulter and Duval occupy the position of the narrator interchangeably, meshing into one another but also questioning the coherence of any unified 'I' that remains fixed through time and experience. She/they suggest, in no uncertain terms, that the talent and artistic labour of the kind of people like them (namely, women of colour, 'primitive but very pretty' and likely to be cast in the role of a muse), are exploited as a matter of course, and that collaboration among unequals will surely bear the signature of the Master. These truths should be acknowledged but only so that they can be challenged. There are no damsels in distress nor villains in this story, because ultimately this is no melodrama, despite the name: just heroic poets, full of passion and with no regrets.

> See me, I'm a heroic poet and I don't care who knows it. And I chose my own kind and in doing so apparently consigned myself to a footnote in history. And so you know, if that is the choice I would do it again. Frankly, I couldn't give a damn. (Sulter 2003, p. 60)

The works discussed in this chapter obviously differ in tone and context but are all in some way inflected by 'the moral urgency ascribed to archival art' (Cherry 2013a, p. 159), as well as the vertiginous unravelling of identity, identification and subjectivity, in which psychoanalytic theory played such a decisive role. Memory-making and the unmaking of history come together in an ambivalent and unstable alliance: neither ever quite fills the other's gaps, unhinging each other instead into a permanent state of volatility.

7

Postscripts

'To conclude would be premature'

Susan Hiller

As this book suggests, the feminist uncanny is the accidental and probably unwanted offspring of the unhappy marriage between feminism and psychoanalysis. Despite the widespread cultural overdetermination of the significance of origins, however, an overdetermination in which psychoanalysis is heavily complicit, the feminist uncanny has not fared badly. In addition to having emerged as a key strategy for the articulation of second-wave feminist dissent in both theory and practice, it continues to resonate in contemporary art practice directly or indirectly informed by feminism, without necessarily paying homage to the second wave. In other words, the feminist uncanny lives on, in different guises, still as unsettling as it was in its nascent state.

What follows is a double postscript. 'Enduringly Feminist, Still Uncanny' presents some contemporary examples of the uncanny in art practice informed by feminism post-second wave. The second postscript reflects on melancholia as an uncanny feminist strategy and ends with a reflection on haunting and history in the work of Monica Ross. Rather than vertical genealogies, the feminist uncanny reveals clusters of intersecting relationships and overlapping temporalities: an exploded sisterhood, diverse and centrifugal yet united in its commitment to a persistently subversive return of the repressed.

Postscript A: Enduringly feminist, still uncanny

We Go to the Gallery is an unprepossessing little book that could easily be mistaken for a piece of British conservative nostalgia, which has seen an ideological boom under austerity over the past few years. Emulating the format and tone of the famous Ladybird books, *We Go to the Gallery* transports a well-dressed mother with her son and daughter from the early 1960s to the fictional but typical contemporary art exhibition 'The Death of Meaning', installed in a white cube inside a brutalist grey box suspiciously reminiscent of the Southbank Centre in London. The book uncovers the crucial role that contemporary art itself and emergent conventions of how we engage with and talk about it both play in the acquisition of national identity and class in contemporary Britain. Glibness, aloofness, a well-hidden but unmistakable anti-intellectualism and, ultimately, diffidence and self-contempt, are all treacherously packaged in the comically idealized middle-class performance of taking one's children to the gallery, perhaps the highest-ranking among the edifying extra-curricular activities favoured by aspirational and conscientious parents. Just like the original Ladybird books, a richly illustrated, simple story dominated by dialogue is printed in large letters for the benefit of early readers, and accompanied by select 'new words' on every page. Coming across an installation that reproduces a domestic interior, the following exchange takes place between mother and son:

> 'Gosh! The living room is in the gallery!' says John.
> 'And irony is in our living room,' says Mummy.
> John feels violated.
> New words: violate; living room; irony.
>
> Elia and Elia 2014, p. 40

I classify Elia's book as uncanny rather than merely satirical, not only because it masquerades as something long familiar, which it proceeds to ruthlessly and cuttingly defamiliarize, but also because it targets the very readership that it represents, in a cruelly distorted but unnervingly recognizable mirror image. It is feminist, because it addresses the respectable but ultimately dreary and marginalized business of early education in the family, the highest point of which is represented by the books that *We Go to the Gallery* mimics, which yet also relies on the less creative but necessary labour of mothers tirelessly reading the books to their offspring time after time and fielding endless questions. Furthermore, under the satire of contemporary middle-class parenting lies a statement about an even more insidious aspect of the ideological instruction of the young and propaganda in general. In the press release for the book's relaunch following a legal battle with Ladybird/Penguin, the 'education enforcement officer' of Dung Beetle books promises a lecture by the artist explaining 'our mission to make all children think in the exact same way' (Elia 2015), while in 'The History of Dung

Beetle books' we learn that the made-up publisher's first success came in 1938 with *Why We Burn Books*; later publications included *Blitzkrieg for under 5s*, *Let's Learn about Radiation Sickness* and *There's an Immigrant in my Café* (Elia and Elia 2014, p. 46).[1]

Infecting the familiar with the unfamiliar and the seemingly innocuous with the shock of unexpected dread is a strategy often employed by artist and designer Freddie Robins, whose mission is to make knitting dangerous:

> What I am much more concerned with is the stereotypical image that craft, and in particular knitting, has, of being a passive, benign activity. How would it be if craft was considered as dangerous or subversive? Since conceiving of this piece [*Craft Kills* 2002] the world suffered the events of September 11th and its aftermath. You can no longer fly with knitting needles in your hand luggage. Knitting is now classed as a dangerous activity. (Robbins on *Craft Kills* 2015)

Like craft, women are also associated with nurturing domesticity and are gravely punished when their actions challenge such assumed associations. *Knitted Homes of Crime* (2002), a series of hand-knitted, fabric-lined sculptures replicating the homes in which convicted female killers lived and/or committed their crimes, explores the tension between cultural expectations and individual

Figure 7.1 Freddie Robins, *Ethel – Knitted Homes of Crime* 2002. Knitted wool, quilted lining fabric, 260 × 180 × 160mm. Hand-knitted by Jean Arkell. Photograph by Douglas Atfield. Courtesy of the artist.

transgressions in a medium that is also informed by and amplifies this tension. Short narratives of the murders accompany the knitted homes, as well as the time it took to make each of them, ranging from ten to forty-two hours. Citing the duration of the craft labour invested in each work evokes the idea of 'doing time' but also underlines the character of knitting as labour rather than mere pastime, let alone a labour of love that is by definition impossible to track, quantify or remunerate. The size and shape of the sculptures allude to the exaggerated and stylized domesticity of the tea cosy, often made in the shape of a house, while the softness of the knitted walls both resonate with and offset the violence of the stories to which they refer: 'As knitted pieces, they are wobbly and uncontrollable – almost as though what has happened to them has made them unstable' (Robins 2002, n. p.). Treacherous domesticity that revolts against itself remains a feminist – art – issue, as the pieced and appliqued blankets of Tracey Emin also suggest by repeatedly staging confrontations, in methods, materials and 'subject matter', between the homely connotations of home and its uncanny accommodation of emotional and physical distress, vulnerability and violence.

Whether the works of Elia and Robbins invite psychoanalytic interpretations isn't as important as the point that they convey understandings of the world which are fluently conversant with psychoanalysis. *We Go to the Gallery* and *Knitted Homes of Crime* engage both the individual and cultural unconscious, borrow from the poetics of fantasy and dreams, and lend themselves to a collective visual and material vernacular in which the repressed is not only allowed to return but does so with noteworthy cultural and political consequences. Unexpected, eccentric and potentially transgressive uses of psychoanalysis are at the core of Zoe Beloff's practice, particularly the magnificent research project and installation *Dreamland: The Coney Island Amateur Psychoanalytic Society and their Circle 1926-1972* (2009–10). A multimedia installation celebrating the centennial of Freud's visit to Coney Island, it features 'dream films' made by members of the society, a working model of an amusement park designed to illustrate Freud's theories by the society's founder Albert Grass, as well as drawings, letters and other artefacts. Although the Coney Island Amateur Psychoanalytic Society did exist and Beloff's project is based on detailed archival research, the installation is suspended between history and fiction, collective fantasy, the retrospective realization of the society's ambitious visions and fragments of a peculiarly dream-like amusement park that interrupt the studious viewer's examination of the Society's archive by triggering personal reverie.

Delving into 'a kind of intimate politics of desire' (Beloff 2010), *Dreamland* does not quarrel with psychoanalysis, like feminism often does, but helps reinvent it on a mass scale, as an outsider method of therapeutic self-examination in and through popular visual culture and folkore, and a way of collectively and boldly making sense out of all that lies out of the reach of the rational mind and bourgeois morality. These devoted and intuitively incisive amateurs did not merely subvert but advanced psychoanalytic thought outside the clinic, by anticipating some of the most provocative insights that were later articulated in the encounter between film theory and psychoanalysis (Beloff 2009, p. 66). Aaron Beebe, director of the Coney Island Museum describes the exhibitions by artists invited to work with the museum's archives as 'at one and the same time educational, life saving, prurient and obscene' (2009, p. 11), an opportune description that would also apply to psychoanalysis as it was transformed in the hands of the Coney Island Society. Similar to Susan Hiller, Beloff challenges the orthodoxies of psychoanalytic rationalism, by showing Freud's science to be closer to spiritualism, the occult, folklore and low culture, and mines the darker recesses of the history of psychoanalysis, which turns out to be the most colourful and full of exciting potential. A kind of alternative, inclusive, fluid and disorderly para-psychoanalytic tradition emerges, in which the feminist uncanny would find itself right at home.

Postscript B: The melancholic one[2]

Time gets endlessly complicated in and by feminism and not only in terms of genealogies. Feminist practice since the second wave has sought to capture, preserve, revitalize, revise and extend the contributions of those who came before it. Since feminist research is openly and self-reflectively inflected by the researcher's desire, her interest and personal involvement, interruptions and discontinuities acquire also personal meaning and affective weight. If the first part of this double postscript dutifully made the point that the feminist uncanny lives on, this second part melancholically dwells on losses, both literal and metaphorical, personal and political. Following two short anecdotes, which highlight the continuing relevance and distinctiveness of feminist practice, I will consider some instances of melancholia in feminist theory and end with a short examination of temporality in the work of Monica Ross (1950–2013), and the resonantly preposterous figure of 'the daughter-ghost'.

Anecdote one: 'Don't mourn, organise'

The first anecdote stems from a social media exchange in which I was involved about obstacles to access to higher education in the UK, both financial and social. We, all female academics, were pondering on how fast government targets shifted in the UK since the Aimhigher programme for widening participation, launched in 2003 and defunct since 2011, when Higher Education Funding Council for England (HEFCE) funding for it ceased.[3] Eventually, a male Facebook friend, also an academic, posted in the thread: 'Don't mourn, organise.' There the discussion ended. I bristled at this halting intervention, not only because of the imperative grammatical mood and its corrective tone, nor because, probably unintentionally, it ground the conversation to a halt, but because I didn't think I or any of the other participants were 'mourning' the loss of the Aimhigher initiative, nor of widening access through whatever means, by simply discussing it. 'Don't mourn, organise' is a widely used quote, the famous last words of activist songwriter Joe Hill, spoken shortly before his death by execution in Utah in 1915, after being wrongfully charged with murder. 'Don't mourn, organise' has since been elevated to a multifunctional slogan in the expanded left, stressing the need for continuing and even reinvigorated struggle in the face of adversity, losses and defeats. Most recently it was used in the aftermath of the Scottish independence referendum by the Edinburgh Anarchist Federation (2014) and it is even the name of a Utah handmade leather goods shop, in acknowledgement perhaps of its significance in the State's history. Even so, the presumption of inaction, of being mired in an excess of debilitating affect (mourning) struck me as both unfair and implicitly sexist. Mourning is, after all, a highly gendered activity, and has historically even been a paid occupation, overwhelmingly performed by mature women. I failed or rather refused to see 'mourning', if this is indeed what we were doing on that Facebook thread, and self-organizing as mutually exclusive. And then I remembered that there is a whole feminist tradition that doesn't regard them as incommensurable either.

In December 1977, the bodies of ten strangled women were found on the sides of roads in Los Angeles, murdered by a serial killer dubbed the 'Hill-side Strangler'. Media sensationalized these victims' lives while at the same time focusing on the random nature of the attacks, contributing to a climate of fear and ignoring a growing body of literature on the politics of crimes against women. *In Mourning and In Rage* was a performance by Suzanne Lacy and Leslie Labowitz offering an alternative interpretation of this case, informed by a feminist analysis of violence. Participants from a range of organizations including the Woman's Building, the Rape Hotline Alliance and City Council joined with the feminist community and families of the victims in creating a public ritual of rage as well as grief. Ten very tall mourning women robed in black climbed from the hearse. At the front steps of City Hall, the performers each spoke of a different form of violence against women, connecting these as part of a fabric of social consent for such crimes (Lacy 2015).

Anecdote two: Angry melancholia

On 6 June 2014, Sutapa Biswas gave a 'Feminist Tour' of the Tate Collection, as part of the 'Late at Tate Britain' programme of events, organized by the Tate Collective and student ambassadors from the widening participation programmes of University of the Arts London (UAL). The theme of the evening was 'Inhabit' and its stated aim 'to occupy space through sound and visuals focusing on issues of displacement, marginalisation, and feminism' (Tate Britain and UAL 2014). Biswas's tour, billed as an exploration of 'the representation of women in the Tate collection, contemporary issues relating to the art market plus questions about feminism, gender and identity' (ibid.), was given the title 'Hanging in the Balance' on the day by the tour guide herself.

Biswas paused in front of Rose Finn-Kelsey's *The Restless Image*, a black-and-white silver gelatin print from 1975. Already an arresting image, this photographic self-portrait of Finn-Kelsey doing a handstand on a Kent beach where she used to spend her summer holidays as a child, explores the 'Discrepancy Between the Felt Position and the Seen Position', which is deeply charged for women artists especially those who started their careers in the 1970s. In the tour, *The Restless Image* became a spring board for exploring the difficult question of the gender and racial politics of acquisitions by major public art collections. Biswas, a personal friend of the artist, spoke of Finn-Kelsey's worries about her artistic legacy of the fate of her oeuvre, especially as recognition came so late in her lifetime. In his obituary for the artist, who passed away in February 2014, Guy Brett suggests just what hangs in the balance, remarking that Finn-Kelsey 'fell ill just after the publication of a comprehensive book on her work' in 2013, a book sorely needed particularly because so much of it was ephemeral (2014).

Biswas brought along precious ephemera from her own archive to the tour, including personalized occasion cards from fellow artist and friend Donald Rodney made and sent during Rodney's stays in hospital. Rodney's photograph *In the House of my Father* (1996–97) was another station in the tour and spurred the narration of the apocryphal story of its acquisition by the Tate. According to Biswas, the Tate tried to also purchase the sculpture of the house along with the photograph but were refused. The sculpture exists as an independent work (*My Mother. My Father. My Sister. My Brother* 1996–97) and remains with the Rodney Estate; it is made out of Rodney's skin, removed during one of the many operations he underwent to combat sickle cell anaemia. The tour was dominated by a pronounced anxiety over value, recognition, making it (or not), making a living (or not), knowledge and its circulation, subjected to and edited through structures of power. Its tone was tinged with urgency, exasperation as well as a palpable melancholia, the source of which was not merely grief over departed friends but also over losses, past, imminent or threatened, which are only partially personified. This was not a pathological melancholia that mires its subjects in self-destructive inertia but a different, energizing kind, an emergent feminist and decolonial angry melancholia, which draws attention to and refuses to let go of its hurt, and which transforms mourning into protest.

Preposterous ghosts

In *The Aftermath of Feminism* (2008, pp. 111–23), Angela McRobbie develops her own version of melancholia by revisiting Judith Butler's notion of 'heterosexual melancholia'. In her reading of Joan Riviere's 'Womanliness as Masquerade' (1929), Butler probes the complexity and ambivalence of desire in masquerade and recasts the acquisition of gender identity within a binary heteronormative matrix as contingent upon an original sacrifice of one's first love object, which is the same as oneself. In this sense, identity is founded upon loss and is furthermore

> rooted in unresolved homosexual cathexis. The melancholy refusal/domination of homosexuality culminates in the incorporation of the same-sexed object of desire and re-emerges in the construction of discrete sexual 'natures' that require and institute their opposites through exclusion. (Butler 1990, p. 54)

Not only homosexuality but woman-to-woman sociality (Irigaray 1985b and 1993) is hereby also denounced. This prohibited sociality that feminism sought to recover requires an intergenerational dimension in order to rewrite the mother – daughter plot as one that is not dominated by maternal jealousy and daughterly contempt. It is relevant that Finn-Kelsey's self-portrait was inspired by coming across a photograph of her mother as a young girl doing handstands on a beach with a friend (Taylor 2003). There is a distinct tradition within feminism of casting one's autobiography as the biography of one's mother, from Michelle Wallace, her own mother Faith Ringgold, to Alice Walker and Carolyn Steedman. It appears that writing oneself can only go through the other woman, the (m)Other.

McRobbie's melancholia stems from the postfeminist masquerade that attempts to hide from young women both feminism and its loss, thus preventing them from mourning it and from potentially – hopefully – reviving it. The subversive potential of this melancholia is noted in McRobbie's book, although she sees it as being terminally frustrated into manifestations of dis-ease. 'This melancholia lurks beneath the surface, threatening to transmogrify into rage' (McRobbie 2009, p. 68). 'Even when it's reviled or ignored, feminism has some kind of shadow presence' (p. 98). McRobbie's thoughts on 'postfeminist' melancholia, although so recently published already seem a little outdated, thanks to the flurry of feminist activity over the past few years. It would appear that postfeminist melancholia has already transmogrified into a revived feminist rage, active, articulate and organized. There is a temporal dimension in melancholia, the protracted work of mourning gone wrong or taking a deliberate detour to air grievances, and put wrongs right. But also, charting different melancholias begins to outline an informal historiography of recent feminist thought and action: I'm tempted to suggest that a history of feminism could well consist of the story of its melancholias.

> Working across and between generations can both historicise recent art and reinvigorate our understanding of earlier art practices in a way that aids, rather than obscures, an appreciation of the contexts in which they were made. Far from being ahistorical this approach suggests alternative historical affinities.' (Johnson 2013, p. 10)

Clare Johnson draws on Mieke Bal's notion of 'preposterous history', which liberates comparative discussion from the limitations of origins and sequence. Bal argues that when a contemporary work of art quotes past practices or alludes to past artworks, this does not hold significance only for the new artwork but also the one quoted from, because the interpretation of the quoted work will have to take heed of its own quotations hereafter: 'This reversal, which puts what came chronologically first ("pre") as an aftereffect behind ("post") its later recycling, is what I would like to call *preposterous history*' (Bal 1999, p. 7, emphasis in the original). As Johnson notes, this reversal of pre and post (or rather, their untethering from a sequential order) 'can lead to the dissolution of matrilineal logic' and, like Foucauldian genealogy, it draws attention to 'the dissipation of events outside of any search for origins' (Johnson 2013, p. 69).

Related to the concept of 'preposterous history' is another that emerged in the recent writing and art practice of Mieke Bal: anachronism as 'a tool to understand things not "as they really were" but as how things from the past make sense to us today' (2011).

Bal has elsewhere pointed to the generative potential of breaking disciplinary and scholarly rules, for example, in her formulation of 'travelling concepts', which highlights the transformative impact of transdisciplinary cultural practice on its shared repertory of accumulated theoretical resources (2002); when exhaustive coverage of the object of study – itself a transdisciplinary constellation rather than a coherent object – can no longer be expected, some common methodological ground should be created in its place.

My response to this exciting theoretical terrain will not take place in philosophy or critical theory but by considering time as one of the artist's materials, not just the medium or vehicle, let alone container of artistic practice. Through a cursory overview of temporality in the work of Monica Ross, I hope to suggest that time as material can be both angrily melancholic and preposterous in its disregard for sequence.

In a previous article on the series of individual and collective performances *Anniversary – an act of memory* by Monica Ross and co-recitors (2008–) I considered apparent inactivity as action, waiting as preparation, repetition as rehearsal (Kokoli 2012b). I turned to psychoanalysis, not only because it elaborates the links between remembering and repetition, but also because, in clinical practice, it both requires and values a great deal of waiting. In 'Remembering, Repeating and Working Through' (1914), a paper on technique, Freud defends waiting to reassure inexperienced analysts that what seems like inaction is a necessary gathering of momentum to work things through; that silences reverberate with potential. Departing from the strict confines of the analytical situation, Jean Laplanche uses the shape of the spiral as a metaphor for both the development of psychoanalytic thought through time and the unfolding of each analysis: in a sequence of gravitational pulls and windows of opportunity, not every opportunity will prove fruitful but one must wait for and take the one that will. The connecting principle of the Declaration of Human Rights in these collective recitations, I suggested, was an admonition for a tolerant, patient waiting for the other to recall and hesitantly play their part, and the transformative aspiration that the right repetition may bring forth change. Time, and especially seemingly dead time, was as important a material as the labour and commitment of Monica Ross and her co-recitors. The project took place in the aftermath of and as a reaction to, if not exactly mourning for, the fatal shooting of Charles de Menezes by police in 2005.

When I visited the Monica Ross archive in Brighton in the summer of 2014,[4] I was struck by the urgency of her art practice on nuclear disarmament in the 1980s. As part of the collective Sister Seven, Ross contributed to a series of consciousness-raising posters, in which a sense of impending doom by nuclear war invites urgent action. It is of course not surprising that activist works invite action, but that a profoundly pessimistic outlook on the future appears to not be incommensurable with a romantic belief in the power of art to change people's minds.

Ross was always keen to point out that *Feministo*, a.k.a. *The Women's Postal Art Event* (cf. Chapter 4) began as a postal art project, a 'correspondence' (2000b). There are multiple temporal dimensions in this project, most obviously in the process of correspondence, the gaps of anticipation between sending, receiving and responding to someone else's artwork. Originally conceived as a means of sustaining a friendship after a house move, Kate Walker invited more women to join in as a way of making art that in its form, content, circulation networks and significance challenged the Western canons from which women were traditionally excluded. Although small in size and cheap to post, many of the artworks exchanged in the Women's Postal Art Event took time and effort to make and allowed their makers to use the craft skills passed on from generation to generation subversively, towards aims for which they weren't originally intended (cf. Chapter 4). In a talk at a conference accompanying a major survey of conceptualism, Monica Ross drew attention to the marginalia of *Live in your Head* (Whitechapel Gallery 2000), the works and practices that were left out. In her poetic text, simultaneously melancholic and assertively revisionist, Monica reflects on 'these gaps, these distances … these not enoughs' of survey exhibitions such as *Live in your Head*. The fragmentary, stream of consciousness style of the talk performs the dilemma of its title, 'history or not', while the Women's Postal Art Event is described in terms of its rhythms, the time it took to make it, precious stolen moments, paired with the passionate urgency of the dialogue that generated it (Ross 2000a).

Triple Transformations, a residency at the Rochdale Gallery with Shirley Cameron and Evelyn Silver in August 1985, took place mere months after the end of the miners' strike, with the aim of exploring the links between women, art and ideology, and forging a new audience for socially engaged performance art. The beginning and end of the residency were celebrated by specially scripted

Figure 7.2 Monica Ross, *Ghost in the Spinning Mill* performance, Rochdale Gallery, 1985. Original photograph by Patsy Mullan, scanned and processed by Bernard G. Mills. Courtesy of the Monica Ross Archive and Bernard G. Mills.

Figure 7.3 Monica Ross, *Ghost in the Spinning Mill* performance, Rochdale Gallery, 1985. Original photograph by Patsy Mullan, scanned and processed by Bernard G. Mills. Courtesy of the Monica Ross Archive and Bernard G. Mills.

performances, underlining its duration. In her performances in the Foundry and Barchant Mill, Besco, Ross set out to mark recent changes in these historic industries. *Ghost in the Spinning Mill* was envisioned as 'an emotional space in which to honour women's experience' of past generations, save it from obscurity, and restore it 'in the memories of the women working there today'. Ross aimed to

> retrieve and re-vive visual and oral aspects of working class (sub)culture. … As the daughter/ghost of my female predecessors I worked through the stairwell and across two floors of the disused Spinning Mill, to re-create aspects of the sounds, movements and visual language of their working lives. (Rochdale Art Gallery 1985, n.p.)

The ghost of the spinning mill, the daughter of 'the ghosts whose love haunts me', the 'daughter/ghost' whose name is Monica, which was also the artist's mother's name, wanders through the abandoned mill covered in fluff,[5] invoking the ancestors of her family, her class and also slavery and colonialism in their well-documented interweavings with cotton farming and the textile industry, performing what Abigail Solomon-Godeau calls 'tactical haunting' (2006), another oxymoron that feminist poetics not only makes possible but highly effective. The performance poses questions about the relationship – and crucially – the desire for (some) continuity between the present and the past that resonate in feminist art history, theory and practice.

Following Walter Benjamin, whose writing Ross always admired and to which she returned, Giorgio Agamben begins his essay 'The Melancholic Angel'[6] by describing the melancholy of Benjamin's Angel of History (based on Paul Klee's monoprint *Angelus Novus* 1920), which is a reflection of the awareness that to *apprehend* the past as such comes with the unbearable condition of acknowledging and performing one's decisive separation from it. Agamben argues that art has traditionally found in aesthetics a negative compensation for the fundamental intransmissibility of culture, while contemporary, post-aesthetic art bravely offers no compensation for intransmissibility whatsoever, no suture but an open space, in which the problem of transmissibility and its impossibility is finally laid out, for visual and intellectual contemplation.

> By transforming the principle of man's [sic] delay before truth into a poetic process and renouncing the guarantees of truth for the love of transmissibility, art succeeds once again in transforming man's inability to exit his historical status, perennially suspended in the inter-world between old and new, past and future, into the very space in which he can take the original measure of

> his dwelling in the present and recover each time the meaning of his action. (Agamben 1999, p. 114)

The desire for transmissibility, like any and all desire, is founded in lack first and foremost. The ambiguous figure of the daughter/ghost offers another solution to the dilemma between transmissibility and aesthetics, love and truth: in her twisted, preposterous temporality, she hovers over the ruins of a disused textile factory, picking up the fragments of life stories and shared history, channelling those who inhabited it both as a real and as a symbolic space. Now 'preserved' in a digital archive, she is no longer there but she will be, a ghost to be summoned in moments still to come, revived each time she is revisited.

Notes

Acknowledgements

1 This material was originally published as: Kokoli, A. (2004), 'Undoing "homeliness" in feminist art: *Feministo: Portrait of the Artist as a Housewife* (1975–77)', *n.paradoxa*, 13, issue 'Domestic Politics', 75–83; and Kokoli, A. (2011), 'Moving Sideways and Other Sleeping Metaphors: Susan Hiller's Paraconceptualism', in Ann Gallagher (ed.) *Susan Hiller* (London: Tate Publishing, pp. 143–53).

Introduction

1 The first issue of bi-monthly *Sorcières* (1976–81) had a drawing of a witch on a broomstick by Leonor Fini on the cover. Themes of the rest of its issues included: food, to prostitute oneself ('se prostituer'), smells, voice, blood (with an article on performance artist Gina Pane), art and women (on Lyubov Popova, Jacqueline Delaunay, Françoise Ménages et al. and topics including contemporary tapestry), theory, spaces and places, dolls, desires, death and murdered nature ('la nature assassinée'). The final issue appropriately focuses on myths and nostalgia, and asks questions about the future of feminism as a movement as well as the fate of the feminist press. Although viewing itself as a typically 1970s project, *Sorcières* also asserts its enduring impact, not least on the lives of the women in its editorial collective (no. 24, p. 3).

2 'Phallogocentrism' was a widely used composite in feminist writing that drew on and contributed to deconstruction and the linguistic turn in psychoanalytic theory. Originally coined by Jacques Derrida, 'phallogocentrism' underlines the interdependence and complicity between phallocentrism and logocentrism. While phallocentrism transforms sexual difference into a hierarchical binary that privileges men and masculinity, logocentrism 'gives independent existence to concepts, which are no more than an effect of linguistic difference … find[ing] the guarantee of truth outside language' (Belsey and Moore 1997, p. 255). The term 'phalloculologocentrism' (Robinson 2006) suggests that the gender asymmetry

of phallogocentrism also pervades the field of vision (see also Chapter 5 'Dinner Parties').

3 *Feministo* is discussed in detail in Chapter 4: 'Squats and Evictions: The Uncanny as Unhomely'.

4 The marriage metaphor is obviously – perhaps even ostentatiously – (hetero?) normative and its negative deployment in this context embraces and exploits its sexist and patriarchal foundations. The complex relationship between feminism and Marxism falls outside the scope of this book, although their 'unhappy marriage' evokes the foundational work of American economist Heidi Hartmann (1981) and the discussions that ensued (e.g. Sargent 1986; Bryson 2004). While Hartmann addresses Marxism principally as political economy, Rowbotham, Segal and Wainright (1979) reflect on the politics and practices of the British and international left more broadly, and suggest that to speak of a relationship between the two (feminism and the left) as though they were wholly distinct could be misleading. I think that the marriage metaphor is far more fitting for feminism and psychoanalysis, considering their common preoccupation with sexuality and family structures.

5 Gallop also discusses Mitchell and feminism's engagement with Lacanian psychoanalysis in 'Juliet Mitchell and the Human Sciences' (1991).

6 For a discussion of the deconstructive and postcolonial meanings of 'catachresis', notably in Spivak and Derrida, see Morton, 2003, pp. 33–5.

7 I am not suggesting that these exhibitions and activities are similar in their assumptions, perspective and impact. See Robinson (2013) for a comparative discussion.

8 Kokoli (2008) is based on the papers presented at this conference with some notable additions.

9 Conversation in the offices of the Women's Leadership Caucus. *West Wing*, Season 3, Episode 9: 'The Women of Kumar'. The evocation of this television series here should not be interpreted as an endorsement, particularly not of this particular neo-orientalist episode.

Chapter 1

1 I wish to thank Maria Walsh for bringing this book to my attention.

2 In his masterful study *The Uncanny*, Nicholas Royle also notes: 'The idea of an index to a study of "the uncanny" is perhaps manifestly insane. This is especially clear in the case of an "index of topics", which is bound to be violently selective, arbitrary and misleading' (Royle 2003, p. 334).

3 I am mindful that I cannot do justice to Laplanche's interpretation within the scope of this chapter (1976, esp. 'Why the Death Drive?'). Laplanche interprets the

death drive of the 'death drive' in the context of Freud's concurrent developments in his theory of the ego and narcissism. 'In the face of this triumph of the vital and the homeostatic, it remained for Freud, in keeping with the structural necessity of his discovery, to reaffirm, not only within psychoanalysis, but even within biology (by means of a categorical disregard for epistemological distinctions), a kind of antilife as sexuality, frenetic enjoyment [jouissance], the negative, the repetition compulsion' (Laplanche 1976, p. 124).

4 'Since the Greeks were in the main strongly homosexual, it was inevitable that we should find among them a representation of woman as a being who frightens and repels because she is castrated' (Freud 1940, p. 274).

5 This 'interlude' is loosely based on a talk I gave at the event 'Ab/Using Freud', a profoundly ambivalent celebration of the 150th anniversary of Freud's birth at the Philosophical Society, School of Historical and Critical Studies (since renamed as School of Humanities), University of Brighton, 11 May 2006.

6 Jacqueline Rose discusses the function of oneness in reference to both the subject and sexual difference in 'Feminine Sexuality – Jacques Lacan and the *école freudienne*' (1986, pp. 49–81).

7 I am here alluding to Freud's famous dictum 'wo es war soll Ich werden', which roughly translates as 'where the id was, the ego shall be'. See 'The Instance of the Letter in the Unconscious, or reason since Freud' (Lacan 2001, pp. 161–97) and also the section 'The Uncanny and Anxiety' in this chapter.

8 I am indebted to Roberto Harari's comprehensive book *Lacan's Seminar on "Anxiety": An Introduction*, especially since the full edited text of Lacan's seminar became available only recently.

9 Compare Lacan's statement on the function of vision: 'We shall then see emerging on the basis of vision, not the phallic symbol, the anamorphic ghost, but the gaze as such, in its pulsatile, dazzling and spread out function' (1998, p. 89).

10 The relationship between abjection and the uncanny in Julia Kristeva's *Powers of Horror* and other feminist texts is discussed in the next chapter, 'The Feminist Uncanny'.

Chapter 2

1 See also my entry on this essay in *Fifty Texts in Art History* (Kokoli 2012, pp. 149–52).

2 See also Cixous, *Le livre de Promethea* (*The Book of Promethea*), in which the negativity of this kind of painful waiting organized around absence, hatred and the violence of the (male) mother/lover/god that dominates *Angst* is gradually replaced by the positivity of a 'happy expectation', like that of the pregnant woman (Andermatt Conley 1984, pp. 159–60).

3 Cf. Jo Anna Isaak's amazing book *Feminism and Contemporary Art: The Revolutionary Power of Women's Laughter* (1996). The uncanny shares many features with humour, at least in its Freudian analysis.
4 On the relationship between artistic creation and procreation, see also Kofman 1988. 'What men find charming in art is the illusion it gives them of being masters of creation and, by that very means, of procreation, the illusion of being able to dominate death and to be the *causa sui*' (p. 171). In a sense, the uncanny emerges when the fabric of this illusion, as Kofman describes it, wears thin.
5 For an important reading of Creed and Kristeva's work on abjection and its application to women's art practice in the 1990s, see Betterton 1996, pp. 132–60.
6 On the relationship between the feminine and the sacred, see also Pollock and Sauron (2007), a collection of essays which, among other things, also tackles the rarely discussed discrepancy between culturally Protestant and culturally Catholic perspectives on femininity, the sacred, the field of vision and their relationship.
7 Another dimension of vampirism that cannot be adequately addressed in this context relates to HIV/AIDS activism and the acknowledgement that LGBTQ communities were losing their members at such a pace through the 1980s that they could be described as uncannily hybrid, including both the living and the dead. On the relationship between HIV/AIDS and the uncanny, see Ultra Red 2005.
8 I am here evoking Nirmal Puwar's figure of the 'space invader', which reflects on the unsettling implications of women and minorities entering fields where white male power is firmly entrenched (2004).
9 According to Nicholas Royle, Cixous' essay 'Fiction and its Phantoms' 'brings out the queerness of Freud's text' (2003, p. 42). More importantly, Royle suggests that the simultaneous emergence of queer and the uncanny at the end of the twentieth century points to an important affinity between them, although 'their explicit conjunction might be another way of defining the emergence of what is called modernism' (p. 43).

Chapter 3

1 A version of this chapter up to the section 'Uncanny Voices', has previously been published as Kokoli (2011). 'Moving Sideways and Other Sleeping Metaphors: Susan Hiller's Paraconceptualism.' In Ann Gallagher (ed.), *Susan Hiller*, London: Tate Publishing, pp. 143–53. I am grateful to Tate Publishing for permission to reuse it.
2 The suggestion that Freud's essay 'The "Uncanny"' is itself an example of the uncanny thanks to its form and telling silences was originally put forward by Cixous (1976a). See Chapters 2 and 3 in this book.

3 Hiller, *Sisters of Menon* 1972/1979, 'Translation 5.79 and Installation Notes.' All automatic script 'translations' come from this part of the installation, bottom left of the horizontal axis, also included in Hiller, 1983.
4 I am indebted to feminist readings of Hiller's production of the seventies and eighties, including: Bosch 1985; Butler 1994; Lippard 1986; Kenrick 1994.
5 Stuart Morgan, 'Beyond Control: An Interview with Susan Hiller', in Fiona Bradley et al., *Susan Hiller* exh. cat., Liverpool: Tate Gallery Liverpool 1996, p. 42.
6 Morgan 1996, p. 41.
7 I am correcting Hiller's transcript '--/we are your sisters from Thebes/Thebes' (Hiller 1983, n.p.), which conceals the different spellings of the name of the city in the automatic script.
8 For a discussion of the possible reasons for the denigration of Grant in American politics and history, see Bouie 2015.
9 See Peirce 1990. For a wider discussion of indexicality in relation to the work of Susan Hiller, see Kokoli 2013.
10 Parts of this section on *The Last Silent Movie* and *Monument* are drawn from a previously published article (Kokoli 2013).
11 See also Godfrey 2008, p. 2.
12 On sound in Hiller's work, see Horlock 2004; and Hiller 2009, pp. 233–8.

Chapter 4

1 Mignon Nixon (2005) writes a far more complicated tale of the relationship between Bourgeois and feminism, in a book that also stages a confrontation between psychoanalysis, feminism and the discipline of art history. In the words of Alison Rowley (2007, p. 1):

> Thus framed, not only did Bourgeois come to be a figure of transference for feminism, but also feminism in the 1970s and 1980s provided Bourgeois with a meaningful context for reworking unassimilated psychic material from much earlier experiences involving crises of positioning both as a daughter in the family in childhood and as a young woman in her profession as an artist in relation to the surrealists.

2 From interviews with Bernard Marcadé and Jerry Govoroy for the film *Louise Bourgeois*, dir. by Camille Guichard, co-produced by Terra Luna Films and Centre Georges Pompidou, Paris 1993; quoted in Bernadac 1995, p. 24, my translation. On this issue, see also Huhn 1996.
3 Before the Married Women's Property Act of 1870 and its extension in 1882, women in England, for example, would lose ownership of any savings and real

estate to their husbands upon marriage and would not be entitled to keep any earnings or property in their name while married.

4 In 'Signature', Levinas spells out his departure from the *Dasein* with great directness: 'In the place of ontology – of the Heideggerian comprehension of the Being of being – is substituted as primordial the relation of a being to a being, which is none the less not equivalent to a rapport between subject and object, but rather to a proximity, to a relation with the Other [*Autrui*]' (Levinas 1990, p. 293).

5 Elizabeth Wright also notes that Freud's 'The "Uncanny"' lends itself to interpretations that posit it as an example of 'a failure of theory in practice' (1998, p. 128), which is precisely what has made the text so appealing to deconstruction.

6 See Lacan, 'Seminar of 21 January 1975' (Mitchell and Rose 1982, p. 168). It needs to be noted that *the objet a* forms part of the subject but is also detachable – hence the fluidity of desire; while *a* is impossible to properly incorporate, it is similarly unseverable. See also Grosz 1990, p. 75.

7 The conceptual interdependency between woman and the dwelling is also elaborated to much the same effect in 'Judaism and the Feminine Element', where Levinas' disagreement with Heidegger on the origins of the dwelling is spelt out (Levinas 1990, pp. 30–8).

8 See, for example, Chalier, 'Ethics and the Feminine' (pp. 119–29), Chanter, 'Antigone's Dilemma' (pp. 130–46) and Irigaray, 'Questions to Emmanuel Levinas', (pp. 109–18), all in Bernasconi and Critchley 1991; Irigaray 1993, pp. 185–217; and especially Ainley 1996, pp. 7–20.

9 My analysis of *Feministo* was originally published in *n.paradoxa* as Kokoli (2004). Some changes have been made to this version.

10 For a representative example, see Kasic 2003.

11 See, for example, Papastergiadis 1993, which admittedly aims to problematize the concept of 'home' but only does so by focusing on the metaphorical weight of 'exile' – implicitly confirming their opposition (home – exile/stasis – crisis). One of the principal starting points of this debate is Nietzsche 1974, p. 340ff.

12 Betty Friedan's thoughts on these issues are revealing, if controversially exaggerated: 'The conditions which destroyed the human identity of so many prisoners [in Nazi concentration camps] were not the torture and the brutality, but conditions similar to those which destroy the identity of the American housewife' (Friedan 1986, p. 265).

13 The names of all the participants are listed on http://womanhouse.refugia.net/

14 Although many contributions to *Women and Craft* (Elinor 1987) support the model of transmission of craft skills across generations of women, Su Richardson has often pointed out that she had to teach herself crocheting as her own mother was far more concerned with skills that would help her daughter go into paid employment rather than become a good housewife.

15 In reconstructing the origins and workings of this art event, the articles reprinted in Parker and Pollock (1987) have been invaluable, especially since the original publications in which some of them appeared are either difficult or impossible to trace: Phil Goodall, '"Feministo: Portrait of the Artist as a Young Woman"', p. 206; R. Parker, 'Portrait of the Artist as a Housewife', pp. 207–10; Monica Ross, 'Portrait of the artist as a young woman: a postal event', p. 211; Phil Goodall, 'Growing point/Pains in "Feministo"', pp. 213–14 (Parker and Pollock 1987). At least half of *MAMA!: Women Artists Together* (MAMA 1977) were devoted to the women's postal art event. In addition to my printed sources, I was fortunate enough to have been granted interviews with Kate Walker (2000) and Monica Ross (2000b), to whom I am deeply indebted for their insights and encouragement.

16 Kate Walker preferred the title *Portrait of the Artist as a Young Woman* all along because it alluded to James Joyce's first novel *Portrait of the Artist as a Young Man*, in which – against feminist aesthetics and politics – the artist is cast as the outsider *par excellence*, an enemy of the people and martyr for his art. (Yet it is worth pointing out that Joyce's writing is counted among the examples of feminine writing regardless of the writer's gender by Hélène Cixous.) The title was changed to '... as a Housewife' only after much debate and to Kate Walker's intense frustration, who characteristically said of her younger collaborators at the time that 'irony is wasted on the young' (Walker 2000). The changed version '... as a Housewife' that was finally used for the ICA installation; yet in the *Feministo* literature I came across the composite 'Portrait of the Artist as a Young Housewife', used as a variant, which suggests a compromise of sorts.

17 The slide collection at the Women's Art Library/MAKE is free for research use but not licensed for publication, as the artists who deposited their work with the collection did not transfer copyright. Obtaining permissions for works in *Feministo* from both the artists and the photographers has been extremely challenging as so many of them are now impossible to trace.

18 For a discussion of possible reconfigurations of community, home(land) and second-wave feminism, see Martin and Mohanty 1986. On the uses and meanings of home in contemporary art, see Perry 2014, in which gender is consistently taken into consideration although the author's focus is on irony, parody and play rather than the uncanny.

19 For example, Margaret Benston, 'The Political Economy of Women's Liberation', in Malos 1980, pp. 119–29. The issue of the productivity of women's labour at home is also examined in Hartmann 1981; Mitchell 1984; and Rubin 1975.

20 Goodall, '"Feministo: Portrait of the Artist as a Young Woman"', p. 206; and Parker, 'Portrait of the Artist as a Housewife', p. 208, both in Parker and Pollock 1987.

21 Many of these issues as well as the history of using craft in feminist art are discussed in detail in two special issues of *Feminist Art News: Women's Craft Issue*, vol. 1, n. 4 (1981) and *Craft!*, vol. 2, n. 6 (1987).

22 Gaie Davidson, 'Interview with Monica Ross' (pamphlet) (Birmingham 1982); Parker, 'Housework', in *Framing Feminism*, p. 200.

Chapter 5

1 I am here alluding to the title of Marianne Hirsch's important book, in which she argued that the maternal had been repressed in second-wave feminist narratives in favour of the distinctly daughterly, dominant perspective (1989). The 'mother – daughter plot' as a symptom of a more widespread attachment to generational models of historical and critical enquiry has been widely criticized for obfuscating the diversity of feminist approaches that defy containment within chronological periods, and for undermining the experience of those who may have come to feminism at different moments in time and in different cultural contexts, regardless of their biological age (e.g. Pollock 1996 and Tickner 2006). In the past few years, the maternal has emerged as an exciting and expanding strand of feminist art historical research (e.g. Liss 2008 and Betterton 2014).

2 I am grateful to Felicity Allen for reminding me of this important aspect of Rosler's work.

3 Through a close reading of texts on the mechanics of identification by Freud and Lacan, Judith Butler locates some potential for rewriting the phallocentric script not by replacing the phallus with a feminine equivalent but by 'offering the lesbian phallus' as a signifier that has 'come to signify in excess of its structurally mandated position' (Butler 1993, p. 90; see also Reich 1992). Although Butler and Reich clearly have the advantage in terms of theoretical sophistication and overcoming binary oppositions (which is still viewed as a great virtue in principle and very often is conceptually and politically valuable too), I don't think that the (merely superficial) essentialism of the feminist art practice under consideration here automatically invalidates it.

4 If 'phallogocentrism' underlines the interdependence and complicity between phallocentrism and logocentrism ('Introduction', n. 2), 'phalloculologocentrism' (as used e.g. in Robinson 2006) suggests that their shared gender asymmetry is reproduced in and supported by a heteronormative division of labour by which the right to look is claimed by masculinity while femininity is cast in the role of being looked at (cf. Mulvey 2009). The deeply ingrained associations between reason and (clear) vision, which are evident in a series of lexicalized metaphors that connect seeing, knowing, understanding and controlling, serve to consolidate and legitimate such asymmetries.

5 I have not been able to find a reference for Greer's prevarication about the cover of *The Whole Woman* but I remember it being discussed in the media at the time. The famous photograph of Greer pretending to bite off Barbie's head isn't that

easy to find either, but at the moment it is available on a Russian website: http://ec-dejavu.ru/b-2/barbie-4.html (accessed 1 March 2015).

6 It is no exaggeration to claim that representing female genitalia can be a dangerous business. At the time of writing, artist Megumi Igarashi, a.k.a. Rokudenashiko, is on trial in her native Japan accused of distribution of obscene materials, for which she could face up to two years in prison and a fine of approximately £14,200, if found guilty. Rokudenashiko (the artist's assumed name which roughly translates as 'good-for-nothing girl'), crowdfunded the making of a kayak modelled on her vulva and distributed smaller 3D models of it as acknowledgement for large contributions (McCurry 2015). On a crowdfunding website, the artist explains her motivations: 'Pussy has been thought to be obscene because it's been overly hidden although it is just a part of women's body. I wanted to make Pussy more casual and pop' [sic; translation by Google] (Rokudenashiko 2015).

7 Patricia White (1992) writes of lesbian spectators as the repressed revenant of second-wave feminist film theory, just as lesbian characters were repressed in Hollywood cinema. From that perspective, if the feminist uncanny is the repressed of Freudian theory, lesbian hauntings emerge as doubly uncanny, evoking what arguably remains repressed in many feminist reconsideration of psychoanalysis.

8 It is important for all art informed by feminism but especially artworks that have attained such iconic status to continue to be interpreted in different contexts and from different perspectives, if they are to escape the unenviable fate of becoming focilized illustrations of the Women's Liberation Movement. Helen Molesworth's reconsideration of *The Dinner Party* alongside Mary Kelly's *Post-Partum Document* and Mierle Laderman's maintenance performances offer a new reading of Chicago's worth in reference to (if not as) Minimalism (1999, esp. pp. 118–19).

9 Irigaray often returns to the importance of establishing a genealogy of women. See, for example, *Je, tu, nous: Toward a Culture of Difference,* trans. by A. Martin (New York and London: Routledge, 1993) and 'Women-amongst-themselves: Creating a woman-to-woman sociality', trans. by David Macey, in *The Irigaray Reader*, ed. by Margaret Whitford (Oxford: Blackwell, 1991), pp. 190–8.

10 I owe the idea of cloth patterns serving as clues to Beckett and Cherry 1994.

11 I have consulted the following general sources on the goddess Kali: Mookerjee 1988; Kinsley 1975; Sykes 1995; Leeming 1994; Ann and Myers Imel 1993.

Chapter 6

1 A range of feminist initiatives and practices that drew on psychoanalysis but also departed from it (not least its emphasis on personal history and trauma as opposed to social context and oppression) both influenced and were influenced

by consciousness raising. The Women's Therapy Centre and Red Therapy were launched in the mid-1970s as both an antidote to mainstream psychotherapy and forms of feminist left-wing activism.

2 My reading of *The Only Woman* is heavily indebted to Pollock (1998, pp. 181–7) but also departs from it insofar as, for Pollock, the work exemplifies a feminist Brechtian position, in which affect is systematically underplayed, whereas I think that this work's affect spills over from the personal to the public and the political.

3 I use a single stroke to denote a line break within the same strip of text and a double stroke for a new strip within the same panel.

4 Deleuze and Guattari have developed a definition of 'minority/minoritarian' on the basis not of numbers but ideological and sociopolitical subjugation (1986).

5 This incident is reminiscent of Roland Barthes's reflections upon discovering a photograph of his mother at the age of five, the infamous Winter Garden photograph (1993, pp. 67–71), while also throwing into relief the significant intersectional differences between Stevens and Barthes. It is moreover doubtful that, for Stevens, her mother's 'unbearable' photograph achieved 'utopically, the impossible science of the unique being' (p. 71); rather, it is ultimately the inadequacy of photographs that *Ordinary/Extraordinary* affirms.

6 On the 'productive ambivalence' of the object of colonial discourse, see Bhabha 1994, p. 67.

7 An earlier and shorter version of this section was presented at the annual conference of the Association of Art Historians in 2005. I thank the organizers and audience for the opportunity to develop my ideas and for their helpful feedback.

8 Unfortunately, story quilts from *The French Collection* aren't illustrated in this book as I could not afford the quoted reproduction fees. Some of the quilts can be viewed online through the artist's website (http://faithringgold.com/ringgold/images.htm) and other pages.

9 All story quilt transcripts are taken from Dan Cameron et al. (1998), *Dancing at the Louvre: Faith Ringgold's French Collection and Other Story Quilts*, Berkeley: University of California Press, pp. 129–48.

10 On the 'time-lag' and/as postcolonial critique, see Bhabha 1994, p. 247: 'The challenge to modernity comes in redefining the signifying relation to a disjunctive "present": staging the past as *symbol*, myth, memory, history, the ancestral – but a past whose iterative *value as sign* reinscribes the "lessons of the past" into the very textuality of the present that determines both the identification with, and the interrogation of, modernity' (emphasis in the original).

11 *The Fae Richards Photo Archive* is not illustrated as I have been unable to establish contact with the license holders. Copies of individual photographs as well as installation views from the Whitney Museum's 1997 Biennial are freely available on the internet. What is more, the content in this case matters less than its framing as archive, to the limited degree to which the two may be distinguished.

12 See, notably, the exhibition *Maud Sulter: Passion*, Street Level Photoworks, Glasgow, 25 April-20 June, curated by Deborah Cherry, as well as Cherry 2013a, 2013b, 2015; and Himid 2011.

13 My discussion of Sulter's work on and with Jeanne Duval is indebted to the scholarship and writing of Deborah Cherry, esp. Cherry 2013a. Cherry also includes *Syrcas* (1994) in Sulter's Jeanne Duval cycle.

14 In Angela Carter's short story 'Black Venus' (1980), in preparation for which the author consulted with Sulter (2003, p. 14), Duval is portrayed as an exoticized, sensual, broken and frustrated creature, much closer to her representation in Baudelaire's poetry. Carter's Duval speaks French poorly (1996, p. 9) and she is shown asking Baudelaire for handouts (p. 7) whereas according to Sulter's research she was the one who provided for them both. Although Carter's Duval remains problematic for these reasons, 'Black Venus' both performs and spells out Duval's predicament, namely her imposed disappearance: 'She had been deprived of history, she was the pure child of the colony' (1996, p. 8). For criticisms of Carter's story, see Cherry 2013a, p. 149.

Postscript

1 The latest instalment to the Dung Beetle series, *We sue an artist (And then rip off her idea)*, responds to the legal threats from Ladybird/Penguin and points out the suspect similarities between Elia's project and a recent series of spoofs commissioned by Ladybird itself as part of its centenary celebrations, with volumes including 'Mindfulness' and 'The Hipster'.

2 This postscript is loosely based on my contribution to Monica Ross: A Symposium, 28 November 2014, British Library, in celebration of Ross's life and work, and the acquisition of her digital archive by the British Library.

3 A new incarnation of this programme was launched in January 2015 as National Networks for Collaborative Outreach (NNCO) with funding for only two years.

4 While the British Library holds Monica Ross's digital archive, non-digital materials are held in her old studio in Brighton.

5 I am grateful to Monica's brother Gerald Ross for identifying a possible reference to their family's experience of growing up in Rochdale. When textile workers finished their shift, buses would become covered in fluff transferred from their clothes and hair and would stick on other passengers. Whether one worked in the mills or not, the whole city would get covered in fluff on a daily basis, a badge of its industrial identity.

6 I wish to thank my colleague Alberto Duman for bringing Agamben's essay to my attention.

Bibliography

NOTE: Freud's works are listed by the date of their original publication, rather than the date of the reprint/edition consulted. The Penguin Freud Library has been used as the default source where possible, for reasons explained in Chapter 2: The Feminist Uncanny.

A People is Missing (2013). 'Revisiting Womanhouse'. http://lemagazine.jeudepaume.org/blogs/beatrizpreciado/2013/10/03/revisiting-womanhouse/ (Accessed 22 April 2015).

Adams, P., Delmar, R. and Lipshitz, S. (1987). 'Using psychoanalytic theory'. In Rozsika Parker and Griselda Pollock (eds), *Framing Feminism: Art and the Women's Movement, 1970-1985*. London: Pandora, p. 205.

Agamben, G. (1999). 'The Melancholic Angel'. In Georgia Albert (trans.), *The Man Without Content*. Stanford: Stanford University Press, pp. 104–15.

Ahmed, S. (2010). 'Feminist Killjoys (And Other Willful Subjects)'. *The Scholar and Feminist Online*, 8.3, Polyphonic Feminisms: Acting in Concert, pp. 1–1. Available online: http://sfonline.barnard.edu/polyphonic/print_ahmed.htm (Accessed 20 November 2014).

Ainley, A. (1996). 'The Feminine, Otherness, Dwelling: Feminist Perspectives on Levinas'. In S. Hand (ed.), *Facing the Other: The Ethics of Emmanuel Levinas*. Richmond: Curzon, pp. 7–20.

Aleci, L. S. (2002). 'In a Pig's Eye: The Offence of Some Living American Women Artists'. In *The Art of Mary Beth Edelson*, exh. cat. New York: Seven Cycles. Reproduced online: http://www.marybethedelson.com/essay_pigeye.html (Accessed 23 February 2015).

Andermatt Conley, V. (1984). *Hélène Cixous: Writing the Feminine*. Lincoln: University of Nebraska Press.

Ann, M. and Myers Imel, D. (eds) (1993). *Goddesses in World Mythology*. Santa Barbara: ABC-CLIO.

Apter, E. (2006). 'Responding: A Referendum on Theory and Feminism'. In C. Armstrong and C. de Zegher (eds), *Women Artists at the Millenium*. Cambridge, MA: MIT Press, pp. 327–34.

Arendt, H. (1998). *The Human Condition*, 2nd edn. Chicago: Chicago University Press.

Baker, B. (2007). 'Chronicle of Selected Artworks, 1972-2007'. In Michelle Barrett and Bobby Baker (eds), *Bobby Baker: Redeeming Features of Daily Life*. London: Routledge, pp. 28–78.

Bal, M. (1991). *Reading Rembrandt: Beyond the Word-Image Opposition*. Cambridge: Cambridge University Press.

Bal, M. (2002). *Travelling Concepts in the Humanities: A Rough Guide*. Toronto: University of Toronto Press, 2002.

Bal, M. (2011). 'Frankfurt' [blog post]. http://www.miekebal.org/news-events/2011/09/29/frankfurt/ (Accessed 2 November 2014).

Bammer, A. (1991). *Partial Visions: Feminism and Utopianism in the 1970s*. London: Routledge.

Barnard, I. (1994). 'Macho Sluts: Genre-Fuck, S/M Fantasy, and the Reconfiguration of Political Action'. *Genders* 19: 265–91.

Barthes, R. (1993). *Camera Lucida: Reflections on Photography*. Trans. Richard Howard. London: Vintage.

Battersby, C. (1989). *Gender and Genius: Towards a Feminist Aesthetics*. Bloomington: Indiana University Press.

Baumgardner, J. and Richards, A. (2010). *Manifesta: Young Women, Feminism and the Future*, rev. edn. New York: Farrar, Straus and Giroux.

Beckett, J. and Cherry, D. (1994). 'Clues to Events'. In Mieke Bal and Inge Boer (eds), *The Point of Theory*. Amsterdam: Amsterdam University Press, pp. 48–55.

Beebe, A. (2009). 'The Coney Island Museum: A Brief History of the Way Things That Weren't Separate Are Separate Now'. In Zoe Beloff (ed.), *The Coney Island Amateur Psychoanalytic Society and its Circle*. New York: Christine Burgin, pp. 9–11.

Beloff, Z. (2009). 'An Introduction to the Coney Island Amateur Psychoanalytic Society'. In Zoe Beloff (ed.), *The Coney Island Amateur Psychoanalytic Society and its Circle*. New York: Christine Burgin, pp. 51–69.

Beloff, Z. (2010). 'Dreamland: The Intimate Politics of Desire – Zoe Beloff in conversation with Niels van Tomme'. *Art Papers*, 26–31.

Belsey, C. and Moore, J. (eds) (1997). *The Feminist Reader*. Malden, MA: Blackwell.

Berlant, L. and Warner, M. (1998). 'Sex in Public', *Critical Inquiry* 24 (2): 547–66.

Bernadac, M.-L. (1995). *Louise Bourgeois*. Paris: Flammarion.

Bernasconi, R. and Critchley, S. (eds) (1991). *Re-Reading Levinas*. Bloomington: Indiana University Press.

Bernheimer, C. and Kahane, C. (1985). *In Dora's Case: Freud, Hysteria, Feminism*. London: Verso.

Betterton, R. (1996). *Intimate Distance: Women, Artists and the Body*. London: Routledge.

Betterton, R. (2004). 'Susan Hiller's Painted Works: Bodies, Aesthetics and Feminism'. In James Lingwood (ed.), *Susan Hiller: Recall: Selected Works, 1969-2004*. Gateshead: Baltic, 2004, pp. 15–20.

Betterton, R. (2014). *Maternal Bodies in the Visual Arts*. Manchester: Manchester University Press.

Bhatia, S. (2012). 'She is Strong'. *Writerspoint*. http://shivesh-writerspoint.blogspot.co.uk/2012/01/she-is-strong.html (Accessed 19 February 2015).

Biography.com Editors (2015). 'Ulysses S. Grant Biography'. http://www.biography.com/people/ulysses-s-grant-9318285 (Accessed 22 December 2015).

Birmingham City University Art and Design Archives (2015). Archives and Creative Practice: Zoe Leonard and Cheryl Dunye. http://www.archivesandcreativepractice.com/zoe-leonard-cheryl-dunye/ (Accessed 2 April 2015).

Biswas, S. (2014a). [Email to the author]. 14 August.

Biswas, S. (2014b). [Artist's talk]. School of Art and Design, Middlesex University. 10 December.

Blackledge, C. (2003). *The Story of V: Opening Pandora's Box*. London: Weidenfeld and Nicolson.

Borzello, F. (2010). *The Artist's Model*. London: Faber & Faber.

Bouie, J. (2015). 'The Unlikely Paths of Grant and Lee'. *Slate*, 9 April 2015. http://www.slate.com/articles/news_and_politics/history/2015/04/appomattox_how_did_ulysses_s_grant_become_an_embarrassment_of_history_and.html (Accessed 10 April 2015).

Brett, G. (2014). 'Rose Finn-Kelcey obituary'. *The Guardian*, 24 February. http://www.theguardian.com/artanddesign/2014/feb/24/rose-finn-kelcey (Accessed 3 November 2014).

Bronfen, E. (1992a). *Over Her Dead Body: Death, Femininity and the Aesthetic*. Manchester: Manchester University Press.

Bronfen, E. (1992b). 'The Death Drive (Freud)'. In Elizabeth Wright (ed.), *Feminism and Psychoanalysis: A Critical Dictionary*. Oxford: Blackwell, pp. 52–7.

Brooklyn Museum (2015). *The Dinner Party*. http://www.brooklynmuseum.org/eascfa/dinner_party/ (Accessed 8 March 2015).

Brooks, P. (1992). *Reading for the Plot: Design and Intention in Narrative*. Cambridge, MA: Harvard University Press.

Bryson, N. (1990). *Looking at the Overlooked: Four Essays on Still-Life Painting*. London: Reaktion.

Bryson, V. (2004). 'Marxism and feminism: can the "unhappy marriage" be saved?'. *Journal of Political Ideologies* 9 (1): 13–30.

Butler, J. (1990). *Gender Trouble: Feminism and the Subversion of Identity*. London: Routledge.

Butler, J. (1993). *Bodies that Matter: On the Discursive Limits of 'Sex'*. London: Routledge.

Butler, S. (1994). 'Subject-to-Change'. *Women's Art Magazine* 59: 23–6.

Carter, A. (1979). *The Sadeian Woman: An Exercise in Cultural History*. London: Virago.

Carter, A. (1996). 'Black Venus' (1980). In *Black Venus*. London: Vintage, pp. 1–14.

Castle, T. (1995). *The Female Thermometer: 18th-century Culture and the Invention of the Uncanny*. Oxford: Oxford University Press.

Cavarero, A. (2009). *Horrorism: Naming Contemporary Violence*. Trans. William McCuaig. New York: Columbia University Press.

Cherry, D. (1998). 'Troubling Presence: Body, Sound and Space in Installation Art of the mid-1990s'. *RACAR* XXV (1–2): 12–30.

Cherry, D. (2013a). 'Image-Making with Jeanne Duval in Mind: Photoworks by Maud Sulter: 1989-2003'. In Marsha Meskimmon and Dorothy Rowe (eds), *Women, Art and Globalisation: Eccentric Encounters*. Manchester: Manchester University Press, pp. 145–68.

Cherry, D. (2013b). 'With Her Fingers on the Political Pulse: The Transnational Curating of Maud Sulter'. In Angela Dimitrakaki and Lara Perry (eds), *Politics in a Glass Case: Feminism, Exhibition Cultures and Curatorial Transgressions*. Liverpool: Liverpool University Press, pp. 205–26.

Cherry, D. (2015a). 'The Ghost Begins by Coming Back: Revenants and Returns in Maud Sulter's Photomontages'. In A. Lepine, M. Lodder and R. McKeever (eds), *Revival: Memories, Identities, Utopias*. London: Courtauld Books Online, pp. 29–44.

Cherry, D. (2015b). 'Poetry – In Motion'. In Deborah Cherry (ed.), *Maud Sulter: Passion*. Altitude Editions, pp. 8–19.

Chicago, J. (1996). *The Dinner Party*. London: Penguin.

Chicago, J. (2006). *Through the Flower: My Struggle as a Woman Artist*. Lincoln, NE: Authors Choice Press.

Chicago, J. (2015). *Through the Flower: About Through the Flower*. http://www.throughtheflower.org/about (Accessed 6 March 2015).

Churchill, C. (2008). *Top Girls*. Ed. Bill Naismith and Nick Worrall. London: Methuen.

Cixous, H. (1976a). 'Fiction and Its Phantoms: A Reading of Freud's Das Unheimlich (The "uncanny")'. *New Literary History* 7 (3): 525–48.

Cixous, H. (1976b). 'The Laugh of the Medusa'. Trans. Keith Cohen and Paula Cohen. *Signs* 1 (4): 875–93.

Cixous, H. (1981). 'Castration or Decapitation?'. Trans. Annette Kuhn, *Signs* 7 (1): 41–55.

Cixous, H. (1985). *Angst*. Trans. Jo Levy. London: John Calder.

Cixous, H. (1991). 'Coming to Writing'. In Deborah Jenson (ed.), *'Coming to Writing' and Other Essays*. Cambridge, MA: Harvard University Press, pp. 1–58.

Clément, C. and Cixous, H. (1986). *The Newly Born Woman*. Trans. Betsy Wing. Minneapolis: University of Minnesota Press.

Cottingham, L. (1996). 'Eating from the *Dinner Party* Plates and Other Myths, Metaphors, and Moments of Lesbian Enunciation in Feminism and Its Art Movement'. In Amelia Jones (ed.), *Sexual Politics: Judy Chicago's Dinner Party in Feminist Art History*. Los Angeles: Hammer Museum of Art and Berkeley: University of California Press, pp. 208–28.

Cottingham, L. (2002). 'Shifting Signs'. In *The Art of Mary Beth Edelson*, exh. cat. New York: Seven Cycles. Reproduced online: http://www.marybethedelson.com/essays.html (Accessed 23 February 2015).

Creed, B. (1993). *The Monstrous Feminine*. London: Routledge.

Creed, B. (2005). *Phallic Panic*. Melbourne: Melbourne University Press.

Davis, A. J. (2007). 'Martha Rosler's Fighting Legions: *Semiotics of the Kitchen* (1975/2003) – Performance and the (Video) Document'. In Jonathan Harris (ed.),

Dead History, Live Art? Spectacle, Subjectivity and Subversion in Visual Culture Since the 1960s. Liverpool: Liverpool University Press and Tate Publishing, pp. 209–32.

Deepwell, K. (1998–). 'Why n.paradoxa?' [editorial statement]. *n.paradoxa* 1–: 1.

Deepwell, K. (2007). 'Feminist Models: Now and in the Future'. In Heike Munder (ed.), *It's Time for Action (There's No Option): About Feminism*. Zurich: Migros museum & JRP Ringier, pp. 190–208.

Deleuze, G. and Guattari, F. (1986). *Kafka: Towards a Minor Literature*. Trans. Dana Polan. Minneapolis: University of Minnesota Press.

Derrida, J. (1982). 'White Mythology: Metaphor in the Text of Philosophy'. In Alan Bass (trans. and annotated), *Margins of Philosophy*. Chicago: Chicago University Press, pp. 207–71.

Derrida, J. (1987). 'To Speculate – on "Freud"'. In Alan Bass (trans.), *The Post Card*. Chicago: University of Chicago Press, pp. 257–409.

Derrida, J. (1994). *Specters of Marx: The State of the Debt, the Work of Mourning, and the New International*. Trans. Peggy Kamuf. London: Routledge, 1994.

Deutsche, R. (1996). *Evictions: Art and Spatial Politics*. Cambridge, MA: MIT Press.

Dimitrakaki, A. (2013). *Gender, artWork and the Global Imperative: A Materialist Feminist Critique*. Manchester: Manchester University Press.

Dolar, M. (1991). '"I Shall Be with You on Your Wedding-Night": Lacan and the Uncanny'. *October* 58: 5–23.

Duncan, C. (1989). 'The MoMA's Hot Mamas'. *Art Journal* 48 (2): 171–8.

Edelman, L. (2004). *No Future: Queer Theory and the Death Drive*. Durham, NC: Duke University Press.

Edelson, M. B. (2015). 'Direct Access: Edelson Comments on The Last Supper and other posters'. http://www.marybethedelson.com/essay_pigeye.html (Accessed 12 March 2015).

Edinburgh Anarchist Federation (2014). 'Don't Mourn. Organise.'. https://libcom.org/library/dont-mourn-organise (Accessed 2 November 2014).

Elia, M. (2015). Artist's website. http://miriamelia.co.uk/ (Accessed 25 April 2015).

Elia, M. and Elia, E. (2014). *We Go to the Gallery*. London: Dung Beetle.

Elinor, G., Richardson, S., Scott, S., Thomas, A. and Walker, K. (eds) (1987). Women and Craft. London: Virago.

Enwezor, O. (2008). *Archive Fever: Uses of the Document in Contemporary Art*. New York: International Center of Photography.

Evans, J. (2005). 'Against Decorum! Jo Spence: A Voice on the Margins'. In Mela Dávila (ed.), *Jo Spence: Beyond the Perfect Image: Photography, Subjectivity, Antagonism*. Barcelona: MACBA, pp. 34–62.

Felski, R. (1989). *Beyond Feminist Aesthetics*. Cambridge, MA: Harvard University Press.

Ferris, L. (2002). 'Cooking up the self: Bobby Baker and Blondell Cummings "Do" the Kitchen'. In Sidonie Smith and Julia Watson (eds), *Interfaces: Women/Autobiography/Image/Performance*. Ann Arbor: Michigan University Press, pp. 186–210.

Firestone, S. (2003 [1970]). *The Dialectic of Sex: The Case for Feminist Revolution.* New York: Farrar, Strauss and Giroux.

Freud, S. (1913). 'The Theme of the Three Caskets' (1913). In *Art and Literature, Penguin Freud Library*, vol. 14, pp. 233–47.

Freud, S. (1953a). 'Remembering, Repeating and Working-Through (Further Recommendations on the Technique of Psycho-analysis II)' (1914). In James Strachey (ed.), *The Standard Edition of the Complete Psychological Works of Sigmund Freud*, vol. XII. London: Hogarth Press and the Institute of Psycho-Analysis, pp. 147–56.

Freud, S. (1953b). 'The Handling of Dream-Interpretation in Psycho-analysis' (1911). In James Strachey (ed.), *The Standard Edition of the Complete Psychological Works of Sigmund Freud*, vol. XII. London: Hogarth Press and the Institute of Psycho-Analysis, pp. 89–96.

Freud, S. (1958). 'Medusa's Head' (1940 [1922]). In *The Standard Edition of the Complete Psychological Works of Sigmund Freud*, Ed. James Strachey, vol. XVIII. London: Hogarth Press and the Institute of Psycho-Analysis, pp. 273–4.

Freud, S. (1976). *The Interpretation of Dreams* (1900), *Penguin Freud Library*, vol. 4 London: Penguin.

Freud, S. (1983a). 'The Dissolution of the Oedipus Complex' (1924c). In *On Sexuality, Penguin Freud Library*, vol. 7. Harmondsworth: Penguin, pp. 313–22.

Freud, S. (1983b). 'Family Romances' (1909 [1908]). In *On Sexuality, Penguin Freud Library*, vol. 7. Harmondsworth: Penguin, pp. 221–5.

Freud, S. (1983c). 'Fetishism' (1927). In *On Sexuality, Penguin Freud Library*, vol. 7. Harmondsworth: Penguin, pp. 351–7.

Freud, S. (1983d). 'The Infantile Genital Organisation (An Interpolation into the Theory of Sexuality)' (1923b). In *On Sexuality, Penguin Freud Library*, vol. 7. Harmondsworth: Penguin, pp. 303–12.

Freud, S. (1983e). 'Some Psychical Consequences of the Anatomical Distinction Between the Sexes' (1925). In *On Sexuality, Penguin Freud Library*, vol. 7. Harmondsworth: Penguin, pp. 330–43.

Freud, S. (1983f). 'The Taboo of Virginity' (1918 [1917]). In *On Sexuality, Penguin Freud Library*, vol. 7. Harmondsworth: Penguin, pp. 261–83.

Freud, S. (1990a). 'Fragment of an Analysis of a Case of Hysteria ("Dora")' (1905 [1901]). In *Case Histories I, Penguin Freud Library*, vol. 8. London: Penguin, pp. 31–164.

Freud, S. (1990b). 'On Transience' (1916 [1915]). In *Art and Literature, Penguin Freud Library*, vol. 14, pp. 283–90.

Freud, S. (1990c). 'The "Uncanny"' (1919). In *Art and Literature, Penguin Freud Library*, vol. 14, pp. 335–76.

Freud, S. (1991a). 'Beyond the Pleasure Principle' (1920). In *On Metapsychology, Penguin Freud Library*, vol. 11. London: Penguin, pp. 269–338.

Freud, S. (1991b). 'The Ego and the Id' (1923a). In *On Metapsychology, Penguin Freud Library*, vol. 11. London: Penguin, pp. 350–407.

Freud, S. (1991c). 'Femininity' (1933 [1932]). In *New Introductory Lectures on Psychoanalysis, Penguin Freud Library*, vol. 2. London: Penguin, pp. 145–66.

Freud, S. (1991d). 'Mourning and Melancholia' (1917 [1915]). In *On Metapsychology, Penguin Freud Library*, vol. 11. London: Penguin, pp. 245–68.

Freud, S. (1993a). 'The Loss of Reality in Neurosis and Psychosis' (1924b). In *On Psychopathology, Penguin Freud Library*, vol. 10. London: Penguin, pp. 219–26.

Freud, S. (1993b). 'Neurosis and Psychosis' (1924a). In *On Psychopathology, Penguin Freud Library*, vol. 10. London: Penguin, pp. 209–18

Freud, S. (2001 [1913]). *Totem and Taboo*. London: Routledge Classics.

Friedan, B. (1986). *The Feminine Mystique*. Harmondsworth: Penguin.

Frye, M. (1983). *The Politics of Reality: Essays in Feminist Theory*. New York: Crossing Press.

Fuss, D. (1992). 'Fashion and the Homospectatorial Look', *Critical Inquiry* 18 (4): 713–32.

Fuss, D. (1995). *Identification Papers*. London: Routledge.

Gallop, J. (1982). *The Daughter's Seduction: Feminism and Psychoanalysis*. Ithaca, NY: Cornell University Press.

Gallop, J. (1985). *Reading Lacan*. Ithaca, NY: Cornell University Press.

Gallop, J. (1991). 'Juliet Mitchell and the Human Sciences'. In Alexandre Leupin (ed.), *Lacan and the Human Sciences*. Lincoln and London: University of Nebraska Press, pp. 123–40.

Garber, M. and Vickers, N. J. (eds) (2003). *The Medusa Reader*. London: Routledge.

Gerhard, J. F. (2013). *The Dinner Party: Judy Chicago and the Power of Popular Feminism, 1970-2007*. Athens and London: The University of Georgia Press.

Gibson, A. (1998). 'Picasso's Studio'. In Dan Cameron (ed.), *Dancing at the Louvre: Faith Ringgold's French Collection and Other Story Quilts*. Berkeley: University of California Press, pp. 64–73.

Godfrey, M. (2008). *The Last Silent Movie*. London: Matt's Gallery.

Gordon, A. (1997). *Ghostly Matters: Haunting and the Sociological Imagination*. Minneapolis: University of Minnesota Press.

Gouma-Peterson, T. (1998). 'Faith Ringgold's Journey: From Greek Busts to African American Dilemma Tales'. In Dan Cameron (ed.), *Dancing at the Louvre: Faith Ringgold's French Collection and Other Story Quilts*. Berkeley: University of California Press, pp. 39–48.

Goux, J.-J. (1993). *Oedipus Philosopher*. Trans. Catherine Porter. Stanford, CA: Stanford University Press.

Grosz, E. (1990). *Jacques Lacan: A Feminist Introduction*. London and New York: Routledge.

Grosz, E. (1995). *Space, Time and Perversion*. London: Routledge.

Grudin, E. U. (1990). 'Essay'. In *Stitching Memories: African-American Story Quilts*. Williamstown, MA: Williams College Museum of Art, pp. 13–17.

Gunnarsson, L. (2011). 'A defence of the category "women"'. *Feminist Theory* 12: 23–37.

Halberstam, J. (2011). *The Queer Art of Failure*. Durham. NC: Duke University Press.

Harari, R. (2000). *Lacan's Seminar on "Anxiety": An Introduction*. New York: Other Press.

Hartmann, H. (1981). 'The Unhappy Marriage of Marxism and Feminism'. In Lydia Sargent (ed.), *Woman and Revolution*. London: Pluto, pp. 1–4.

Harvey, D. (1989). *Condition of Postmodernity: An Enquiry into the Origins of Cultural Change*. Oxford: Blackwell.

Heiser, J. (2007). 'A Romantic Measure'. In Christine Kintisch and Ellen Seifermann (eds), *Romantischer Konzeptualismus/Romantic Conceptualism*, Nürnberg: Kunsthalle and Vienna: BAWAG Foundation, pp. 134–49.

Hiller, S. (1983). *Sisters of Menon*. London: Coracle Press for Gimpel Fils.

Hiller, S. (1993). 'In Conversation with Andrew Renton'. In Adrian Searle (ed.), *Talking Art I*. London: ICA, pp. 85–99.

Hiller, S. (1996). *Thinking About Art: Conversations with Susan Hiller*. Ed. Barbara Einzig. Manchester: Manchester University Press.

Hiller, S. (2009). *The Provisional Texture of Reality: Selected Texts and Interviews, 1977-2007*, edited, introduced and annotated by A. M. Kokoli. Zurich: JRP|Ringier.

Hiller, S. and Parker, R. (1996). 'Looking at New Work: An Interview with Rozsika Parker'. In *Thinking About Art*, pp. 51–9.

Himid, L. (2011). *Thin Black Line(s): Tate Britain 2011/2012*. Preston: Making Histories Visible Project, Centre for Contemporary Art, UCLAN.

Hirsch, M. (1989). *The Mother/Daughter Plot: Narrative, Psychoanalysis, Feminism*. London: John Wiley & Sons.

Hodgetts, V. (1972). 'Eggs to Breasts'. *Womanhouse*. http://womanhouse.refugia.net/ (Accessed 26 February 2015).

Hoffmann, E. T. A. (2010). 'The Sandman'. In John Oxenford (trans.), *Tales from the German, Comprising specimens from the most celebrated authors*, Gutenberg ebook. http://www.gutenberg.org/files/32046/32046-h/32046-h.htm#sandman. (Accessed 17 November 2014).

Hoggets, V. (1972). Eggs to Breasts, Womanhouse Catalogue. Available online: http://womanhouse.refugia.net/ (Accessed 10 September 2014).

Holland, P. (1991). 'Introduction: History, Memory and the Family Album'. In Jo Spence and Patricia Holland (eds), *Family Snaps: The Meanings of Domestic Photography*. London: Virago, pp. 1–14.

Horlock, M. (2004). 'Susan Hiller with Mary Horlock: Interview'. In Jim Drobnick (ed.), *Aural Cultures*. Banff: YYZ Books/Walter Phillips Gallery Editions.

Huhn, R. (1996). 'Louise Bourgeois: Deconstructing the Phallus within the Exile of the Self'. In Catherine de Zegher (ed.), *Inside the Visible: An Elliptic Traverse of Twentieth-Century Art in, of, and from the Feminine*. Cambridge MA: MIT Press, pp. 135–43.

Humes, C. A. (2003). 'Wrestling with Kali: South Asian and British Constructions of the Dark Goddess'. In Rachel Fell McDermott and Jeffrey J. Kripal (eds), *Encountering Kali: In the Margins, at the Center, in the West*. Berkeley: University of California Press, pp. 145–68.

Irigaray, L. (1985a). *Speculum of the Other Woman*. Trans. Gillian C. Gill. Ithaca, NY: Cornell University Press.

Irigaray, L. (1985b). *This Sex Which Is Not One*. Trans. Catherine Porter with Carolyn Burke. Ithaca, NY: Cornell University Press.

Irigaray, L. (1991). *The Irigaray Reader*. Ed. Margaret Whitford. Oxford: Blackwell.

Irigaray, L. (1993). *An Ethics of Sexual Difference*. Trans. Carolyn Burke and Gillian C. Gill. London: Athlone.

Isaak, J. A. (1996). *Feminism and Contemporary Art: The Revolutionary Power of Women's Laughter*. London: Routledge.

Jackson, S. (2010). 'The Desire for Freud: Psychoanalysis and Feminism' (1983). In Deborah Cameron and Joan Scanlon (eds), *The Trouble and Strife Reader*. London: Bloomsbury Academic, pp. 123–33.

Jardine, A. (1985). *Gynesis: Configurations of Woman and Modernity*. Ithaca, NY: Cornell University Press.

Jay, M. (1994). *Downcast Eyes: The Denigration of Vision in Twentieth-Century French Thought*. Berkeley: University of California Press.

Jay, M. (1998). *Cultural Semantics: Keywords of Our Time*. London: Athlone Press.

Jentsch, E. (1995). 'On the psychology of the uncanny'. *Angelaki* 2: 7–16.

Johnson, B. (1987). 'My Monster/My Self'. In *A World of Difference*. Baltimore: John Hopkins University Press, pp. 144–54.

Jonte-Pace, D. (2001). *Speaking the Unspeakable: Religion, Misogyny and the Uncanny Mother in Freud's Cultural Texts*. Berkeley: University of California Press.

Jones, A. (1994). 'Postfeminism, Feminist Pleasures, and Embodied Theories of Art'. In J. Frueh, C. L. Langer and A. Raven (eds), *New Feminist Criticism: Art, Identity, Action*. New York: IconEdition/HarperCollins, pp. 16–41.

Jones, A. (1996). *Sexual Politics: Judy Chicago's Dinner Party in Feminist Art History*. Los Angeles: Hammer Museum of Art and Berkeley: University of California Press.

Jones, A. (2006). *Self/Image: Technology, Representation and the Contemporary Subject*. London: Routledge.

Jones, A. (2012). *Seeing Differently: A History and Theory of Identification in the Visual Arts*. London: Routledge.

Kaplan, E. A. (2002). 'Mary Beth Edelson: Trickster and Gunslinger'. In *The Art of Mary Beth Edelson*, exh. cat. New York: Seven Cycles. Reproduced online: http://www.marybethedelson.com/essays.html (Accessed 23 February 2015).

Kasic, B. (2003). 'Re-thinking the Imaginary of Home(s)', *n.paradoxa*, vol. 11, pp. 30–7.

Kenrick, P. (1994). 'Susan Hiller, Automatic Writing and Images of Self'. In Gabrielle Griffin (ed.), *Difference in View: Women and Modernism*. London: Taylor and Francis, pp. 108–29.

Kinsley, D. R. (1975). *The Sword and the Flute: Kali and Krsna, Dark Visions of the Terrible and the Sublime in Hindu Mythology*. Dehli: Vikas.

Kittler, F. A. (1999). *Gramophone, Film, Typewriter*. Trans. Geoffrey Winthrope-Young and Michael Wutz. Stanford, CA: Stanford University Press.

Knabb, K. (ed.) (2006). *Situationist International Anthology* (revised and expanded edition). [No location provided]: Bureau of Public Secrets. Excerpts available online: http://www.bopsecrets.org/SI/index.htm (Accessed 5 August 2014).

Kofman, S. (1985). *The Enigma of Woman: Woman in Freud's Writings*. Trans. Catherine Porter. Ithaca: Cornell University Press.

Kofman, S. (1988). *The Childhood of Art: An Interpretation of Freud's Aesthetics*. Trans. Winifred Woodhull. New York: Columbia University Press.

Kofman, S. (1991). *Freud and Fiction*. Trans. Sarah Wykes. Cambridge: Polity Press.

Kokoli, A. (2004). 'Undoing "homeliness" in feminist art: *Feministo: Portrait of the Artist as a Housewife* (1975–7)', *n.paradoxa*, 13, issue 'Domestic Politics', pp. 75–83.

Kokoli, A. (ed.) (2008). *Feminism Reframed: Reflections on Art and Difference*. Newcastle: Cambridge Scholars Publishing.

Kokoli, A. (2011). 'Moving Sideways and Other Sleeping Metaphors: Susan Hiller's Paraconceptualism'. In Ann Gallagher (ed.), *Susan Hiller*. London: Tate Publishing, pp. 143–53.

Kokoli, A. (2012a). 'Laura Mulvey, "Visual Pleasure and Narrative Cinema (1975)"'. In Diana Newall and Grant Pooke (eds), *Fifty Texts in Art History*. London: Routledge, pp. 144–8.

Kokoli, A. (2012b). 'Remembering, repeating and working through in *Anniversary – An Act of Memory* by Monica Ross and co-recitors (2008-)', *Performance Research*, 17(5), issue 'On Duration': 24–30.

Kokoli, A. (2013). 'The voice as uncanny index in Susan Hiller's *The Last Silent Movie*', *The Art Journal* 72 (2): 6–15.

Korsmeyer, C. (2004). *Gender and Aesthetics: An Introduction*. London: Routledge.

Krauss, R. (1985). 'Notes on the Index' (Parts I & II). In *The Originality of the Avant-Garde and Other Modernist Myths*. Cambridge, MA: MIT Press, pp. 196–220.

Kripal, J. J. (2003). 'Why the Tantrika is a Hero: Kali in the Psychoanalytic Tradition'. In Rachel Fell McDermott and Jeffrey J. Kripal (eds), *Encountering Kali: In the Margins, at the Center, in the West*. Berkeley: University of California Press, pp. 196–222.

Kristeva, J. (1980). *Desire in Language: A Semiotic Approach to Literature and Art*. Ed. Leon S. Roudiez. New York: Columbia University Press.

Kristeva, J. (1982). *Powers of Horror: An Essay on Abjection*. New York: Columbia University Press.

Kristeva, J. (1984). *Revolution in Poetic Language*. New York: Columbia University Press.

Kristeva, J. (1986). 'Women's Time'. In Toril Moi (ed.), *The Kristeva Reader*. Oxford: Blackwell, pp. 187–213.

Kristeva, J. (1992). *Black Sun: Depression and Melancholia*. New York: Columbia University Press.

Kristeva, J. (1994). *Strangers to Ourselves*. New York: Columbia University Press.

Lacan, J. (1982). 'The Meaning of the Phallus'. In J. Mitchell and J. Rose (eds), *Feminine Sexuality: Jacques Lacan and the école freudienne*. London: Macmillan, pp. 74–85.

Lacan, J. (1998). *The Four Fundamental Concepts of Psychoanalysis*. Ed. Jacques-Alain Miller and Trans. Alan Sheridan. London: Vintage.

Lacan, J. (1999). *The Seminar of Jacques Lacan, Book XX: On Feminine Sexuality, the Limits of Love and Knowledge, 1972-1973 (Encore)*. Ed. Jacques-Alain Miller and Trans. with notes by Bruce Fink. London: Norton.

Lacan, J. (2001). *Écrits: A Selection*. London: Routledge.

Lacan, J. (2014). *The Seminar of Jacques Lacan, Book X: Anxiety*. Ed. Jacques-Alain Miller and Trans. A. R. Price. Cambridge: Polity.

Lacy, S. (2015). '*In Mourning and In Rage* (1977)', Suzanne Lacy and Leslie Labowitz, http://www.suzannelacy.com/in-mourning-and-in-rage-1977/ (Accessed 22 April 2015).

Laplanche, J. (1976). *Life and Death in Psychoanalysis*. Trans. and with an introduction by Jeffrey Mehlman. Baltimore: Johns Hopkins University Press.

Laplanche, J. (1989). *New Foundations for Psychoanalysis*. Trans. David Macey. Oxford: Blackwell.

Laplanche, J. (1999). *Essays on Otherness*. Ed. John Fletcher. London: Routledge.

Laplanche, J. and Pontalis, J.-B. (1973). *The Language of Psychoanalysis*. London: Karnac Books.

Lavin, M. (1995). *Cut with the kitchen knife: Weimar Photomontages of Hannah Hoch*. New Haven: Yale University Press.

Lavin, M. (2010). *Push Comes to Shove: New Images of Aggressive Women*. Cambridge, MA: MIT Press.

Leader, D. (2000). *Freud's Footnotes*. London: Faber & Faber.

Leeming, D. and M. (1994). *A Dictionary of Creation Myths*. Oxford: Oxford University Press.

Leighten, P. (2001). 'Colonialism, *l'art nègre*, and *Les Demoiselles d'Avignon*'. In Christopher Green (ed.), *Picasso's Les Demoiselles d'Avignon*. Cambridge: Cambridge University Press, pp. 77–103.

Levinas, E. (1979). *Totality and Infinity: An Essay on Exteriority*. Trans. Alphonso Lingis. The Hague: Martinus Nijhoff.

Levinas, E. (1990). *Difficult Freedom: Essays on Judaism*. Trans. Seán Hand. London: Athlone Press.

Liddell, H. G. and Scott, R. (1940). *Greek-English Lexicon*, 9th edn. Oxford: Clarendon Press.

Linville, S. E. (2004). *History Films, Women and Freud's Uncanny*. Austin, TX: University of Texas Press.

Lippard, L. (1976). *From the Center: Feminist Essays on Women's Art*. New York: Dutton.

Lippard, L. (1986). *Out of Bounds*. London: ICA.

Liss, A. (2008). *Feminist Art and the Maternal*. Minneapolis: University of Minnesota Press.

Lyon, J. (1999). *Manifestoes: Provocations of the Modern*. Ithaca, NY: Cornell University Press.

Lyons, K. (2015). 'I think Germaine Greer is wrong on trans issues – but banning her isn't the answer', *Guardian*, 27 October http://www.theguardian.com/commentisfree/2015/oct/27/germaine-greer-transphobia-cardiff-feminism-inclusive (Accessed 11 December 2015).

Mainardi, P. (1982). 'Quilts: The Great American Art'. In Norma Broude and Mary Garrard (eds), *Feminism and Art History*. New York: Harper and Row, pp. 85–99.

Malos, E. (ed.) (1980). *The Politics of Housework*. London: Allison & Busby.

MAMA Collective (1977). *MAMA! Women Artists Together*. Birmingham: MAMA Collective.

Margantin, L. (2013). 'Jeanne Duval photographiée par Nadar', *Oeuvres ouvertes*. http://www.oeuvresouvertes.net/spip.php?article2142 (Accessed 7 April 2015).

Margolies, I. (2009). 'A Matter of Time: Jeanne Dielman, 23, quai du Commerce, 1080 Bruxelles'. *The Criterion Collection Film Essays*. http://www.criterion.com/current/posts/1215-a-matter-of-time-jeanne-dielman-23-quai-du-commerce-1080-bruxelles (Accessed 27 February 2015).

Mark, L. G. (ed.) (2007). *WACK! Art and the Feminist Revolution*. Los Angeles: MoCA.

Marks, L. U. (2000). *The Skin of the Film: Intercultural Cinema, Embodiment, and the Senses*. Durham, NC: Duke University Press.

Martin, B. and Mohanty, C. T. (1986). 'Feminist Politics: What's Home Got to Do with It?'. In Teresa de Lauretis (ed.), *Feminist Studies, Critical Studies*. Bloomington: Indiana University Press, pp. 191–212.

Martin, E. (1991). 'The Egg and the Sperm: How Science Has Constructed a Romance Based on Stereotypical Male-Female Roles', *Signs* 16 (3): 485–501.

Masschelein, A. (2011). *The Unconcept: The Freudian Uncanny in Late-Twentieth-Century Theory*. Albany: SUNY Press.

Mastai, J. (1995). 'Though Shalt Not … The Law of the Mother'. In *Women and Paint*. Saskatoon: Mendel Art Gallery, pp. 8–14.

McCurry, J. (2015). 'Japanese artist goes on trial over "vagina selfies"'. *The Guardian* 15 April. (Accessed 15 April 2015).

McRobbie, A. (2009). *The Aftermath of Feminism: Gender, Culture, and Social Change*. London: Sage.

Mehlman, J. (1972). 'French Freud …'. *Yale French Studies* 48: 5–9.

Mehlman, J. (1977). *Revolution and Repetition: Marx/Hugo/Balzac*. Berkeley: University of California Press.

'Melodrama' (2015). *Encyclopaedia Britannica Online*. http://www.britannica.com/EBchecked/topic/374063/melodrama (Accessed 7 April 2015).

Meskimmon, M. (2011). *Contemporary Art and the Cosmopolitan Imagination*. London: Routledge.

Miller, C., Nead, L. and Pollock, G. (1989). *Images of Women*. Leeds: Leeds City Art Galleries.

Miller, J.-A. (1988). 'Extimité'. Trans. Françoise Massardier-Kenney, *Prose Studies* 11 (3): 121–31.

Mitchell, J. (1984). 'Women: The Longest Revolution'. In *Women: The Longest Revolution*. London: Virago, pp. 17–54.
Mitchell, J. and Rose, J. (eds) (1982). *Feminine Sexuality: Jacques Lacan and the école Freudienne*. Trans. Jaqueline Rose. London: Macmillan.
Moi, Toril (2001). *'What is a Woman?' and Other Essays*. Oxford: Oxford University Press.
Molesworth, H. (1999). 'Cleaning Up in the 1970s: The Work of Judy Chicago, Mary Kelly and Mierle Laderman Ukeles'. In Michael Newman and John Bird (eds), *Rewriting Conceptual Art*. London: Reaktion, pp. 107–22.
Mookerjee, A. (1988). *Kali: The Feminine Force*. London: Thames & Hudson.
Morgan, S. (1996). 'Beyond Control: An Interview with Susan Hiller'. In Fiona Bradley (ed.), *Susan Hiller*. Liverpool: Tate Gallery Liverpool, pp. 34–45.
Morris III, C. E. and Nakayama, T. K. (2014). [Editorial Statement], *QED: A Journal in GLBTQ Worldmaking*. Available online: http://msupress.org/journals/qed/ (Accessed 18 November 2014).
Morton, S. (2003). *Gayatri Chakravorty Spivak*. Hove: Psychology Press.
Mother Tongue (2013). *The White Aesthetic Necessitated by the 'Glasgow Miracle': Two Invisible Case Studies*, Parts I & II. Pamphlet published by Mother Tongue in line with the exhibition *24 Spaces: A Cacophony*, Malmö Konsthall, 14 May–18 August 2013.
Mother Tongue (2014). *A Thousand of Him, Scattered: Relative Newcomers in Diaspora*. London: TrAIN, in partnership with Edinburgh: Stills.
Müller, U. (2015). *Re:tracing the Feminist Art Programme*. http://www.encore.at/retracing/index2.html Published c.1997 (Accessed 19 April 2015).
Mulvey, L. (1993). 'Some Thoughts on Theories of Fetishism in the Context of Contemporary Culture', *October* 65: 3–20.
Mulvey, L. (1996). *Fetishism and Curiosity*. Bloomington: Indiana University Press/London: BFI.
Mulvey, L. (2009). *Visual and Other Pleasures*, 2nd edn. Basingstoke: Palgrave Macmillan.
Munford, R. and Melanie Waters (2013). *Feminism and Popular Culture: Investigating the Postfeminist Mystique*. London: IB Tauris.
Muñoz, J. E. (1999). *Dissidentifications: Queers of Color and the Performance of Politics*. Minneapolis: Minnesota University Press.
Nead, L. (1988). *Myths of Sexuality: Representations of Women in Victorian Britain*. Oxford: Blackwell.
Nead, L. (1992). *The Female Nude: Art, Obscenity and Sexuality*. London: Routledge.
Nicoletta, J. (2005). 'Louise Bourgeois's Femmes-Maisons'. In Norma Broude and Mary D. Garrard (eds), *Reclaiming Female Agency: Feminist Art History After Postmodernism*. Berkeley: University of California Press, pp. 361–71.
Nietzsche, F. (1974). *The Gay Science*. Trans. W. Kaufmann. New York: Vintage.
Nixon, M. (2005). *Fantastic Reality: Louise Bourgeois and a Story of Modern Art*. Cambridge, MA: MIT Press.

Nixon, M. (2006). '*The She-Fox*: Transference and the "Woman Artist"'. In C. Armstrong and C. de Zegher (eds), *Women Artists at the Millenium*. Cambridge, MA: MIT Press, pp. 275–303.

Nochlin, L. (1989). 'Why Have There Been No Great Women Artists?' (1971). In *'Women, Art, and Power' and Other Essays*. London: Thames & Hudson, pp. 145–78.

O'Grady, L. (2012). 'This Will Have Been: My 1980s'. *Art Journal* 71 (2): 7–17.

Pagels, E. (1989). *The Gnostic Gospel*. London: Vintage.

Papastergiadis, N. (1993). *Modernity as Exile: The Stranger in John Berger's Writing*. Manchester: Manchester University Press.

Parker, R. (2010). *The Subversive Stitch*, rev. edn. London: IB Tauris.

Parker, R. and Pollock, G. (1981). *Old Mistresses: Women, Art and Ideology*. London: Routledge & Kegan Paul.

Peirce, C. S. (1990). 'The Icon, Index and Symbol'. In Charles Harthorne and Paul Weiss (eds), *The Collected Papers of Charles Sanders Peirce*, vol. 2. Cambridge, MA: Belknap, pp. 156–73.

Perry, G. (2014). *Playing at Home: The House in Contemporary Art*. London: Reaktion.

Pines, M. (2008). 'Shame: What Psychoanalysis does and does not say'. In Claire Pajaczkowska and Ivan Ward (eds), *Shame and Sexuality: Psychoanalysis and Visual Culture*. London: Routledge, pp. 93–106.

Pollock, G. (1988). *Vision and Difference: Femininity, Feminism and the Histories of Art*. London: Routledge.

Pollock, G. (1989). 'Whose Images of Women?'. In Corinne Miller, Lynda Nead and Griselda Pollock (eds), *Images of Women*. Leeds: Leeds City Art Galleries, pp. 6–10.

Pollock, G. (ed.) (1996). *Generations and Geographies in the Visual Arts: Feminist Readings*. London: Routledge.

Pollock, G. (1999a). *Differencing the Canon: Feminist Desire and the Writing of Art's Histories*. London: Routledge.

Pollock, G. (1999b). 'Still Working on the Subject: Feminist Poetics at its Avant-Garde Moment'. In S. Breitwieser (ed.), *Reading the Post-Partum Document: Mary Kelly*. Vienna: Generali Foundation, pp. 236–60.

Pollock, G. (2004). 'Tracing Figures of Presence: Naming Ciphers of Absence/ Feminism, Imperialism and Postmodernity: The Work of Sutapa Biswas'. In *Sutapa Biswas*. London: inIVA, pp. 22–41.

Pollock, G. (2007a). *Encounters in the Virtual Feminist Museum: Time, space and the archive*. London: Routledge.

Pollock, G. (2007b). 'Kitchen Show'. In Michelle Barrett and Bobby Baker (eds), *Bobby Baker: Redeeming Features of Daily Life*. London: Routledge, pp. 178–83.

Pollock, G. (2008). 'The Visual Poetics of Shame'. In Claire Pajaczkowska and Ivan Ward (eds), *Shame and Sexuality: Psychoanalysis and Visual Culture*. London: Routledge, pp. 109–27.

Pollock, G. (2013). 'From Horrorism to Compassion: Re-facing Medusan Otherness in Dialogue with Adriana Caverero and Bracha Ettinger'. In Griselda Pollock (ed.),

Visual Politics of Psychoanalysis: Art and the Image in Post-traumatic Cultures. London: IB Tauris, pp. 159–89.

Pollock, G. and Sauron, V. (eds) (2007). *The Sacred and the Feminine: Imagination and Sexual Difference*. London: IB Tauris.

Puwar, N. (2004). *Space Invaders: Race, Gender and Bodies out of Place*. Oxford: Berg.

Rege, S. (2013). *Writing Caste/Writing Gender: Narrating Dalit Women's Testimonies*. New Delhi: Zubaan.

Reich, J. L. (1992). 'Genderfuck: The Law of the Dildo'. *Discourse* 15 (1): 112–27.

Rich, A. (1993). '"When We Dead Awaken": Writing as Revision'. In Barbara Charlesworth Gelpi and Albert Gelpi (ed.), *Adrienne Rich's Poetry and Prose*. New York: Norton Press, pp. 166–77.

Richardson, M. (2011). 'Sculptor's Death Date Unearthed: Edmonia Lewis Died in London in 1907'. *Artfix Daily Blogs*. http://www.artfixdaily.com/blogs/post/51-sculptors-death-unearthed-edmonia-lewis-died-in-london-in-1907 (Accessed 4 April 2015).

Richardson, S. and Davidson, G. (1987). 'Crocheted Strategies: A new audience for women's work'. In Gillian Elinor, Su Richardson, Sue Scott, Angharad Thomas and Kate Walker (eds), *Women and Craft*. London: Virago, pp. 37–41.

Riley, Denise (2003). *Am I That Name? Feminism and the Category of 'Women' in History*. Minneapolis: University of Minnesota Press.

Ring, J. (2015). Artist's website. http://www.jonathanring.co.uk/ (Accessed 1 March 2015).

Roberts, J. (2005). 'Jo Spence: Photography, Empowerment and the Everyday'. In Mela Dávila (ed.), *Jo Spence: Beyond the Perfect Image. Photography, Subjectivity, Antagonism*. Barcelona: MACBA, pp. 66–84.

Robins, F. (2002). 'Cosy: Keep in Under your Jumper – In Conversation with Linda Theophilus'. *Cosy*. Colchester: firstsite, n.p.

Robins, F. (2015). Artist's website. http://www.freddierobins.com/ (Accessed 24 April 2015).

Robinson, H. (2006). *Reading Art, Reading Irigaray: The Politics of Art by Women*. London: IB Tauris.

Robinson, H. (2013). 'Feminism meets the big exhibition: 2005 onwards'. *Anglo Saxonica* 3 (6): 129–51.

Robinson, H. (2015). 'Institutional Time: A Critique of Studio Art Education, by Judy Chicago (2014)' [book review]. *International Journal of Education Through Art*, 11: 1.

Rochdale Art Gallery (1985). *Triple Transformations: Shirley Cameron, Monica Ross and Evelyn Silver* (exhibition catalogue). [Monica Ross Archive].

Rochdale Art Gallery (1986). *The Issue of Painting, Sutapa Biswas, Margaret Harrison, Glenys Johnson* (press release). [National Art Library Information File on Sutapa Biswas].

Rochefort, C. (1981). 'Are Women Writers still Monsters?' (1975) [excerpts]. In Elaine Marks and Isabelle de Courtivron (eds), *New French Feminisms: An Anthology*. Brighton: Harvester Press, pp. 183–6.

Rokudenashiko (2015). *Support MK Boat Project -! The World's First 3D Scanned Peach on the Beach-* [sic]. Trans. Google, http://6d745.com/en-campfire/ (Accessed 15 April 2015).
Rose, B. (2001). 'Vaginal Iconology'. In Hilary Robinson (ed.), *Feminism-Art-Theory*. Oxford: Blackwell, pp. 573–7.
Rose, J. (1986). *Sexuality in the Field of Vision*. London: Verso.
Rose, J. (2014). *Women in Dark Times*. London: Bloomsbury.
Ross, M. (2000a). 'History of Not'. http://www.gold.ac.uk/media/Ross_Monica_History_Or_Not.pdf (Accessed 24 April 2015).
Ross, M. (2000b). Unpublished interview with the author.
Rosser, P. (1994). 'There's No Place Like Home'. In J. Frueh, C. L. Langer and A. Raven (eds), *New Feminist Criticism: Art, Identity, Action*. New York: IconEdition/HarperCollins, pp. 60–79.
Roth, M. (1995). 'Reading Between the Lines: The Imprinted Spaces of Sutapa Biswas'. In Katy Deepwell (ed.), *New Feminist Art Criticism*. Manchester: Manchester University Press, 1995, pp. 31–50.
Roth, M. (1998). 'Of Cotton and Sunflower Fields: The Making of *The French* and *The American Collection*'. In Dan Cameron (ed.), *Dancing at the Louvre: Faith Ringgold's French Collection and Other Story Quilts*. Berkeley: University of California Press, pp. 49–63.
Rowbotham, S., Segal, L. and Wainright, H. (1979). *Beyond the Fragments: Feminism and the Making of Socialism*. Rev. edn. London: Merlin Press.
Rowley, A. (2007). 'Fantastic Reality: Louise Bourgeois and a Story of Modern Art by Mignon Nixon (book review)'. *Papers of Surrealism*, 5. http://www.surrealismcentre.ac.uk/papersofsurrealism/journal5/acrobat%20files/book%20reviews/Rowleypdf.pdf (Accessed 1 December 2015).
Rowley, S. (1994). 'Going Public: Getting Personal'. In Catriona Moore (ed.), *Dissonance: Feminism and the Arts, 1970-90*. St. Leonards: Allen & Unwin in association with Artspace, pp. 213–27.
Royle, N. (2003). *The Uncanny*. Manchester: Manchester University Press.
Rubin, G. (1975). 'The Traffic in Women'. In Rayna R. Reiter (ed.), *Toward an Anthropology of Women*. New York: Monthly Review, pp. 157–210.
Rubin, W. (1984). *'Primitivism' in 20th c. Art: Affinity of the Tribal and the Modern*. New York: MoMA.
Russo, M. (1994). *The Female Grotesque: Risk, Excess and Modernity*. London: Routledge.
Saltzman, L. (2006). *Making Memory Matter: Strategies of Remembrance in Contemporary Art*. Chicago: University of Chicago Press.
Sargent, L. (ed.) (1986). *The Unhappy Marriage of Marxism and Feminism: A Debate on Class and Patriarchy*. London: Pluto Press.
Schallhorn, K. (2015). 'University of the South celebrates women with giant golden clitoris sculpture in library'. *Campus Reform: News*. http://www.campusreform.org/?ID = 6319 (Accessed 1 March 2015).

Scheman, N. (1980). 'Anger and the Politics of Naming'. In Sally McConnell-Ginet, Ruth Barker and Nelly Fur man (eds), *Women and Language in Literature and Society*. New York: Praeger, pp. 174–87.

Schor, M. (1997). *Wet: On Painting, Feminism, and Art Culture*. Durham, NC: Duke University Press.

Schor, M. (2014). 'The Feminist Wheel'. In *A Year of Positive Thinking* [blog], 20 September. http://ayearofpositivethinking.com/2014/09/20/the-feminist-wheel/ (Accessed 19 April 2015).

Sebeok, T. E. (1986). *I Think I Am a Verb: More Contributions to the Doctrine of Signs*. New York: Plenum Press.

Siopis, P. (2008). 'Shame in Three Parts at the Freud Museum'. In Claire Pajaczkowska and Ivan Ward (eds), *Shame and Sexuality: Psychoanalysis and Visual Culture*. London: Routledge, pp. 143–58.

Sjöholm, C. (2005). *Kristeva and the Political*. Hove: Psychology Press.

Solomon-Godeau, A. (2006). 'Taunting and Haunting: Critical Tactics in a "Minor" Mode'. In C. Armstrong and C. de Zegher (eds), *Women Artists at the Millenium*. Cambridge, MA: MIT Press, pp. 371–401.

Spence, J. (1988). *Putting Myself in the Picture: A Political, Personal and Photographic Autobiography*. Seattle: The Real Comet Press.

Spence, J. (1995). *Cultural Sniping: The Art of Transgression*. London: Routledge.

Spender, D. (1985). *For the Record: The Making and Meaning of Feminist Knowledge*. London: The Women's Press.

Spinifex Press (2015). 'Feminist Publishing in India: Kali for Women'. http://www.spinifexpress.com.au/fasiapub/india/kali.htm (Accessed 19 February 2015).

Spitz, E. H. (1991). *Image and Insight: Essays in Psychoanalysis and the Arts*. New York: Columbia University Press.

Spivak, G. C. (1992). 'The Politics of Translation'. In Michèle Barrett and Anne Phillips (eds), *Destabilising Theory: Contemporary Feminist Debates*. Cambridge: Polity Press, pp. 177–200.

Stone, A. (2007). 'On the Geneaology of Women: A Defence of Anti-Essentialism'. In Stacy Gillis, Gillian Howie and Rebecca Munford (eds), *Third Wave Feminism: A Critical Exploration*. London: Palgrave, pp. 16–29.

Sulter, M. (ed.) (1990). *Passion: Discourses on Blackwomen's Creativity*. Hebden Bridge: Urban Fox Press.

Sulter, M. (2003). *Jeanne Duval: A Melodrama*. Edinburgh: National Galleries of Scotland.

Sykes, E. (ed.) (1995). *Who's Who in Non-Classical Mythology*. London: Routledge.

Szasz, T. (1979). 'Psychiatry and Matrimony: Arrangements for Living'. In *Schizophrenia: The Sacred Symbol of Psychiatry*. Oxford: Oxford University Press, pp. 139–84.

Szymczyk, A. (2006). 'The Archive and its Lacunae'. In *Susan Hiller*, exh. cat., 'Concept, Body and Dream' series, Rivoli: Castello di Rivoli and Turin: Museo d'Arte Contemporanea, n.p.

Tate Britain and UAL (2014). *Late at Tate Britain: Inhabit, Friday 6 June 2014* [leaflet].

Tawadros, G. (1989). 'Beyond the Boundary: The Work of Three Black Women Artists in Britain', *Third Text* 8 (9): 121–50.

Taylor, G. (2002). *Castration: An Abbreviated History*. London: Routledge.

Taylor, R. (2003). 'Rose Finn-Kelcey, The Restless Image – A Discrepancy Between the Felt Position and the Seen Position. Self Portrait 1975. Summary'. Tate Online. http://www.tate.org.uk/art/artworks/finn-kelcey-the-restless-image-a-discrepancy-between-the-felt-position-and-the-seen-p78607/text-summary (Accessed 2 November 2014).

Tickner, L. (1996). 'May Stevens' (1981). In Block Editorial Board (eds), *The Block Reader in Visual Culture*. London: Routledge, pp. 21–30.

Tickner, L. (2006). 'Mediating Generation: The Mother-Daughter Plot'. In C. Armstrong and C. de Zegher (eds), *Women Artists at the Millenium*. Cambridge, MA: MIT Press, pp. 84–120.

Tyler, I. (2009). 'Against Abjection'. *Feminist Theory* 10 (1): 77–98.

Ultra Red (2005). 'Time for the Dead to Have a Word with the Living: The AIDS Uncanny'. *The Journal of Aesthetics and Protest* 1 (4): 82–94.

Van den Bosch, A. (1985). 'Susan Hiller: Resisting Representation'. *Artscribe* 46: 44–8.

Verhaeghe, P. and De Ganck, J. (2012). 'Beyond the return of the repressed: Louise Bourgeois' chthonic art'. In *Louise Bourgeois: The Return of the Repressed*. Buenos Aires: PROA Foundation, 2012) http://proa.org/eng/exhibition-louise-bourgeois-textos.php (Accessed 18 January 2015).

Vidler, A. (1992). *The Architectural Uncanny: Essays in the Modern Unhomely*. Cambridge, MA: MIT Press.

Voegelin, S. (2010). *Listening to Noise and Silence: Towards a Philosophy of Sound Art*. London: Continuum.

Waddell, M. and Wandor, M. (1987). 'Mystifying Theory'. In Rozsika Parker and Griselda Pollock (eds), *Framing Feminism: Art and the Women's Movement, 1970-1985*. London: Pandora, p. 204.

Wagner, A. (1996). *Three Artists [Three Women]*. Berkeley: University of California Press.

Walker, K. (1980). 'Feministo: A Portrait of the Artist as a Young Housewife'. *Heresies* 4 (1): 34.

Walker, K. (2000). Unpublished interview with the author.

Wallace, M. (1998). '*The French Collection*: Momma Jones, Mommy Fay, and Me'. In Dan Cameron (ed.), *Dancing at the Louvre: Faith Ringgold's French Collection and Other Story Quilts*. Berkeley: University of California Press, pp. 14–25.

Wallace, S. (2015). Cliteracy. http://www.sophiawallace.com/cliteracy-100-natural-laws. (Accessed 1 March 2015).

Walsh, M. (2013). *Art and Psychoanalysis*. London: IB Tauris.

Warner, M. (2007). 'Bobby Baker: The Rebel at the Heart of the Joker'. In Michelle Barrett and Bobby Baker (eds), *Bobby Baker: Redeeming Features of Daily Life*. London: Routledge, pp. 95–107.

Weber, S. (1973). 'The Sideshow, or: Remarks on a Canny Moment'. *Modern Language Notes* 88: 1102–33.

White, P. (1992). 'Female Spectator, Lesbian Specter: The Haunting'. In Beatriz Colomina (ed.), *Sexuality and Space*. Princeton NJ: Princeton Architectural Press, pp. 131–61.

White House Historical Association (2015). 'Ulysses S. Grant'. https://www.whitehouse.gov/1600/presidents/ulyssessgrant (Accessed 22 December 2015).

Wigley, M. (1993). *The Architecture of Deconstruction: Derrida's Haunt*. Cambridge, MA: MIT Press.

Wilding, F. (1972). Crocheted Environment. http://womanhouse.refugia.net/ (Accessed 22 April 2015).

Wilding, F. and Double, X. (1977). 'By our own Hands'. http://womanhouse.refugia.net/ (Accessed 22 April 2015).

Williamson, J. (1998). *Decoding Advertisements*. London: Maryon Boyars.

Woolf, V. (1957). *A Room of One's Own* (1929). San Diego: HBJ.

Woolf, V. (2012). 'Professions for Women' (1931). In *The Death of the Moth and Other Essays*. Project Gutenberg Australia. http://gutenberg.net.au/ebooks12/1203811h.html#ch-28 (Accessed 20 April 2015).

Wright, E. (1998). *Psychoanalytic Criticism: A Reappraisal*, 2nd edn. Cambridge: Polity Press.

Yates, M. (2015). Artist's website. http://www.users.otenet.gr/~myates/ (Accessed 5 April 2015).

Zapperi, G. (2013). 'Woman's Reappearance: Rethinking the archive in contemporary art – Feminist perspectives'. *Feminist Review* 105: 21–47.

Žižek, S. (1989). *The Sublime Object of Ideology*. London: Verso.

Žižek, S. (1997). *The Indivisible Remainder: An Essay on Schelling and Related Matters*. London: Verso.

Index

www.ingramcontent.com/pod-product-compliance
Ingram Content Group UK Ltd.
Pitfield, Milton Keynes, MK11 3LW, UK
UKHW020140290926
15471UKWH00003B/601

9 781350 060784